Caste

The Origins
of Our
Discontents

By Isabel Wilkerson

The Warmth of Other Suns:
The Epic Story of America's Great Migration

Caste: The Origins of Our Discontents

Caste

The Origins
of Our
Discontents

Adapted for Young Adults

Isabel Wilkerson

EMBER

All rights reserved. Published in the United States by Ember, an imprint of
Random House Children's Books, a division of Penguin Random House LLC, New York.
Originally published in hardcover in the United States by Delacorte Press, an imprint of
Random House Children's Books, a division of Penguin Random House LLC, New York, in 2022.

This work is based on *Caste: The Origins of Our Discontents*, copyright © 2020 by Isabel Wilkerson.
Originally published in 2020 in hardcover by Random House,
an imprint and division of Penguin Random House LLC.

Ember and the E colophon are registered trademarks of Penguin Random House LLC.

Visit us on the Web! GetUnderlined.com

Educators and librarians, for a variety of teaching tools, visit us at RHTeachersLibrarians.com

The Library of Congress has cataloged the hardcover edition of this work as follows:
Names: Wilkerson, Isabel, author.
Title: Caste: the origins of our discontents: adapted for young adults / Isabel Wilkerson.
Description: First edition. | New York: Delacorte Press, [2022] | Includes index. |
Audience: Ages 12 and up | Summary: "This work is based on *Caste: The Origins of Our Discontents*,
copyright © 2020. Originally published in the United States in hardcover by Random House, an
imprint and division of Penguin Random House LLC, New York, in 2020"— Provided by publisher.
Identifiers: LCCN 2022012485 (print) | LCCN 2022012486 (ebook) |
ISBN 978-0-593-42794-1 (hardcover) | ISBN 978-0-593-42795-8 (library binding) |
ISBN 978-0-593-42796-5 (ebook)
Subjects: LCSH: Caste—United States—Juvenile literature. | Social stratification—
United States—Juvenile literature. | Ethnicity—United States—Juvenile literature. | Power (Social
sciences)—United States—Juvenile literature. | United States—Race relations—Juvenile literature.
Classification: LCC HT725.U6 W56 2022 (print) | LCC HT725.U6 (ebook) | DDC 305.5/122

ISBN 978-0-593-42797-2 (paperback)

Printed in the United States of America
2nd Printing
First Ember Edition 2023

To the memory of my parents
who survived the caste system
and to the memory of Brett
who defied it

Because even if I should speak,
no one would believe me.
And they would not believe me precisely because
they would know that what I said was true.

—James Baldwin

If the majority knew of the root of this evil,
then the road to its cure would not be long.

—Albert Einstein

Contents

The Man in the Crowd

There is a famous black-and-white photograph from the era of the Third Reich. It is a picture taken in Hamburg, Germany, in 1936, of shipyard workers, a hundred or more, facing the same direction in the light of the sun. They are heiling in unison, their right arms rigid in outstretched allegiance to the Führer.

If you look closely, you can see a man in the upper right who is different from the others. His face is gentle but unyielding. Modern-day displays of the photograph will often add a helpful red circle around the man or an arrow pointing to him. He is surrounded by fellow citizens caught under the spell of the Nazis. He keeps his arms folded to his chest, as the stiff palms of the others hover just inches from him. He alone is refusing to salute. He is the one man standing against the tide.

Looking back from our vantage point, he is the only person in the entire scene who is on the right side of history. Everyone around him is tragically, fatefully, categorically wrong. In that moment, only he could see it.

His name is believed to have been August Landmesser. At the time, he could not have known the murderous path the hysteria around him would lead to. But he had already seen enough to reject it.

He had joined the Nazi Party himself years before. By now though, he knew firsthand that the Nazis were feeding Germans lies about Jews, the outcastes of his era, that, even this early in the Reich, the Nazis had caused terror, heartache, and disruption. He knew that Jews were anything but Untermenschen, *that they were German citizens, human as anyone else. He was an Aryan in love with a Jewish woman, but the recently enacted Nuremberg Laws had made their relationship illegal. They were forbidden to marry or to have sexual relations, either of which amounted to what the Nazis called "racial infamy."*

His personal experience and close connection to the scapegoated caste allowed him to see past the lies and stereotypes so readily embraced by susceptible members—the majority, sadly—of the dominant caste. Though Aryan himself, his openness to the humanity of the people who had been deemed beneath him gave him a stake in their wellbeing, their fates tied to his. He could see what his countrymen chose not to see.

In a totalitarian regime such as that of the Third Reich, it was an act of bravery to stand firm against an ocean. We would all want to believe that we would have been him. We might feel certain that, were we Aryan citizens under the Third Reich, we surely would have seen through it, would have risen above it like him, been that person resisting authoritarianism and brutality in the face of mass hysteria.

We would like to believe that we would have taken the more difficult path of standing up against injustice in defense of the outcaste. But unless people are willing to transcend their fears, endure discomfort and derision, suffer the scorn of loved ones and neighbors and coworkers and friends, fall into disfavor of perhaps everyone they know, face exclusion and even banishment, it would be numerically impossible, humanly impossible, for everyone to be that man. What would it take to be him in any era? What would it take to be him now?

Part One

———

A Structure Built Long Ago

CHAPTER ONE

———

The Afterlife of Pathogens

In the haunted summer of 2016, an unaccustomed heat wave struck the Siberian tundra on the edge of what the ancients once called the End of the Land. Above the Arctic Circle, the heat rose beneath the earth's surface and bore down from the sky, the air reaching an inconceivable 95 degrees on the Russian peninsula of Yamal. Wildfires flared, and pockets of methane gurgled beneath the normally frozen soil in the polar region.

Soon, the children of the indigenous herdsmen fell sick from a mysterious illness that many people alive had never seen and did not recognize. A twelve-year-old boy developed a high fever and acute stomach pangs, and passed away. Russian authorities declared a state of emergency and began airlifting hundreds of the sickened herding people, the Nenets, to the nearest hospital in Salekhard.

Scientists then identified what had afflicted the Siberian settlements. The aberrant heat had chiseled far deeper into the Russian permafrost than was normal and had exposed a toxin that had been encased since 1941, when the world was last at war. It was the pathogen anthrax, which had killed herds of reindeer all those decades ago and lain hidden in the animal carcasses long since buried in the permafrost. A thawed and tainted carcass rose to the surface that summer, the pathogen awakened, intact and as powerful as it had ever been. The pathogen spores seeped into the grazing land and infected the reindeer and spread to the herders who raised and relied upon them. The anthrax, like the reactivation of the human pathogens of hatred and tribalism in this evolving century, had never died. It lay in wait, sleeping, until extreme circumstances brought it to the surface and back to life.

On the other side of the planet, the United States, the world's oldest and most powerful democracy was in spasms over an election that would transfix the Western world and become a psychic break in American history, one that will likely be studied and dissected for generations.

For the first time in history, a woman was running as a major party candidate for president of the United States. A household name, the candidate was a no-nonsense national figure overqualified by some estimates, conventional and measured if uninspiring to her detractors, with a firm grasp of any policy or crisis that she might be called upon to address. Her opponent was a blunt-spoken billionaire, a reality television star prone to assailing most anyone unlike himself, who had never held public office and who pundits believed had no chance of winning his party's primaries much less the presidency.

On the face of it, what is commonly termed race in America was not at issue. Both candidates were white, born to the country's historic dominant majority. But the woman candidate represented the more liberal party made up of a patchwork of coalitions of, roughly speaking, the humanitarian-minded and the marginalized. The male candidate represented the conservative party that in recent decades had come to be seen as protecting an old social order benefitting and appealing largely to white voters.

Observers the world over recognized the significance of the election. Onlookers in Berlin and Johannesburg, Delhi and Moscow, Beijing and Tokyo, stayed up late into the night or the next morning to watch the returns that second Tuesday in November 2016. Inexplicably to many outside the United States, the outcome would turn not on the popular vote, but on the Electoral College, an American invention from the founding era of slavery by which each state has a say in declaring the winner based on the electoral votes assigned them and the outcome of the popular ballot in their jurisdiction.

By then, there had been only five elections in the country's history in which the Electoral College or a similar mechanism had overruled the popular vote, two such cases occurring in the twenty-first century alone. One of those two was the election of 2016, a collision of unusual circumstance.

The election would set the United States on a course toward isolationism, tribalism, the walling in and protecting of one's own, the worship of wealth and acquisition at the expense of others, even of the planet itself. After the votes had been counted and the billionaire declared the winner, to the shock of the world and of those perhaps less steeped in the country's racial and political history, a man on a golf course in Georgia could feel freer to express himself. He was a son of the Confederacy, which had gone to war against the United States for the right to enslave other humans. The election was a victory for him and for the social order he had been born to. He said to those around him, "I remember a time when everybody knew their place. Time we got back to that."

In the ensuing months, as the new president pulled out of treaties and entreated dictators, many observers despaired of the end of democracy and feared for the republic. On his own, the new leader withdrew the world's oldest democracy from the 2016 Paris Agreement, in which the nations of the world had come together to battle climate change, leaving many to anguish over an already losing race to protect the planet.

What had happened to America? The earth had shifted overnight, or so it appeared. We have long defined earthquakes as arising from the collision of tectonic plates that force one wedge of earth beneath the other, believed that the internal shoving match under the surface is all too easily recognizable. In classic earthquakes, we can feel the ground shudder and crack beneath us, we can see the devastation of the landscape or the tsunamis that follow.

What scientists have only recently discovered is that the more familiar earthquakes, those that are easily measured while in progress and instantaneous in their destruction, are often preceded by longer, slow-moving, catastrophic disruptions rumbling twenty miles or more beneath us, too deep to be felt and too quiet to be measured for most of human history. They are as potent as those we can see and feel, but they have long gone undetected because they work in silence, unrecognized until a major quake announces itself on the surface. Only recently have geophysicists had technology sensitive enough to detect the unseen stirrings deeper in the earth's core. They are called silent earthquakes. And only recently have circumstances forced us, in this current era of human rupture, to search for the unseen stirrings of the human heart, to discover the origins of our discontents.

By the time of the American election that fateful year, back on the northernmost edge of the world, the Siberians were trying to recover from the heat that had stricken them months before. Dozens of the indigenous herding people had been relocated, some quarantined and their tents disinfected. The authorities embarked on mass vaccinations of the surviving reindeer and their herders. They had gone for years without vaccinations because it had been decades since the last outbreak, and they felt the problem was in the past. "An apparent mistake," a Russian biologist told a Russian news site. The military had to weigh how best to dispose of the two thousand dead reindeer to keep the spores from spreading again. It was not safe merely to bury the carcasses to rid themselves of the pathogen. They would have to incinerate them in combustion fields at up to five hundred degrees Celsius, then douse the cinders and surrounding land with bleach to kill the spores to protect the people going forward.

Above all, and more vexing for humanity at large, was the sobering message of 2016 and the waning second decade of a still-new millennium: that rising heat in the earth's oceans and in the human heart could revive long-buried threats, that some pathogens could never be killed, only contained, perhaps at best managed with ever-improving vaccines against their expected mutations.

What humanity learned, one would hope, was that an ancient and hardy virus required perhaps more than anything, knowledge of its ever-present danger, caution to protect against exposure, and alertness to the power of its longevity, its ability to mutate, survive, and hibernate until reawakened. It seemed these contagions could not be destroyed, not yet anyway, only managed and anticipated, as with any virus, and that foresight and vigilance, the wisdom of never taking them for granted, never underestimating their persistence, was perhaps the most effective antidote, for now.

CHAPTER TWO

———

An Old House
and an Infrared Light

The inspector trained his infrared lens onto a misshapen bow in the ceiling, an invisible beam of light searching the layers of lath to test what the eye could not see. This house had been built generations ago, and I had noticed the slightest welt in a corner of plaster in a spare bedroom and had chalked it up to idiosyncrasy. Over time, the welt in the ceiling became a wave that widened and bulged despite the new roof. It had been building beyond perception for years. An old house is its own kind of devotional, a dowager aunt with a story to be coaxed out of her, a mystery, a series of interlocking puzzles awaiting solution. Why is this soffit tucked into the southeast corner of an eave? What is behind this discolored patch of brick? With an old house, the work is never done, and you don't expect it to be.

America is an old house. We can never declare the work over. Wind, flood, drought, and human upheavals batter a structure that is already fighting whatever flaws were left unattended in the original foundation. When you live in an old house, you may not want to go into the basement after a storm to see what the rains have wrought. Choose not to look, however, at your own peril. The owner of an old house knows that whatever you are ignoring will never go away. Whatever is lurking will fester whether you choose to look or not. Ignorance is no protection from the consequences of inaction. Whatever you are wishing away will gnaw at you until you gather the courage to face what you would rather not see.

We in the developed world are like homeowners who inherited a house on a piece of land that is beautiful on the outside, but whose soil is unstable loam and rock, heaving and contracting over generations, cracks patched but the deeper ruptures waved away for decades, centuries even. Many people may rightly say, *"I had nothing to do with how this all started. I have nothing to do with the sins of the past. My ancestors never attacked indigenous people, never owned slaves."* And, yes. Not one of us was here when this house was built. Our immediate ancestors may have had nothing to do with it, but here we are, the current occupants of a property with stress cracks and bowed walls and fissures built into the foundation. We are the heirs to whatever is right or wrong with it. We did not erect the uneven pillars or joists, but they are ours to deal with now.

And any further deterioration is, in fact, on our hands.

• • •

The inspector was facing the mystery of the misshapen ceiling, and so he first held a sensor to the surface to detect if it was damp. The reading inconclusive, he then pulled out the infrared camera to take a kind of X-ray of whatever was going on, the idea being that you cannot fix a problem until and unless you can see it. He could now see past the plaster, beyond what had been wallpapered or painted over, as we now are called upon to do in the house we all live in, to examine a structure built long ago.

Like other old houses, America has an unseen skeleton, a caste system that is as central to its operation as are the studs and joists that we cannot see in the physical buildings we call home. Caste is the infrastructure of our divisions. It is the architecture of human hierarchy, the subconscious code of instructions for maintaining, in our case, a four-hundred-year-old social order. Looking at caste is like holding the country's X-ray up to the light.

A caste system is an artificial construction, a fixed and embedded ranking of human value that sets the presumed supremacy of one group against the presumed inferiority of other groups on the basis of ancestry and often immutable traits, traits that would be neutral in the abstract but are ascribed life-and-death meaning in a hierarchy favoring the dominant caste whose forebears designed it. A caste system uses rigid, often arbitrary boundaries to keep the ranked groupings apart, distinct from one another and in their assigned places.

Throughout human history, three caste systems have stood out. The tragically accelerated, chilling, and officially vanquished caste system of Nazi Germany. The lingering, millennia-long caste system of India. And the shape-shifting, unspoken, race-based caste pyramid in the United States. Each version relied on stigmatizing those deemed inferior to justify the dehumanization necessary to keep the lowest-ranked people at the bottom and to rationalize the protocols of enforcement. A caste system endures because it is often justified as divine will, originating from sacred text or the presumed laws of nature, reinforced throughout the culture and passed down through the generations.

As we go about our daily lives, caste is the wordless usher in a darkened theater, flashlight cast down in the aisles, guiding us to our assigned seats for a performance. The hierarchy of caste is not about feelings or morality. It is about power—which groups have it and which do not. It is about resources—which caste is seen as worthy of them and which are not, who gets to acquire and control them and who does not. It is about respect, authority, and assumptions of competence—who is accorded these and who is not.

As a means of assigning value to entire swaths of humankind, caste guides each of us often beyond the reaches of our awareness. It embeds into our bones an unconscious ranking of human characteristics and sets forth the rules, expectations, and stereotypes that have been used to justify brutalities against entire groups within our species. In the American caste system, the signal of rank is what we call race, the division of humans on the basis of their appearance. In America, race is the primary tool and the visible decoy, the front man, for caste.

What people look like, or, rather, the race they have been assigned or are perceived to belong to, is the visible cue to their caste. It is the historic flash card to the public of how they are to be treated, where they are expected to live, what kinds of positions they are expected to hold, whether they belong in this section of town or that seat in a boardroom, whether they should be expected to speak with authority on this or that subject, whether they will be administered pain relief in a hospital, whether their neighborhood is likely to adjoin a toxic waste site or to have contaminated water flowing from their taps, whether they are more or less likely to survive childbirth in the most advanced nation in the world, whether they may be shot by authorities with impunity.

Caste and race are neither synonymous nor mutually exclusive. They can and do coexist in the same culture and serve to reinforce each other. Race, in the United States, is the visible agent of the unseen force of caste. Caste is the bones, race the skin. Race is what we can see, the physical traits that have been given arbitrary meaning and become shorthand for who a person is. Caste is the powerful infrastructure that holds each group in its place.

Caste is fixed and rigid. Race is fluid and superficial, subject to periodic redefinition to meet the needs of the dominant caste in what is now the United States. While the requirements to qualify as white have changed over the centuries, the fact of a dominant caste has remained constant from its inception—whoever fit the definition of white, at whatever point in history, was granted the legal rights and privileges of the dominant caste. Perhaps more critically and tragically, at the other end of the ladder, the subordinated caste, too, has been fixed from the beginning as the psychological floor beneath which all other castes cannot fall.

Thus we are all born into a silent war-game, centuries old, enlisted in teams not of our own choosing. The side to which we are assigned in the American system of categorizing people is proclaimed by the team uniform that each caste wears, signaling our presumed worth and potential. That any of us manages to create abiding connections across these manufactured divisions is a testament to the beauty of the human spirit.

The use of inherited physical characteristics to differentiate inner abilities and group value may be the cleverest way that a culture has ever devised to manage and maintain a caste system.

"As a social and human division," wrote the political scientist Andrew Hacker of the use of physical traits to form human categories, "it surpasses all others—even gender—in intensity and subordination."

CHAPTER THREE

An American Untouchable

In the winter of 1959, after leading the Montgomery bus boycott that arose from the arrest of Rosa Parks and before the trials and triumphs to come, Martin Luther King, Jr., and his wife, Coretta, landed in India, in the city then known as Bombay, to visit the land of Mohandas Gandhi, the father of nonviolent protest. They were covered in garlands upon arrival, and King told reporters, "To other countries, I may go as a tourist, but to India I come as a pilgrim."

He had long dreamed of going to India, and they stayed an entire month, at the invitation of Prime Minister Jawaharlal Nehru. King wanted to see for himself the place whose fight for freedom from British rule had inspired his fight for justice in America. He wanted to see the so-called Untouchables, the lowest caste in the ancient Indian caste system, whom he had read of and had sympathy for, but who had still been left behind after India gained its independence the decade before.

He discovered that people in India had been following the trials of his own oppressed people in America, knew of the bus boycott he had led. Wherever he went, the people on the streets of Bombay and Delhi crowded around him for an autograph.

One afternoon, King and his wife journeyed to the southern tip of the country, to the city of Trivandrum in the state of Kerala, and visited with high school students whose families had been Untouchables. The principal made the introduction.

"Young people," he said, "I would like to present to you a fellow untouchable from the United States of America."

King was floored. He had not expected that term to be applied to him. He was, in fact, put off by it at first. He had flown in from another continent, had dined with the prime minister. He did not see the connection, did not see what the Indian caste system had to do directly with him, did not immediately see why the lowest-caste people in India would view him, an American Negro and a distinguished visitor, as low-caste like themselves, see him as one of them. "For a moment," he wrote, "I was a bit shocked and peeved that I would be referred to as an untouchable."

Then he began to think about the reality of the lives of the people he was fighting for—20 million people, consigned to the lowest rank in America for centuries, "still smothering in an airtight cage of poverty," quarantined in isolated ghettoes, exiled in their own country.

And he said to himself, "Yes, I am an untouchable, and every Negro in the United States of America is an untouchable."

In that moment, he realized that the Land of the Free had imposed a caste system not unlike the caste system of India and that he had lived under that system all of his life. It was what lay beneath the forces he was fighting in America.

• • •

There was little confusion among some of the leading white supremacists of the previous century as to the connections between India's caste system and that of the American South, where the purest legal caste system existed in the United States. "A record of the desperate efforts of the conquering upper classes in India to preserve the purity of their blood persists until this very day in their carefully regulated system of castes," wrote Madison Grant, a popular eugenicist, in his 1916 best-seller, *The Passing of the Great Race*. "In our Southern States, Jim Crow cars and social discriminations have exactly the same purpose."

A caste system has a way of filtering down to every inhabitant, its codes absorbed like mineral springs, setting the expectations of where one fits on the ladder. "The mill worker with nobody else to 'look down on,' regards himself as eminently superior to the Negro," observed the Yale scholar Liston Pope in 1942. "The colored man represents his last outpost against social oblivion."

It was in 1913 that a prominent southern educator, Thomas Pearce Bailey, took it upon himself to assemble what he called the racial creed of the South. It amounted to the central tenets of the caste system. One of the tenets was "Let the lowest white man count for more than the highest negro."

That same year, a man born to the bottom of India's caste system, born an Untouchable in the central provinces, arrived in New York City from Bombay. That fall, Bhimrao Ambedkar came to the United States to study economics as a graduate student at Columbia, focused on the differences between race, caste, and class. Living just blocks from Harlem, he would see firsthand the condition of his counterparts in America. He completed his thesis just as the film *Birth of a Nation*, the incendiary homage to the Confederate South, premiered in New York City in 1915. He would study further in London and return to India to become the foremost leader of the Untouchables and a preeminent intellectual who would help draft a new Indian constitution. He would work to dispense with the demeaning term *Untouchable*. He rejected the term *Harijans* applied to them by Gandhi, patronizingly so to their minds. He spoke of his people as *Dalits*, meaning "broken people," which, due to the caste system, they were.

It is hard to know what effect his exposure to the social order in America had on him personally. But over the years, he paid close attention, as did many Dalits, to the subordinate caste in America. Indians had long been aware of the plight of enslaved Africans and of their descendants in the pre–Civil War United States. Back in the 1870s, after the end of slavery and during the brief window of black advancement known as Reconstruction, an Indian social reformer named Jotiba Phule found inspiration in the abolitionists. He expressed hope "that my countrymen may take their noble example as their guide."

Many decades later, in the summer of 1946, acting on news that black Americans were petitioning the United Nations for protection as minorities, Ambedkar reached out to the best known African-American intellectual of the day, W.E.B. Du Bois. He told Du Bois that he had been a "student of the Negro problem" from across the oceans and recognized their common fates.

"There is so much similarity between the position of the

Untouchables in India and of the position of the Negroes in America," Ambedkar wrote to Du Bois, "that the study of the latter is not only natural but necessary."

Du Bois wrote back to Ambedkar to say that he was, indeed, familiar with him, and that he had "every sympathy with the Untouchables of India." It had been Du Bois who seemed to have spoken for the marginalized in both countries as he identified the double-consciousness of their existence. And it was Du Bois who, decades before, had invoked an Indian concept in channeling the bitter cry of his people in America: "Why did God make me an outcast and a stranger in mine own house?"

• • •

The American caste system began in the years after the arrival of the first Africans to Virginia colony in the summer of 1619, as the colony sought to refine the distinctions of who could be enslaved for life and who could not. Over time, colonial laws granted English and Irish indentured servants greater privileges than the Africans who worked alongside them, and the Europeans were fused into a new identity, that of being categorized as white, the polar opposite of black. The historian Kenneth M. Stampp called this assigning of race a "caste system, which divided those whose appearance enabled them to claim pure Caucasian ancestry from those whose appearance indicated that some or all of their forebears were Negroes." Members of the Caucasian caste, as he called it, "believed in 'white supremacy,' and maintained a high degree of caste solidarity to secure it."

Thus, throughout this book you will see many references

to the American South, the birthplace of this caste system. The South is where the majority of the subordinate caste was consigned to live for most of the country's history and for that reason is where the caste system was formalized and most brutally enforced. It was there that the tenets of intercaste relations first took hold before spreading to the rest of the country, leading the writer Alexis de Tocqueville to observe in 1831: "The prejudice of race appears to be stronger in the states that have abolished slavery than in those where it still exists; and nowhere is it so intolerant as in those states where servitude has never been known."

To recalibrate how we see ourselves, I use language that may be more commonly associated with people in other cultures, to suggest a new way of understanding our hierarchy: *Dominant caste, ruling majority, favored caste,* or *upper caste* instead of, or in addition to, *white*. *Middle caste* instead of, or in addition to, *Asian* or *Latino*. *Subordinate caste, lowest caste, bottom caste, disfavored caste, historically stigmatized* instead of *African-American*. *Original, conquered,* or *indigenous peoples* instead of, or in addition to, *Native American*. *Marginalized people* in addition to, or instead of, women of any race, or minorities of any kind.

Some of this may sound like a foreign language. In some ways it is and is meant to be. Because, to truly understand America, we must open our eyes to the hidden work of a caste system that has gone unnamed but prevails among us to our collective detriment, to see that we have more in common with each other and with cultures that we might otherwise dismiss, and to summon the courage to consider that therein may lie the answers.

In embarking upon this work, I devoured books about caste

in India and in the United States. Anything with the word *caste* in it lit up my neurons. I discovered kindred spirits from the past—sociologists, anthropologists, ethnographers, writers— whose work carried me through time and across generations. Many had labored against the tide, and I felt that I was carrying on a tradition and was not walking alone.

In the midst of the research, word of my inquiries spread to some Indian scholars of caste, based here in America. They invited me to speak at an inaugural conference on caste and race at the University of Massachusetts in Amherst, the town where W.E.B. Du Bois's papers are kept.

At a closing ceremony that I had not been made aware of ahead of time, the hosts presented to me a bronze-colored bust of the patron saint of the low-born of India, Bhimrao Ambedkar, the Dalit leader who had written to Du Bois all those decades before.

It felt like an initiation into a caste to which I had somehow always belonged. Over and over, they shared scenarios of what they had endured, and I responded in personal recognition, as if even to anticipate some particular turn or outcome. To their astonishment, I began to be able to tell who was highborn and who was low-born among the Indian people among us, not from what they looked like, as one might in the United States, but on the basis of the universal human response to hierarchy—in the case of an upper-caste person, an inescapable certitude in bearing, demeanor, behavior, a visible expectation of centrality.

After one session, I went up to a woman presenter whose caste I had ascertained from observing her interactions. I noticed that she had reflexively stood over the Dalit speaker and had taken it upon herself to explain what the Dalit woman had just said or meant, to take a position of authority as if by second nature, perhaps without realizing it.

We chatted a bit, and then I said to her, "I believe you must be upper caste, are you not?" She looked crestfallen. "How did you know?" she said, "I try so hard." We talked for what seemed an hour more, and I could see the effort it took to manage the unconscious signals of encoded superiority, the presence of mind necessary to counteract the programming of caste. I could see how hard it was even for someone committed to healing the caste divide, who was, as it turned out, married to a man from the subordinate caste and who was deeply invested in egalitarian ideals.

On the way home, I was snapped back to my own world when airport security flagged my suitcase for inspection. The TSA worker happened to be an African-American who looked to be in his early twenties. He strapped on latex gloves to begin his work. He dug through my suitcase and excavated a small box, unwrapped the folds of paper and held in his palm the bust of Ambedkar that I had been given.

"This is what came up in the X-ray," he said. It was heavy like a paperweight. He turned it upside down and inspected it from all sides, his gaze lingering at the bottom of it. He seemed concerned that something might be inside.

"I'll have to swipe it," he warned me. He came back after some time and declared it okay, and I could continue with it on my journey. He looked at the bespectacled face with the receding hairline and steadfast expression, and seemed to wonder why I would be carrying what looked like a totem from another culture.

"So who is this?" he asked. The name Ambedkar alone would

not have registered; I had learned of him myself only the year before, and there was no time to explain the parallel caste system. So I blurted out what seemed to make the most sense.

"Oh," I said, "this is the Martin Luther King of India."

"Pretty cool," he said, satisfied now, and seeming a little proud. He then wrapped Ambedkar back up as if he were King himself and set him back gently into the suitcase.

An Invisible Program

In the imagination of two late-twentieth-century filmmakers, an unseen force of artificial intelligence has overtaken the human species, has managed to control humans in an alternate reality in which everything one sees, feels, hears, tastes, smells, touches is in actuality a program. There are programs within programs, and humans become not just programmed but are in danger of and, in fact, well on their way to becoming nothing more than programs. What is reality and what is a program morph into one. The interlocking program passes for life itself.

The great quest in the film series The Matrix involves those humans who awaken to this realization as they search for a way to escape their entrapment. Those who accept their programming get to lead deadened, surface lives enslaved to a semblance of reality. They are captives, safe on the surface, as long as they are unaware of their captivity. Perhaps it is the unthinking acquiescence, the blindness to one's imprisonment, that is the most effective way for human beings to remain captive. People who do not know that they are captive will not resist their bondage.

But those who awaken to their captivity threaten the hum of the matrix. Any attempt to escape their imprisonment risks detection, signals *a breach in the order, exposes the artifice of unreality that has been imposed upon human beings. The Matrix, the unseen master program fed by the survival instinct of an automated collective, does not react well to threats to its existence.*

In a crucial moment, a man who has only recently awakened to the program in which he and his species are ensnared consults a wise woman, the Oracle, who, it appears, could guide him. He is uncertain and wary, as he takes a seat next to her on a park bench that may or may not be real. She speaks in code and metaphor. A flock of birds alights on the pavement beyond them.

"See those birds," the Oracle says to him. "At some point a program was written to govern them."

She looks up and scans the horizon. "A program was written to watch over the trees and the wind, the sunrise and sunset. There are programs running all over the place."

Some of these programs go without notice, so perfectly attuned they are to their task, so deeply embedded in the drone of existence. "The ones doing their job," she tells him, "doing what they were meant to do, are invisible. You'd never even know they were here."

So, too, with the caste system as it goes about its work in silence, the string of a puppet master unseen by those whose subconscious it directs, its instructions an intravenous drip to the mind, caste in the guise of normalcy, injustice looking just, atrocities looking unavoidable to keep the machinery humming, the matrix of caste as a facsimile for life itself and whose purpose is maintaining the primacy of those hoarding and holding tight to power.

Part Two

The Arbitrary Construction

of Human Divisions

CHAPTER FOUR

___

A Long-Running Play and the Emergence of Caste in America

Day after day, the curtain rises on a stage of epic proportions, one that has been running for centuries. The actors wear the costumes of their predecessors and inhabit the roles assigned to them. The people in these roles are not the characters they play, but they have played the roles long enough to incorporate the roles into their very being, to merge the assignment with their inner selves and how they are seen in the world.

Over the run of the show, the cast has grown accustomed to who plays which part. For generations, everyone has known who is center stage in the lead. Everyone knows who the hero is, who the supporting characters are, who is the sidekick good for laughs, and who is in shadow, the undifferentiated chorus with no lines to speak, no voice to sing, but necessary for the production to work.

The roles become sufficiently embedded into the identity of the players that the leading man or woman would not be expected so much as to know the names or take notice of the people in the back, and there would be no need for them to do so. Stay in the roles long enough, and everyone begins to believe that the roles are preordained, that each cast member is best suited by talent and temperament for their assigned role, and maybe for only that role, that they belong there and were meant to be cast as they are currently seen.

The social pyramid known as a caste system is not identical to the cast in a play, though the similarity in the two words hints at a tantalizing intersection. When we are cast into roles, we are not ourselves. We are not supposed to be ourselves. We are performing based on our place in the production, not necessarily on who we are inside. We are all players on a stage that was built long before our ancestors arrived in this land. We are the latest cast in a long-running drama that premiered on this soil in the early seventeenth century.

It was in late August 1619, a year before the Pilgrims landed at Plymouth Rock, that a Dutch man-of-war ship set anchor at the mouth of the James River, at Point Comfort, in the wilderness of what is now known as Virginia. We know this only because of a haphazard line in a letter written by the early settler John Rolfe. This is the oldest surviving reference to Africans in the English colonies in America, people who looked different from the colonists and who would ultimately be assigned by law to the bottom of an emerging caste system. Rolfe mentions them as merchandise and not necessarily the merchandise the English settlers had been expecting. The ship "brought not anything but 20 and odd Negroes," Rolfe wrote, "which the Governor and Cape Marchant bought for victualles."

These Africans had been captured from a slave ship bound for the Spanish colonies but were sold farther north to the British. Historians do not agree on what their status was, if they were bound in the short term for indentured servitude or relegated immediately to the status of lifetime enslavement, the condition that would befall most every human who looked like them arriving on these shores or born here for the next quarter millennium.

The few surviving records from the time of their arrival show they "held at the outset a singularly debased status in the eyes of white Virginians," wrote the historian Alden T. Vaughan. If not yet consigned formally to permanent enslavement, "black Virginians were at least well on their way to such a condition."

In the decades to follow, colonial laws herded European workers and African workers into separate and unequal queues and set in motion the caste system that would become the cornerstone of the social, political, and economic system in America. This caste system would trigger the deadliest war on U.S. soil, lead to the ritual killings of thousands of subordinate-caste people in lynchings, and become the source of inequalities that becloud and destabilize the country to this day.

With the first rough attempts at a colonial census, conducted in Virginia in 1630, a hierarchy began to form. Few Africans were seen as significant enough to be listed in the census by name, as would be the case for the generations to follow, in contrast to the majority of European inhabitants, indentured or not. The Africans were not cited by age or arrival date as were the Europeans, information vital to setting the terms and time frame of indenture for Europeans, or for Africans, had they been in the same category, been seen as equal, or seen as needing to be accurately accounted for.

Thus, before there was a United States of America, there was the caste system, born in colonial Virginia. At first, religion, not race as we now know it, defined the status of people in the colonies. Christianity, as a proxy for Europeans, generally exempted European workers from lifetime enslavement. This initial distinction is what condemned, first, indigenous people, and, then, Africans, most of whom were not Christian upon arrival, to the lowest rung of an emerging hierarchy before the concept of race had congealed to justify their eventual and total debasement.

The creation of a caste system was a process of testing the bounds of human categories and not the result of a single edict. It was a decades-long sharpening of lines whenever the colonists had a decision to make. When Africans began converting to Christianity, they posed a challenge to a religion-based hierarchy. Their efforts to claim full participation in the colonies was in direct opposition to the European hunger for the cheapest, most pliant labor to extract the most wealth from the New World.

The strengths of African workers became their undoing. British colonists in the West Indies, for example, saw Africans as "a civilized and relatively docile population," who were "accustomed to discipline," and who cooperated well on a given task. Africans demonstrated an immunity to European diseases, making them more viable to the colonists than were the indigenous people the Europeans had originally tried to enslave.

More pressingly, the colonies of the Chesapeake were faltering and needed manpower to cultivate tobacco. The colonies farther south were suited for sugarcane, rice, and cotton—crops with which the English had little experience, but that Africans had either cultivated in their native lands or were quick to master. "The colonists soon realized that without Africans and the skills that they brought, their enterprises would fail," wrote the anthropologists Audrey and Brian Smedley.

In the eyes of the European colonists and to the Africans' tragic disadvantage, they happened to bear an inadvertent birthmark over their entire bodies that should have been nothing more than a neutral variation in human appearance, but which made them stand out from the English and Irish indentured servants. The Europeans could and did escape from their masters and blend into the general white population that was hardening into a single caste. "The Gaelic insurrections caused the English to seek to replace this source of servile labor entirely with another source, African slaves," the Smedleys wrote.

The colonists had been unable to enslave the native population on its own turf and believed themselves to have solved the labor problem with the Africans they imported. With little further use for the original inhabitants, the colonists began to exile them from their ancestral lands and from the emerging caste system.

This left Africans firmly at the bottom, and, by the late 1600s, Africans were not merely slaves; they were hostages subjected to unspeakable tortures that their captors documented without remorse. And there was no one on the planet willing to pay a ransom for their rescue.

Americans are loath to talk about enslavement in part because what little we know about it goes against our perception of our country as a just and enlightened nation, a beacon of democracy for the world. Slavery is commonly dismissed as a "sad, dark chapter" in the country's history. It is as if the greater the distance we can create between slavery and ourselves, the better to stave off the guilt or shame it induces.

But in the same way that individuals cannot move forward, become whole and healthy, unless they examine the domestic violence they witnessed as children or the alcoholism that runs in their family, the country cannot become whole until it confronts what was not a chapter in its history, but the basis of its economic and social order. For a quarter millennium, slavery *was* the country.

Slavery was a part of everyday life, a spectacle that public officials and European visitors to the slaving provinces could not help but comment on with curiosity and revulsion.

In a speech in the House of Representatives, a nineteenth-century congressman from Ohio lamented that on "the beautiful avenue in front of the Capitol, members of Congress, during this session, have been compelled to turn aside from their path, to permit a coffle of slaves, *males and females chained to each other by their necks,* to pass on their way to this *national slave market.*"

The secretary of the U.S. Navy expressed horror at the sight of barefoot men and women locked together with the weight of an ox-chain in the beating sun, forced to walk the distance to damnation in a state farther south, and riding behind them, "a white man on horse back, carrying pistols in his belt, and who, as we passed him, had the impudence to look us in the face without blushing."

The Navy official, James K. Paulding, said: "When they [the slaveholders] permit such flagrant and indecent outrages upon humanity as that I have described; when they sanction a villain, in thus marching half naked women and men, loaded with chains, without being charged with a crime but that of being *black,* from one section of the United States to another, hundreds of miles in the face of day, they disgrace themselves, and the country to which they belong."

• • •

American slavery, which lasted from 1619 to 1865, was not the slavery of ancient Greece or the illicit sex slavery of today. The abhorrent slavery of today is unreservedly illegal, and any current-day victim who escapes, escapes to a world that recognizes her freedom and will work to punish her enslaver. American slavery, by contrast, was legal and sanctioned by the state and a web of enforcers. Any victim who managed to escape, escaped to a world that not only did not recognize her freedom but would return her to her captors for further unspeakable horrors as retribution. In American slavery, the victims, not the enslavers, were punished, subject to whatever atrocities the enslaver could devise as a lesson to others.

What the colonists created was "an extreme form of slavery that had existed nowhere in the world," wrote the legal historian Ariela J. Gross. "For the first time in history, one category of humanity was ruled out of the 'human race' and into a separate subgroup that was to remain enslaved for generations in perpetuity."

The institution of slavery was, for a quarter millennium, the conversion of human beings into currency, into machines who existed solely for the profit of their owners, to be worked as long as the owners desired, who had no rights over their bodies or loved ones, who could be mortgaged, bred, won in a bet, given as wedding presents, bequeathed to heirs, sold away from spouses or children to cover an owner's debt or to spite a rival or to settle an estate. They were regularly whipped, raped, and branded, subjected to any whim or distemper of the people who owned them. Some were castrated or endured other tortures too grisly for these pages, tortures that the Geneva Conventions would have banned as war crimes had the conventions applied to people of African descent on this soil.

"The slave is doomed to toil, that others may reap the fruits" is how a letter writer identifying himself as Judge Ruffin testified to what he saw in the Deep South.

"The slave is entirely subject to the will of his master," wrote William Goodell, a minister who chronicled the institution of slavery in the 1830s. "What he chooses to inflict upon him, he must suffer. He must never lift a hand in self-defense. He must utter no word of remonstrance. He has no protection and no redress," fewer than the animals of the field. They were seen as "not capable of being injured," Goodell wrote. "They may be punished at the discretion of their lord, or even put to death by his authority."

As a window into their exploitation, consider that in 1740, South Carolina, like other slaveholding states, finally decided to limit the workday of enslaved African-Americans to fifteen hours from March to September and to fourteen hours from September to March, double the normal workday for humans who actually got paid for their labor. In that same era, prisoners found guilty of actual crimes were kept to a maximum of ten hours per workday. Let no one say that African-Americans as a group have not worked for our country.

For the ceaseless exertions of their waking hours, many subsisted on a peck of corn a week, which they had to mill by hand at night after their labors in the field. Some owners denied them even that as punishment and allowed meat for protein only once a year. "They were scarcely permitted to pick up crumbs that fell from their masters' tables," George Whitefield wrote. Stealing food was "a crime, punished by flogging."

"Your slaves, I believe, work as hard, if not harder, than the horses whereon you ride," Whitefield wrote in an open letter to the colonies of the Chesapeake in 1739. "These, after their work is done, are fed and taken proper care of."

Enslavers bore down on their hostages to extract the most profit, whipping those who fell short of impossible targets, and whipping all the harder those who exceeded them to wring more from their exhausted bodies.

"Whipping was a gateway form of violence that led to bizarrely creative levels of sadism," wrote the historian Edward Baptist. Enslavers used "every modern method of torture," he observed, from mutilation to waterboarding.

Slavery made the enslavers among the richest people in the world, granting them "the ability to turn a person into cash at the shortest possible notice." But from the time of enslavement, southerners minimized the horrors they inflicted and to which they had grown accustomed. "No one was willing," Baptist wrote, "to admit that they lived in an economy whose bottom gear was torture."

• • •

The vast majority of African-Americans who lived in this land in the first 246 years of what is now the United States lived under the terror of people who had absolute power over their bodies and their very breath, subject to people who faced no sanction for any atrocity they could conjure.

"This fact is of great significance for the understanding of racial conflict," wrote the sociologist Guy B. Johnson, "for it means that white people during the long period of slavery became accustomed to the idea of 'regulating' Negro insolence and insubordination by force with the consent and approval of the law."

Slavery so perverted the balance of power that it made the degradation of the subordinate caste seem normal and righteous. "In the gentlest houses drifted now and then the sound of dragging chains and shackles, the bay of the hounds, the report of pistols on the trail of the runaway," wrote the southern writer Wilbur J. Cash. "And as the advertisements of the time incontestably prove, mutilation and the mark of the branding iron."

The most respected and beneficent of society people oversaw forced labor camps that were politely called plantations, concentrated with hundreds of unprotected prisoners whose crime was that they were born with dark skin. Good and loving mothers and fathers, pillars of their communities, personally inflicted gruesome tortures upon their fellow human beings.

"For the horrors of the American Negro's life," wrote James Baldwin, "there has been almost no language."

This was what the United States was for longer than it was not. It is a measure of how long enslavement lasted in the United States that the year 2022 marks the first year that the United States would be an independent nation for as long as slavery lasted on its soil. No current-day adult will be alive in the year in which African-Americans as a group will have been free for as long as they had been enslaved. That will not come until the year 2111.

• • •

It would take a civil war, the deaths of three-quarters of a million soldiers and civilians, the assassination of a president, Abraham Lincoln, and the passage of the Thirteenth Amendment to bring the institution of enslavement in the United

States of America to an end. For a brief window of time, the twelve years known as Reconstruction, the North sought to rebuild the South and help the 4 million people who had been newly liberated. But the federal government withdrew for political expediency in 1877, and left those in the subordinate caste in the hands of the very people who had enslaved them.

Now, nursing resentments from defeat in the war, people in the dominant caste took out their hostilities on the subordinate caste with fresh tortures and violence to restore their sovereignty in a reconstituted caste system.

The dominant caste devised a labyrinth of laws to hold the newly freed people on the bottom rung ever more tightly, while a popular new pseudoscience called eugenics worked to justify the renewed debasement. People on the bottom rung could be beaten or killed with impunity for any breach of the caste system, like not stepping off the sidewalk fast enough or trying to vote.

The colonists made decisions that created the caste system long before the arrival of the ancestors of the majority of people who now identify as Americans. The dominant caste controlled all resources, controlled whether, when, and if a black person would eat, sleep, reproduce, or live. The colonists created a caste of people who would by definition be seen as dumb because it was illegal to teach them to read or write, as lazy to justify the bullwhip, as immoral to justify rape and forced breeding, as criminal because the colonists made the natural response to kidnap, floggings, and torture—the human impulse to defend oneself or break free—a crime if one was black.

Thus, each new immigrant—the ancestors of most current-day Americans—walked into a preexisting hierarchy, bipolar in construction, arising from slavery and pitting the extremes in human pigmentation at opposite ends. Each new immigrant had to figure out how and where to position themselves in the hierarchy of their adopted new land. Oppressed people from around the world, particularly from Europe, passed through Ellis Island and shed their old selves, and often their old names, to gain admittance to the powerful dominant majority.

Somewhere in the journey, Europeans became something they had never been or needed to be before. They went from being Czech or Hungarian or Polish to white, a political designation that only has meaning when set against something not white. They would join a new creation, an umbrella category for anyone who entered the New World from Europe. Germans gained acceptance as part of the dominant caste in the 1840s, according to immigration and legal scholar Ian Haney López, the Irish in the 1850s to 1880s, and the eastern and southern Europeans in the early twentieth century. It was in becoming American that they became white.

"In Ireland or Italy," López wrote, "whatever social or racial identities these people might have possessed, being White wasn't one of them."

Serbs and Albanians, Swedes and Russians, Turks and Bulgarians, who might have been at war with one another back in their mother countries were fused together, on the basis not of a shared ethnic culture or language or faith or national origin but solely on the basis of what they looked like, in order to strengthen the dominant caste in the hierarchy.

"No one was white before he/she came to America," James Baldwin once said.

Their geographic origin was their passport to the dominant

caste. "The European immigrants' experience was decisively shaped by their entering an arena where Europeanness—that is to say, whiteness—was among the most important possessions one could lay claim to," wrote the Yale historian Matthew Frye Jacobson. "It was their whiteness, not any kind of New World magnanimity, that opened the Golden Door."

To gain acceptance, each fresh infusion of immigrants had to enter into a silent, unspoken pact of separating and distancing themselves from the established lowest caste. Becoming white meant defining themselves as furthest from its opposite— black. They could establish their new status by observing how the lowest caste was regarded and imitating or one-upping the disdain and contempt, learning the epithets, joining in on violence against them to prove themselves worthy of admittance to the dominant caste.

They might have arrived as neutral innocents but would have been forced to choose sides if they were to survive in their adopted land. Here they had to learn how to be white. Thus Irish immigrants, who would not have had anything against any one group upon arrival and were escaping famine and persecution of their own under the British, were pitted against black residents when they were drafted to fight a war over slavery from which they did not benefit and that they did not cause.

Unable to attack the white elites who were sending them to war and who had prohibited black men from enlisting, Irish immigrants turned their frustration and rage against the scapegoats who they by now knew were beneath them in the American hierarchy. They hung black men from lamp poles and burned to the ground anything associated with black people— homes, businesses, churches, a black orphanage—in the Draft

Riots of 1863, considered the largest race riot in American history. A century later and in living memory, some four thousand Italian and Polish immigrants went on a rampage when a black veteran tried to move his family into the all-white suburb of Cicero, Illinois, in 1951. Hostility toward the lowest caste became part of the initiation rite into citizenship in America.

Thus, people who had descended from Africans became the unifying foil in solidifying the caste system, the bar against which all others could measure themselves approvingly. "It was not just that various white immigrant groups' economic successes came at the expense of nonwhites," Jacobson wrote, "but that they owe their now stabilized and broadly recognized whiteness itself in part to those nonwhite groups."

• • •

The institution of slavery created disfigured relationships that were handed down through the generations. The people whose ancestors had put them atop the hierarchy grew accustomed to the unearned deference from the subjugated group and came to expect it. They told themselves that the people beneath them did not feel pain or heartache, were debased machines that only looked human and upon whom one could inflict any atrocity. The people who told themselves these things were telling lies to themselves. Their lives were to some degree a lie and in dehumanizing these people whom they regarded as beasts of the field, they dehumanized themselves.

Americans of today have inherited these distorted rules of engagement whether or not their families had enslaved people or had even been in the United States. Slavery built the man-made chasm between blacks and whites that forces the middle castes of Asians, Latinos, indigenous people, and new immigrants of African descent to navigate what began as a bipolar hierarchy.

Newcomers learn to vie for the good favor of the dominant caste and to distance themselves from the bottom-dwellers, as if everyone were in the grip of an invisible playwright. They learn to conform to the dictates of the ruling caste if they are to prosper in their new land, a shortcut being to contrast themselves with the degraded lowest caste, to use them as the historic foil against which to rise in a harsh, every-man-for-himself economy.

By the late 1930s, as war and authoritarianism were brewing in Europe, the caste system in America was fully in force and into its third century. Its operating principles were evident all over the country, but caste was enforced without quarter in the authoritarian Jim Crow regime of the former Confederacy.

"Caste in the South," wrote the anthropologists W. Lloyd Warner and Allison Davis, "is a system for arbitrarily defining the status of all Negroes and of all whites with regard to the most fundamental privileges and opportunities of human society." It would become the social, economic, and psychological template at work in one degree or another for generations.

• • •

A few years ago, a Nigerian-born playwright came to a talk that I gave at the British Library in London. She was intrigued by the lecture, the idea that 6 million African-Americans had had to seek political asylum within the borders of their own country during the Great Migration, a history that she had not known of. She talked with me afterward and said something that I have never forgotten, that startled me in its simplicity.

"You know that there are no black people in Africa," she said.

Most Americans, weaned on the myth of drawable lines between human beings, have to sit with that statement. It sounds nonsensical to our ears. Of course there are black people in Africa. There is a whole continent of black people in Africa. How could anyone not see that?

"Africans are not black," she said. "They are Igbo and Yoruba, Ewe, Akan, Ndebele. They are not black. They are just themselves. They are humans on the land. That is how they see themselves, and that is who they are."

What we take as gospel in American culture is alien to them, she said.

"They don't become black until they go to America or come to the U.K.," she said. "It is then that they become black."

It was in the making of the New World that Europeans became white, Africans black, and everyone else yellow, red, or brown. It was in the making of the New World that humans were set apart on the basis of what they looked like, identified solely in contrast to one another, and ranked to form a caste system based on a new concept called race. It was in the process of ranking that we were all cast into assigned roles to meet the needs of the larger production.

None of us are ourselves.

CHAPTER FIVE

"The Container We Have Built for You"

Her name is Miss. It is only Miss. It is Miss for a reason. She was born in Texas in the 1970s to parents who came of age under Jim Crow, the authoritarian regime that laid the ground rules for the rest of a willing country. The overarching rule was that the lowest caste was to remain low in every way at all times, at any cost. Every reference was intended to reinforce their inferiority. In describing a train wreck, for instance, newspapers would report, "two men and two women were killed, and four Negroes." Black men were never to be addressed as "Mister," and black women were never to be addressed as "Miss" or "Mrs.," but rather by their first name or "auntie" or "gal," regardless of their age or marital status.

These rules were as basic as the change in the seasons, and a mayoral campaign in Birmingham, Alabama, turned almost entirely on a breach of a sacrosanct protocol. The supremacist police chief, Bull Connor, had a favorite in that 1961 race. He decided to secure the election of the man he wanted to win by framing the man he wanted to lose: he paid a black man to shake the opposing candidate's hand in public as a photographer lay in wait. The story took up a full page in a local newspaper, and the opponent lost the election as Bull Connor knew he would. For white southerners, it was a "cardinal sin," it was "harrowing," wrote the historian Jason Sokol, "to call a black man 'Mister' or to shake hands with him."

A young boy growing up ninety miles south, in Selma, watched white people, complete strangers, children even, call his mother and grandmother by their first names, have the nerve to call out "Pearlie!" to his mother instead of "Mrs. Hale," despite their upright bearing and church gloves and finery. Harold Hale came to hate this presumption of overfamiliarity, their putting his high-minded Mama and Big Mama in their place, and, worse still, knowing that there was nothing he could do about it.

In early 1965, Dr. Martin Luther King, Jr., came to town. It had been one hundred years since the end of the Civil War, and the subordinate caste was still not permitted to vote, despite the Fifteenth Amendment granting that right. Harold Hale signed up for the march Dr. King was planning from Selma to Montgomery.

The Edmund Pettus Bridge that they would have to cross to begin the journey was a few blocks from Hale's house. When he and the six hundred other marchers arrived at the foot of the bridge, a column of state troopers in helmets and on horseback blocked their path. The troopers stormed the protesters. They gassed, beat, and trampled them, "charging horses, their hoofs flashing over the fallen," in the words of the writer George B. Leonard, who watched in horror from his black-and-white television set. ABC News had cut into the middle of *Judgment at Nuremberg,* a movie about Nazi war crimes, to broadcast the grainy footage from Selma, one nightmare fusing into another.

Hale, a teenager far from the leaders up front, was unharmed physically. But he worried now about how long it might take for change to come. He decided then and there that if there was one thing he would do, he would make the dominant caste respect the next generation in his line. He decided he would stand up to the caste system by naming his firstborn daughter, whenever he might be so blessed, "Miss." He would give no one in the dominant caste the option but to call her by the title they had denied his foremothers. Miss would be her name. When his firstborn daughter arrived, his wife, Linda, went along with the plan.

Miss was now seated across from me at her lace-covered dinner table one summer evening. The homemade lasagna and strawberry cake had been put away. The kids and her husband were otherwise occupied, and she was recounting her life, north and south, how her father's dreams have brushed up against caste as she moves about the world.

A white porcelain sugar bowl sat between us on the table. She swept her hand over the top of the bowl. "I find that white people are fine with me," she said, "as long as I stay in my place. As long as I stay in 'the container we have built for you.' "

She tapped the side of the sugar bowl, gentle, insistent taps.

"As soon as I get out of the container," she said, lifting the lid from its bowl, "it's a problem."

She held the lid up to the light and then closed it back in its place.

When she was a little girl, her family moved to a small town in East Texas. They were the only black family on their block. Her father took delight in keeping the front yard pristine and tended to it in his off hours. He would change out the annuals in the flower beds overnight so that people would awaken to the surprise of a practically new yard. One day, a white man who lived in the neighborhood saw her father out front mowing the lawn. The man told her father he was doing a mighty fine job and asked what he was charging for yard work.

"Oh, I don't charge anything," Harold Hale said. "I get to sleep with the lady of the house."

He smiled at the man. "I live here."

Once word got out, people took baseball bats and knocked down the mailbox in front of the Hales' carefully tended garden. So Harold Hale set the next mailbox in concrete. One day, someone rolled by and tried to knock it down again from the car window, and when they did, the family heard a yell from outside. "The person had hurt their arm trying to hurl the bat at the new mailbox," Miss said. "But it was in concrete, and the bat kicked back at them." People left the mailbox alone after that.

The local high schools began permitting the two castes to go to school together in the early 1970s, before the family had arrived. When she was in tenth grade, she and her friends attracted unexpected attention for the walkie-talkies they used during their breaks between classes. This was before cellphones, and it allowed her to keep in touch with her friends, who'd gather at her locker at break time. The principal called her into his office one day, suspicious of the activity and wanting to know why these people were gathered around her locker. She showed him the device.

He asked her name.

"Miss Hale," she said.

"What's your first name?"

"It's Miss."

"I said, what is your first name?"

"My name is Miss."

"I don't have time for this foolishness. What's your real name?"

She repeated the name her father had given her. The principal was agitated now, and told an assistant to get her records. The records confirmed her name.

"Hale. Hale," he repeated to himself, trying to figure out the origins of this breach in protocol. In small southern towns, the white people knew or expected to know all the black people, the majority of whom would be dependent on the dominant caste for their income or survival one way or the other. He was trying to figure out what black family had had the nerve to name their daughter Miss, knowing the fix it would put the white people in.

"Hale. I don't know any Hales," he finally said. "You're not from around here. Where is your father from?"

"He's from Alabama."

"Who does he work for?"

She told him the name of the company, which was based outside of Texas. She told him it was a Fortune 500 company. Her parents had taught her to say this in hopes of giving her some extra protection.

"I knew you weren't from around here," he said. "Know how I know?"

She shook her head, waiting to be excused.

"You looked me in the eye when I was talking," he said of this breach in caste. "Colored folks from around here know better than to do that."

She was finally excused, and when she got home that day,

she told her father what happened. He had waited twenty years for this moment.

"What did he say? And then what did you say? And what did he say after that?"

He could barely contain himself. The plan was working.

He told her over and over that she must live up to the name she was given. "They don't have the corner on humanity," he told her. "They don't have the corner on femininity. They don't have the corner on everything it means to be a whole, admirable, noble, honorable female member of the species. They haven't cornered that."

Years later, Miss had a chance to see life in another part of America. In college, she was invited to spend the summer with the family of a fellow student on Long Island in New York. The family welcomed her and got a kick out of her name and how her family had stuck it to those bigots down South.

She was attentive to the grandmother in the family, so the grandmother grew especially fond of her. Miss had a graceful, easygoing manner, and was respectful toward the elders in the long tradition of black southern life. When the summer came to a close, and it was time to return to school, the grandmother was despondent at her leaving, so attached had she grown to her.

"I wish you would stay," the matriarch said, looking forlorn and hoping to convince her still.

Miss reminded her that she would need to be leaving.

"There was a time," the matriarch said, in warning and regret, "when I could have made you stay." She adjusted herself, her voice trailing off at her impotence. . . .

• • •

Each of us is in a container of some kind. The label signals to the world what is presumed to be inside and what is to be done with it. The label tells you which shelf your container supposedly belongs on. In a caste system, the label is frequently out of sync with the contents, mistakenly put on the wrong shelf, and this hurts people and institutions in ways we may not always know.

Back before Amazon and iPhones, I was a national correspondent at *The New York Times,* based in Chicago. I had decided to do a lighthearted piece about Chicago's Magnificent Mile, a prime stretch of Michigan Avenue that had always been the city's showcase, but now some big names from New York and elsewhere were about to take up residence. I figured New York retailers would be delighted to talk. As I planned the story, I reached out to them for interviews. Everyone I called was thrilled to describe their foray into Chicago and to sit down with the *Times.*

The interviews went as expected until the last one. I had arrived a few minutes early to make sure we could start on time, given the deadline I was facing.

The boutique was empty at this quiet hour of the late afternoon. The manager's assistant told me the manager would be arriving soon from another appointment. I told her I didn't mind the wait. I was happy to get another big name in the piece. She went to a back corner as I stood alone in a wide-open showroom. A man in a business suit and overcoat walked in, harried and breathless. From the far corner she nodded that this was him, so I went up to introduce myself and get started. He was out of breath, had been rushing, coat still on, checking his watch.

"Oh, I can't talk with you now," he said, brushing past me. "I'm very, very busy. I'm running late for an appointment."

I was confused at first. Might he have made another appointment for the exact same time? Why would he schedule two appointments at once? There was no one else in the boutique but the two of us and his assistant in back.

"I think I'm your appointment," I said.

"No, this is a very important appointment with *The New York Times*," he said, pulling off his coat. "I can't talk with you now. I'll have to talk with you some other time."

"But I am with *The New York Times*," I told him, pen and notebook in hand. "I talked with you on the phone. I'm the one who made the appointment with you for four-thirty."

"What's the name?"

"Isabel Wilkerson with *The New York Times*."

"How do I know that?" he shot back, growing impatient. "Look, I said I don't have time to talk with you right now. She'll be here any minute."

He looked to the front entrance and again at his watch.

"But I am Isabel. We should be having the interview right now."

He let out a sigh. "What kind of identification do you have? Do you have a business card?"

This was the last interview for the piece, and I had handed them all out by the time I got to him.

"I've been interviewing all day," I told him. "I happen to be out of them now."

"What about ID? You have a license on you?"

"I shouldn't have to show you my license, but here it is."

He gave it a cursory look.

"You don't have anything that has *The New York Times* on it?"

"Why would I be here if I weren't here to interview you? All of this time has passed. We've been standing here, and no one else has shown up."

"She must be running late. I'm going to have to ask you to leave so I can get ready for my appointment."

I left and walked back to the *Times* bureau, dazed and incensed, trying to figure out what had just happened. This was the first time I had ever been accused of impersonating myself. His caste notions of who should be doing what in society had so blinded him that he dismissed the idea that the reporter he was anxiously awaiting, excited to talk to, was standing right in front him. It seemed not to occur to him that a *New York Times* national correspondent could come in a container such as mine, despite every indication that I was she.

The story ran that Sunday. Because I had not been able to interview him, he didn't get a mention. It would have amounted to a nice bit of publicity for him, but the other interviews made it unnecessary in the end. I sent him a clip of the piece along with the business card that he had asked for. To this day, I won't step inside that retailer. I will not mention the name, not because of censorship or a desire to protect any company's reputation, but because of our cultural tendency to believe that if we just identify the presumed-to-be-rare offending outlier, we will have rooted out the problem. The problem could have happened anyplace, because the problem is, in fact, at the root.

CHAPTER SIX

———

The Measure of Humanity

The idea of race is a recent phenomenon in human history. It dates to the start of the transatlantic slave trade and thus to the subsequent caste system that arose from slavery. The word *race* likely derived from the Spanish word *raza* and was originally used to refer to the "'caste or quality of authentic horses,' which are branded with an iron so as to be recognized," wrote the anthropologists Audrey and Brian Smedley. As Europeans explored the world, they began using the word to refer to the new people they encountered. Ultimately, "the English in North America developed the most rigid and exclusionist form of race ideology," the Smedleys wrote. "Race in the American mind was and is a statement about profound and unbridgeable differences. . . . It conveys the meaning of social distance that cannot be transcended."

Geneticists and anthropologists have long seen race as a man-made invention with no basis in science or biology. The nineteenth-century anthropologist Paul Broca tried to use thirty-four shades of skin color to delineate the races, but could come to no conclusion. If all the humans on the planet were lined up by a single physical trait, say, height or color, in ascending or descending order, tallest to shortest, darkest to lightest, it would confound us to choose the line between these arbitrary divisions. One human would blend into the next and it would be nearly impossible to make the cutoff between, say, the San people of South Africa and the indigenous people along the Marañón River in Peru, who are scientifically measured to be the same color, even though they live thousands of miles apart and do not share the same immediate ancestry.

As a window into the random nature of these categories, the use of the term *Caucasian* to label people descended from Europe is a relatively new and arbitrary practice in human history. The word was not passed down from the ancients but rather sprang from the mind of a German professor of medicine, Johann Friedrich Blumenbach, in 1795. Blumenbach spent decades studying and measuring human skulls—the foreheads, the jawbones, the eye sockets—in an attempt to classify the varieties of humankind.

He coined the term *Caucasian* on the basis of a favorite skull of his that had come into his possession from the Caucasus Mountains of Russia. To him, the skull was the most beautiful of all that he owned. So he gave the group to which he belonged, the Europeans, the same name as the region that had produced it. That is how people now identified as white got the scientific-sounding yet random name Caucasian. More than a century later, in 1914, a citizenship trial was under way in America over whether a Syrian could be a Caucasian (and thus white), which led an expert witness in the case to say of Blumenbach's confusing and fateful discovery: "Never has a single head done more harm to science."

The epic mapping of the human genome and the quieter, long-dreamt-of results of DNA kits ordered in time for a family reunion have shown us that race as we have come to know it is not real. It is a fiction told by modern humans for so long that it has come to be seen as a sacred truth.

Two decades ago, analysis of the human genome established that all human beings are 99.9 percent the same. "Race is a social concept, not a scientific one," said J. Craig Venter, the geneticist who ran Celera Genomics when the mapping was completed in 2000. "We all evolved in the last 100,000 years from the small number of tribes that migrated out of Africa and colonized the world." Which means that an entire racial caste system, the catalyst of hatreds and civil war, was built on what the anthropologist Ashley Montagu called "an arbitrary and superficial selection of traits," derived from a few of the thousands of genes that make up a human being. "The idea of race," Montagu wrote, "was, in fact, the deliberate creation of an exploiting class seeking to maintain and defend its privileges against what was profitably regarded as an inferior caste."

We accept the illogic of race because these are the things we have been told. We see a person with skin that is whiter than that of most "white" people, and we accept that they are not "white" (and thus of a different category) because of the minutest difference in the folds of their eyelids and because perhaps their great-grandparents were born in Japan. We see a person whose skin is espresso, darker than most "black" people in America, and accept that he is, in fact, not "black," absolutely not "black" (and is thus a completely separate category), because his hair has a looser curl and perhaps he was born in Madagascar. We have to be taught this illogic. Small children who have yet to learn the rules will describe people as they see them, not by the political designations of black, white, Asian, or Latino, until adults "correct" them to use the proper caste designations to make the irrational sound reasoned. Color is a fact. Race is a social construct.

"We think we 'see' race when we encounter certain physical differences among people such as skin color, eye shape, and hair texture," the Smedleys wrote. "What we actually 'see' . . . are the learned social meanings, the stereotypes, that have been linked to those physical features by the ideology of race and the historical legacy it has left us."

And yet, observed the historian Nell Irvin Painter, "Americans cling to race as the unschooled cling to superstition."

• • •

The word *caste,* which has become synonymous with India, did not, it turns out, originate in India. It comes from the Portuguese word *casta,* a Renaissance-era word for "race" or "breed." The Portuguese, who were among the earliest European traders in South Asia, applied the term to the people of India upon observing Hindu divisions. Thus, a word we now ascribe to India actually arose from Europeans' interpretations of what they saw; it sprang from the Western culture that created America.

The Indian concept of rankings, however, goes back millennia and is thousands of years older than the European concept of race. The rankings were originally known as *varnas,* the ancient term for the major categories in what Indians have in recent centuries called the caste system. The human impulse to create hierarchies runs across societies and cultures, predates the idea of race, and thus is farther reaching, deeper, and older than raw racism and the comparatively new division of humans by skin color.

Before Europeans expanded to the New World and collided with people who looked different from themselves, the concept of racism as we know it did not exist in Western culture. "Racism is a modern conception," wrote the historian Dante Puzzo, "for prior to the XVIth century there was virtually nothing in the life and thought of the West that can be described as racist."

The R Word

In the half century since civil rights protests forced the United States into making state-sanctioned discrimination illegal, what Americans consider to be racism has shifted, and now the word is one of the most contentious and misunderstood in American culture. For the dominant caste, the word is radioactive— resented, feared, denied, lobbed back toward anyone who dares to suggest it. Resistance to the word often derails any discussion of the underlying behavior it is meant to describe, thus eroding it of meaning.

Social scientists often define racism as the combination of racial bias and systemic power, seeing racism, like sexism, as primarily the action of people or systems with personal or group power over another person or group with less power, as men have power over women, whites over people of color, and the dominant over the subordinate.

But over time, racism has often been reduced to a feeling, a character flaw, conflated with prejudice, connected to whether one is a good person or not. It has come to mean overt and declared hatred of a person or group because of the race ascribed to them, a perspective few would ever own up to. While people will admit to or call out sexism or xenophobia and homophobia, people may immediately deflect accusations of racism, saying they don't have "a racist bone in their body," or are the "least racist person you could ever meet," that they "don't see color," that their "best friend is black," and they may have even convinced themselves on a conscious level of these things.

What does *racist* mean in an era when even extremists won't admit to it? What is the litmus test for racism? Who is racist in a society where someone can refuse to rent to people of color, arrest brown immigrants en masse, or display a Confederate flag, but not be "certified" as a racist unless he or she confesses to it or is caught using derogatory signage or slurs? The fixation with smoking out individual racists or sexists can seem a losing battle in which we fool ourselves into thinking we are rooting out injustice by forcing an admission that (a) is not likely to come, (b) keeps the focus on a single individual rather than the system that created that individual, and (c) gives cover for those who, by aiming at others, can present themselves as noble and bias-free for having pointed the finger first, all of which keeps the hierarchy intact.

Caste, on the other hand, predates the notion of race and has survived the era of formal, state-sponsored racism that had long been openly practiced in the mainstream. The modern-day version of easily deniable racism may be able to cloak the invisible structure that created and maintains hierarchy and inequality. But caste does not allow us to ignore structure. Caste *is* structure. Caste is ranking. Caste is the boundaries that reinforce the fixed assignments based upon what people look like. Caste is a living, breathing entity. It is like a corporation that seeks to sustain itself at all costs. To achieve a truly egalitarian world requires looking deeper than what we think we see. We cannot win against a hologram.

Caste is the granting or withholding of respect, status, honor, attention, privileges, resources, benefit of the doubt, and human kindness to someone on the basis of their perceived rank or standing in the hierarchy. Caste pushes back against an African-American woman who, without humor or apology, takes a seat at the head of the table speaking Russian. It prefers an Asian-American man to put his technological expertise at the service of the company but not aspire to CEO. Yet it sees as logical a sixteen-year-old white teenager serving as store manager over employees from the subordinate caste three times his age. Caste is insidious and therefore powerful because it is not hatred, it is not necessarily personal. It is the worn grooves of comforting routines and unthinking expectations, patterns of a social order that have been in place for so long that it looks like the natural order of things.

What is the difference between racism and casteism? Because caste and race are interwoven in America, it can be hard to separate the two. Any action or institution that mocks, harms, assumes, or attaches inferiority or stereotype on the basis of the social construct of race can be considered racism. Any action or structure that seeks to limit, hold back, or put someone in a defined ranking, seeks to keep someone in their place by elevating or denigrating that person on the basis of their perceived category, can be seen as casteism.

Casteism is the investment in keeping the hierarchy as it is in order to maintain your own ranking, advantage, privilege, or to elevate yourself above others or keep others beneath you. For those in the marginalized castes, casteism can mean seeking to keep those on your disfavored rung from gaining on you, to curry the favor and remain in the good graces of the dominant caste, all of which serve to keep the structure intact.

In the United States, racism and casteism frequently occur at the same time, or overlap or figure into the same scenario. Casteism is about positioning and restricting those positions, vis-à-vis others. What race and its precursor, racism, do extraordinarily well is to confuse and distract from the underlying structural and more powerful Sith Lord of caste. Like the cast on a broken arm, like the cast in a play, a caste system holds everyone in a fixed place.

For this reason, many people—including those we might see as good and kind people—could be casteist, meaning invested in keeping the hierarchy as it is or content to do nothing to change it, but not racist in the classical sense, not active and openly hateful of this or that group. Actual racists, actual haters, would by definition be casteist, as their hatred demands that those they perceive as beneath them know and keep their place in the hierarchy.

In everyday terms, it is not racism that prompts a white shopper in a clothing store to go up to a random black or brown person who is also shopping and to ask for a sweater in a different size, or for a white guest at a party to ask a black or brown person who is also a guest to fetch them a drink, as happened to Barack Obama as a state senator, or even perhaps a judge to sentence a subordinate-caste person for an offense for which a dominant-caste person might not even be charged. It is caste or rather the policing of and adherence to the caste system. It's the autonomic, unconscious, reflexive response to expectations from a thousand imaging inputs and neurological societal downloads that affix people to certain roles based upon what they look like and what they historically have been assigned to or the characteristics and stereotypes by which they have been categorized. No ethnic or racial category is immune to the messaging we all receive about the hierarchy, and thus no one escapes its consequences.

Race and caste are not the cause and do not account for every poor outcome or unpleasant encounter. But caste, along with its faithful servant race, is an x-factor in most any American equation, and any answer one might ever come up with to address our current challenges is flawed without it.

———

CHAPTER SEVEN

Through the Fog of Delhi to the Parallels in India and America

The flight to India landed in a gray veil that hid the terminal and its tower at the international airport in Delhi. It was January 2018, my first moments on the subcontinent. The pilot searched for a jetway through the drapery of mist. It was two in the morning, and it was as if we had landed in a steam kettle, were still airborne in a cloud, the night air pressing against cabin windows, and we could see nothing of the ground. I had not heard of rain in the forecast and was fascinated by this supernatural fog in the middle of the night, until I realized that it was not fog at all, but smoke—from coal plants, cars, and burning stubble—trapped in stagnant wind. The pollution was a shroud at first to seeing India as it truly was.

At daybreak, the sun pushed through the haze, and, once I connected with my hosts, I raced along with them to cross an intersection, an open stretch of asphalt with cars hurtling in every direction with no lanes or speed limits. We made our way along the side streets to the conference we were attending. I saw the wayside altars and mushroom temples with their garlands and silk flowers to the Hindu deities at the base of the sacred fig trees. There, commuters can pause for reflection as they head to work or an exam or a doctor's visit. The sidewalk shrines seemed exotic to me until I thought of the American ritual of spontaneous altars of flowers and balloons at the site of something very different, at the site of an accident or tragedy, as for the young woman killed at the infamous rally in Charlottesville, Virginia, just months before. Both reflect a human desire to connect with and honor something or someone beyond ourselves.

The United States and India are profoundly different from each other—in culture, technology, economics, ethnic makeup. And yet, many generations ago, these two great lands paralleled each other, both protected by oceans and ruled for a time by the British, fertile and coveted. Both adopted social hierarchies and abide great chasms between the highest and the lowest in their respective lands. Both were conquered by people said to be Aryans arriving, in one case, from across the Atlantic Ocean, in the other, from the north. Those deemed lowest in each country would serve those deemed high. The younger country, the United States, would become the most powerful democracy on earth. The older country, India, the largest.

Their respective hierarchies are profoundly different. And yet, as if operating from the same instruction manual translated to fit their distinctive cultures, both countries adopted similar methods of maintaining rigid lines of demarcation and protocols. Both countries kept their dominant caste separate, apart from and above those deemed lower. Both exiled their indigenous peoples—the Adivasi in India, the Native Americans in the United States—to remote lands and to the unseen margins of society. Both countries enacted a fretwork of laws to chain the lowliest group—Dalits in India and African-Americans in the United States—to the bottom, using terror and force to keep them there.

"Perhaps only the Jews have as long a history of suffering from discrimination as the Dalits," wrote the Dalit journalist V. T. Rajshekar. "However, when we consider the nature of the suffering endured by the Dalits, it is only the African American parallel of enslavement, apartheid and forced assimilation that comes to mind."

Both countries have since abolished the formal laws that defined their caste systems—the United States in a series of civil rights laws in the 1960s and India decades before, in the 1940s, but both caste systems live on in hearts and habits, institutions and infrastructures. Both countries still live with the residue of codes that prevailed for far longer than they have not.

This description of caste history from the 2017 Indian book *Ground Down by Growth* could be said of the American caste system with only a few word changes, as noted by parentheses: *"The colonial powers officially abolished slavery in India (the United States) in 1843 (1865), but this simply led to its transformation into bondage through relations of debt, what has been called 'debt peonage' by scholars."*

In both countries and at the same time, the lowest castes toiled for their masters—African-Americans in the tobacco fields along the Chesapeake or in the cotton fields of Mississippi, Dalits plucking tea in Kerala and cotton in Nandurbar. Both worked as enslaved people and later for the right to live on the land that they were farming, African-Americans in the system of sharecropping, Dalits in the Indian equivalent, known as *saldari*, both still confined to their fixed roles at the bottom of their respective worlds.

"Both occupy the lowest positions on the status hierarchies in their societies," wrote Harvard political scientist Sidney Verba and his colleagues in a study of Dalits and African-Americans. Both have been "particularly singled out from other groups" based on characteristics ascribed to them.

While doors have opened to the subordinated castes in India and in America in the decades since discrimination was officially prohibited, the same spasms of resistance have afflicted both countries. What is called "affirmative action" in the United States is called "reservations" in India, and they are equally unpopular with the dominant castes in both countries, language tracking in lockstep, with complaints of reverse discrimination in one and reverse casteism in the other.

There are many overarching similarities but they are not the same in how they are structured or operate. The American system was founded as a primarily two-tiered hierarchy with its contours defined by the uppermost group, those identified as white, and by the subordinated group, those identified as black, with immigrants from outside of Europe forming blurred middle castes that sought to adjust themselves within a bipolar structure.

The Indian caste system, by contrast, is an elaborate fretwork of thousands of subcastes, or *jatis*, correlated to region and village, which fall under the four main *varnas*, Brahmin, Kshatriya, Vaishya, and Shudra, and the excluded fifth, known as Untouchables or Dalits. This hierarchy intensified under British rule and is further complicated by the role of non-Hindus—Muslims, Buddhists, and Christians—who are outside the caste system but have incorporated themselves into the workings of the country and, while eschewing rigid caste, may or may not have informal rankings among themselves and in relation to the *varnas*.

Unlike the United States, which primarily uses physical features to tell the castes apart, in India it is people's surnames that may most readily convey their caste. Dalit names are generally "contemptible" in meaning, referring to the humble or dirty work they were relegated to, while the Brahmins carry the names of the gods. Generally, you must know the significance of the name, learn the occupation of their forefathers, and perhaps know their village or their place in the village to ascertain their caste. But after centuries of forced submission and in-group marriage, they may also be identified by their bearing, accents, and clothing, all of which, over the centuries, were required to be lowly and menial, as well as a tendency to be darker than upper-caste people, though not always.

The Indian caste system is said to be stable and unquestioned by those within it, bound as it is by religion and in the Hindu belief in reincarnation, the belief that one lives out in this life the karma of the previous ones, suffers the punishment or reaps the rewards for one's deeds in a past life, and that the more keenly one follows the rules for the caste they were born to, the higher their station will be in the next life.

Some observers say that this is what distinguishes the Indian caste system from any other, that people in the lowest caste accept their lot, that it is fixed and unbending, that Dalits live out their karma decreed by the gods, and do their lowly work without complaint, knowing not to dream of anything more. In order to survive, some people in a subordinated caste may learn and believe that resistance is futile. But this condescending view disregards generations of resistance, as well as the work of Ambedkar and the reformer Jotiba Phule before him. It was also wrongly assumed of enslaved Africans, and it disregards a fundamental truth of the species, that all human beings want to be free.

The Dalits were no more contented with their lot than anyone would be. In a caste system, conflating compliance with approval can be dehumanizing in itself. Many Dalits looked out beyond their homeland, surveyed the oppressed people all over the world, and identified the people closest to their lamentations. They recognized a shared fate with African-Americans, few of whom would have known of the suffering of Dalits. Some Dalits felt so strong a kinship with one wing of the American civil rights movement and had followed it so closely that, in the 1970s, they created the Dalit Panthers, inspired by the Black Panther Party.

A few years ago, a group of mostly African-American professors made a trip to a rural village in Uttar Pradesh, India. There, hundreds of villagers from the lowliest subcaste, the scavengers, came together for a ceremony to welcome the Americans. The villagers sang Dalit liberation songs for the occasion. Then they turned to their American guests and invited them to sing a liberation song of their own. A law professor from Indiana University, Kenneth Dau Schmidt, began a song that the civil rights marchers sang in Birmingham and Selma before they faced sheriffs' dogs and water hoses. As he reached the refrain, the Dalit hosts joined in and began to sing with their American counterparts. Across the oceans, they well knew the words to "We Shall Overcome."

CHAPTER EIGHT

The Nazis and the
Acceleration of Caste

Berlin, June 1934

In the early stages of the Third Reich, before the world could imagine the horrors to come, a committee of Nazi bureaucrats met to weigh the options for imposing a rigid new hierarchy, one that would isolate Jewish people from Aryans now that the Nazis had taken control. The men summoned in the late spring of 1934 were not, at that time, planning, nor in a position to plan, extermination. That would come years later at a chillingly bloodless and cataclysmic meeting in Wannsee deeper into a world war that had not yet begun.

On this day, June 5, 1934, they were there to debate the legal framework for an Aryan nation, to turn ideology into law, and were now anxious to discuss the findings of their research into how other countries protected racial purity from the taint of the disfavored. They sat down for a closed-door session in the Reich capital that day, and considered it serious enough to bring a stenographer to record the proceedings and produce a transcript. As they settled into their chairs to hash out what would eventually become the Nuremberg Laws, the first topic on the agenda was the United States and what they could learn from it.

The man chairing the meeting, Franz Gürtner, the Reich minister of justice, introduced a memorandum in the opening minutes, detailing the ministry's investigation into how the United States managed its marginalized groups and guarded its ruling white citizenry. The seventeen legal scholars and functionaries went back and forth over American purity laws governing intermarriage and immigration. In debating "how to institutionalize racism in the Third Reich," wrote the Yale legal historian James Q. Whitman, "they began by asking how the Americans did it."

The Nazis needed no outsiders to plant the seeds of hatred within them. But in the early years of the regime, when they still had a stake in the appearance of legitimacy and the hope of foreign investment, they were seeking legal prototypes for the caste system they were building. They were looking to move quickly with their plans for racial separation and purity, and knew that the United States was centuries ahead of them with its anti-miscegenation statutes and race-based immigration bans. "For us Germans, it is especially important to know and see how one of the biggest states in the world with Nordic stock already has race legislation which is quite comparable to that of the German Reich," the German press agency Grossdeutscher Pressedienst wrote as the Nazis were solidifying their grip on the country.

Western Europeans had long been aware of the American paradox of proclaiming liberty for all men while holding subsets of its citizenry in near total subjugation. The French writer Alexis de Tocqueville toured antebellum America in the

1830s and observed that only the "surface of American society is covered with a layer of democratic paint." Germany well understood the U.S. fixation on race purity and eugenics, the pseudoscience of grading humans by presumed group superiority. Many leading Americans had joined the eugenics movement of the early twentieth century, including the inventor Alexander Graham Bell, the auto magnate Henry Ford, and Charles W. Eliot, the president of Harvard University. During the First World War, the German Society for Racial Hygiene applauded "the dedication with which Americans sponsor research in the field of racial hygiene and with which they translate theoretical knowledge into practice."

The Nazis had been especially taken with the militant race theories of two widely known American eugenicists, Lothrop Stoddard and Madison Grant. Both were men of privilege, born and raised in the North and educated in the Ivy League. Both built their now discredited reputations on hate ideology that devised a crude ranking of European "stock," declared eastern and southern Europeans inferior to "Nordics" and advocated for the exclusion and elimination of "races" they deemed threats to Nordic racial purity, foremost among them Jews and "Negroes."

A racial slur that the Nazis adopted in their campaign to dehumanize Jews and other non-Aryans—the word *Untermensch*, meaning "subhuman"—came to them from the New England–born eugenicist Lothrop Stoddard. A 1922 book he wrote carried the subtitle *The Menace of the Under-man*, which translated into *Untermenschen* in the German edition. The Nazis took the word as their own and would most become associated with it. They made Stoddard's book on white supremacy a standard text in the Reich's school curriculum and accorded him a private audience with the purposely remote Adolf Hitler at the Reich Chancellery in December 1939. Well into World War II, Stoddard sat in on Nazi sterilization trials and commended the Nazis for "weeding out the worst strains in the Germanic stock in a scientific and truly humanitarian way." He lamented, though, that, "if anything, their judgments were almost too conservative."

Madison Grant, a leading eugenicist from New York whose social circle included Presidents Theodore Roosevelt and Herbert Hoover, converted his zeal for Aryan supremacy into helping enact a series of American immigration and marriage restrictions in the 1920s, as the Nazi Party was forming across the Atlantic. Grant went far beyond southern segregationists in his contempt for marginalized people. He argued that "inferior stocks" should be sterilized and quarantined in "a rigid system of elimination of those who are weak or unfit" or "perhaps worthless race types." Grant published a rabid manifesto for cleansing the gene pool of undesirables, his 1916 book, *The Passing of the Great Race,* the German edition of which held a special place in the *Führer's* library. Hitler wrote Grant a personal note of gratitude and said, "The book is my Bible."

By the time that Hitler rose to power, the United States "was not just a country with racism," Whitman, the Yale legal scholar, wrote. "It was *the* leading racist jurisdiction—so much so that even Nazi Germany looked to America for inspiration." The Nazis recognized the parallels even if many Americans did not.

• • •

On that day in June 1934, these seventeen Reich bureaucrats and legal scholars were convening at a time of intrigue and upheaval in a country descending into dictatorship. The Nazis were in the final throes of consolidating their power after their takeover the year before. Hitler had been sworn in as chancellor but was not yet the *Führer*. That would not happen until later that summer, in August 1934, when the death of Germany's ailing president, Paul von Hindenburg, the last holdover of the Weimar regime, cleared the way for Hitler to seize total control.

Hitler had made it to the chancellery in a brokered deal that conservative elites agreed to only because they were convinced they could hold him in check and make use of him for their own political aims. They underestimated his cunning and overestimated his base of support, which had been the very reason they had felt they needed him in the first place. At the height of their power at the polls, the Nazis never pulled the majority they coveted and drew only 38 percent of the vote in the country's last free and fair elections at the onset of their twelve-year reign. The old guard did not foresee, or chose not to see, that his actual mission was "to exploit the methods of democracy to destroy democracy."

By the time they recognized their fatal miscalculation, it was too late. Hitler had risen as an outside agitator, a cult figure enamored of pageantry and rallies with parades of people carrying torches that an observer said looked like "rivers of fire." Hitler saw himself as the voice of the *Volk*, of their grievances and fears, especially those in the rural districts, as a god-chosen savior, running on instinct. He had never held elected office before.

As soon as he was sworn in as chancellor, the Nazis unfurled their swastikas, a Sanskrit symbol linking them to their Aryan "roots," and began to close in on the Jews. They stoked ancient resentments that dated back to the Middle Ages but that rose again when the Jews were made the scapegoats for Germany's loss and humiliation at the end of World War I. Seen as dominant in banking and finance, Jews were blamed for the insufficient financial support of the war effort, although historians now widely acknowledge that Germany lost on the battlefield and not solely for lack of funds.

Still, Nazi propaganda worked to turn Germans against Jewish citizens. Nazi thugs taunted and beat up Jews in the streets and any Aryans who were found to be in relationships with them. The regime began restricting Jews from working in government or in high-status professions like medicine or the law, fields that incited jealousy among ordinary Germans who could not afford the expensive cars and villas on the lake that many successful Jews had acquired. This was the middle of the Great Depression, and more than a third of Germans were out of work in 1933, the year the Nazis came to power. The Jews' prestige and wealth were seen as above the station of a group that Nazis decreed were beneath the Aryans.

Mindful of appearances beyond their borders, for the time being at least, the Nazis wondered how the United States had managed to turn its racial hierarchy into rigid law yet retain such a sterling reputation on the world stage. They noticed that in the United States, when it came to these racial prohibitions, "public opinion accepted them as natural," wrote the historian Claudia Koonz.

A young Nazi intellectual named Herbert Kier was tasked with compiling a table of U.S. race laws, and was confounded by the lengths to which America went to segregate its population. He made note that, by law in most southern states, "white children and colored children are sent to different schools" and that most states "further demand that race be given in birth certificates, licenses and death certificates." He discovered that "many American states even go so far as to require by statute segregated facilities for coloreds and whites in waiting rooms, train cars, sleeping cars, street cars, buses, steamboats and even in prisons and jails." In Arkansas, he noted, the tax rolls were segregated. He later remarked that, given the "fundamental proposition of the equality of everything that bears a human countenance, it is all the more astonishing how extensive race legislation is in the USA."

Kier was just one of several Nazi researchers "who thought American law went overboard," Whitman wrote.

With the results of their research laid out before them, the men at the June meeting began debating two main pathways to their version of a caste system: first, creating a legal definition for the categories of Jews and Aryans, and, second, prohibiting intermarriage between the two. Germany had looked at America's miscegenation laws decades before and tested its own intermarriage ban at the turn of the twentieth century, when it forbade its settlers to mix with indigenous people in its colonies in South West Africa. In so doing, Germany went further than most colonial powers, but it did not come close to the American model. Now Nazi extremists pushed for ways to prevent "any further penetration of Jewish blood into the body of the German *Volk*."

What the Nazis could not understand, however, was why, in America, "the Jews, who are also of interest to us, are not reckoned among the coloreds," when it was so obvious to the Nazis that Jews were a separate "race" and when America had already shown some aversion by imposing quotas on Jewish immigration. Aside from what, to the Nazis, was a single vexing omission, "this jurisprudence would suit us perfectly," said the Nazi radical Roland Freisler, who, unbeknownst to those at the table, would one day be in a position to make heartless use of it in his career as the hanging judge of the Reich. "I am of the opinion that we need to proceed with the same primitivity that is used by these American states," he said. "Such a procedure would be crude but it would suffice."

The moderates at the table, including the chair himself, Franz Gürtner, questioned the American statutes. They went back and forth on exactly how a marriage ban would work, parsed the proposed definitions of Jew and Aryan, tried to make sense of the American fraction system. Doubters were disturbed by the idea that people who were half-Jewish and half-Aryan would be cut off from their Aryan side and deprived of caste privileges they would otherwise be accorded. Rather than defining such people as half-Jewish, the skeptics wondered, would they not also be half-Aryan? But one hard-liner, Achim Gercke, referred back to the prototype they had been studying. He proposed a definition of one-sixteenth Jewish for classification of Jews, Koonz wrote, "because he did not wish to be less rigorous than the Americans."

The men debated for ten hours that day and ended without agreement. "We have been talking past one another," Freisler, frustrated by the lack of progress, said toward the end. The moderates had managed for now to contain the radicals who had pushed for the American prototype. But fifteen months later, the radicals would prevail.

In September 1935, Hitler summoned the Reichstag to the annual Nazi rally in Nuremberg to announce new legislation that had been incubating since the Nazi takeover. By then, Hitler had either imprisoned or killed many of his political opponents, including the murders of twelve members of the Reichstag and of his longtime friend Ernst Röhm, the head of a Nazi paramilitary unit, the S.A. All of this rendered the Reichstag a puppet arm of the government, having been intimidated into submission. At that very moment, the Nazis were building concentration camps all over the country. One was soon to open in Sachsenhausen, north of the Reich capital, and would become one of their "showcases."

The plan was to announce the legislation, ultimately known as the Blood Laws, on the final day of the rally. The night before, Hitler directed a small group of deputies to draft a version for him to deliver to the Reichstag to rubber-stamp. The Nazi researchers had come across a provision in some of the U.S. miscegenation laws that could help them define whether a person who was half-Jewish should count as a Jew or an Aryan. It turned out that Texas and North Carolina had an "association clause" in their marriage bans that helped those states decide if an ambiguous person was black or white, privileged or disfavored. Such a person would be counted in the disfavored group if they had been married to or had been known to associate with people in the disfavored group, thus defying caste purity.

This was what Hitler announced that September and expanded in the months to come: The Law for the Protection of

German Blood and German Honor defined a Jew as a person with three Jewish grandparents. It also "counted" as Jewish anyone descended from two Jewish grandparents and who practiced Judaism or was accepted into the Jewish community or was married to a Jew, in line with the Americans' association clause.

Secondly, the law banned marriage and intercourse outside of marriage between Jews and Germans, and it forbade German women under forty-five to work in a Jewish household.

Thus began a campaign of ever-tightening restrictions. Jews were henceforth stripped of citizenship, prohibited from displaying the German flag, denied passports. With that announcement, "Germany became a full-fledged racist regime," the historian George M. Fredrickson wrote. "American laws were the main foreign precedents for such legislation."

But given the Nazis' own fixation on race, the American prototype had its limits. "The scholars who see parallels between the American and Nazi racial classification schemes are to that extent wrong," Whitman said, "but only because they understate the relative severity of American law."

As cataclysmic as the Nuremberg Laws were, the Nazis had not gone as far with the legislation as their research into America had taken them. What did not gain traction on the day of the closed-door session or in the final version of the Nuremberg Laws was one aspect of the American system. While the Nazis praised "the American commitment to legislating racial purity," they could not abide "the unforgiving hardness" under which " 'an American man or woman who has even a drop of Negro blood in their veins' counted as blacks," Whitman wrote. "The one-drop rule was too harsh for the Nazis."

CHAPTER NINE

The Evil of Silence

The ash rose from the crematorium into the air, carried by karma and breeze, and settled onto the front steps and geranium beds of the townspeople living outside the gates of death at Sachsenhausen, north of Berlin. The ash coated the swing sets and paddling pools in the backyards of the townspeople.

There was no denying the slaughter and torment on the other side of the barbed wire. The fruit of evil fell upon villagers like snow dust. They were covered in evil, and some were good parents and capable spouses, and yet they did nothing to stop the evil, which had now grown too big for one person to stop, and thus no one person was complicit, and yet everyone was complicit. It had grown bigger than them because they had allowed it to grow bigger than them, and now it was raining down onto their gingerbread cottages and their lives of pristine conformity.

The dissident theologian Dietrich Bonhoeffer was one of the millions who suffered and perished behind the electrified walls of a Nazi concentration camp, tortured and kept in solitary confinement. Could the townspeople hear the prayers of the innocents? "Silence in the face of evil is itself evil," Bonhoeffer once said of bystanders. "God will not hold us guiltless. Not to speak is to speak. Not to act is to act."

The villagers were not all Nazis, in fact, many Germans were not Nazis. But they followed the Nazi leaders on the radio, waited to hear the latest from Hitler and Goebbels, the Nazis having seized the advantage of this new technology, the chance to reach Germans live and direct in their homes anytime they chose, an intravenous drip to the mind. The people had ingested the lies of an inherent Untermenschen, that these prisoners—Jews, Sinti, homosexuals, opponents of the Reich—were not humans like themselves, and thus the townspeople swept the ash from their steps and carried on with their days. Mothers pulled their children inside when the wind kicked up, hurried them along, to keep them from being covered in the ash of fellow human beings.

• • •

In the middle of Main Street in a southern American town, there stood a majestic old tree, an elm or an oak or a sycamore, that had been planted before modern roads were paved. It held a sacred place in the hearts of the townspeople, though it was an altogether inconvenient location for a shade tree. It blocked traffic, coming and going, and motorists were forced to curve around it to get through town. It was the potential cause of many accidents, given that motorists could not always see past it or know for sure who had the right of way.

And yet it could not be cut down. It was the local lynching tree, and it was performing its duty to "perpetually and eternally" remind the black townspeople of who among them had last been hanged from its limbs and who could be next. The tree was awaiting its appointed hour, and the white townspeople were willing to risk inconvenience, injury, and death, even to themselves, to keep the tree and the subordinate caste in their places. The tree bore silent witness to black citizens of *their eternal lot, and in so doing, it whispered reassurances to the dominant caste of theirs.*

• • •

The townspeople of the East Texas village of Leesburg hammered a buggy axle into the ground to serve as a stake. Then they chained nineteen-year-old Wylie McNeely to it. They collected the kindling they would use for the fire at the base of his feet, despite his protestations of innocence in connection to the white girl they said he had assaulted. Five hundred people gathered that fall in 1921 to see Wylie McNeely burn to death in front of them. But first, the leaders of the lynching had to settle a matter of importance. The leaders drew lots to see who would get which piece of McNeely's body after they had burned him alive, figure out the body parts "which they regarded as the choicest souvenir." This they did in front of the young man facing his final seconds on this earth, there chained up and left to hear of the disposition of his fingers and ears to the men who had kidnapped him outside of the law. The leaders debated this in front of the five hundred people who had come to watch him die and who were impatient for the festivities to begin. After the men had decided and after all was settled, they lit the match.

• • •

The little girls appear to be in grade school, in light cotton dresses with a sailor's collar and their hair cut in precise pageboys just below their ears. In the picture the two younger girls seem to be fidgeting in shadow, close to the women in the group, who were perhaps their mothers or aunts. The girl you notice first, though, looks to be about ten years old, positioned at the front of the group of grown-ups and children, her eyes alert and riveted. A man is at her side, crisp in his tailored white pants, white shirt, and white Panama hat, as if headed to cocktail hour at a boating party, his arms folded, face at rest, unperturbed, vaguely bored.

It is July 19, 1935. They are all standing at the base of a tree in the pine woods of Fort Lauderdale, Florida. Above them hangs the limp body of Rubin Stacy, his overalls torn and bloodied, riddled with bullets, his hands cuffed in front of him, head snapped from the lynching rope, killed for frightening a white woman. The girl in the front is looking up at the dead black man with wonderment rather than horror, a smile of excitement on her face as if show ponies had just galloped past her at the circus. The fascination on her young face set against the gruesome nature of the gathering was captured by a photographer and is among the most widely circulated of all lynching photographs of twentieth-century America.

Lynchings were part carnival, part torture chamber, and attracted thousands of onlookers who collectively became accomplices to public sadism. Photographers were tipped off in advance and installed portable printing presses at the lynching sites to sell to lynchers and onlookers like photographers at a prom. They made postcards out of the gelatin prints for people to send to their loved ones. People mailed postcards of the severed, half-burned head of Will James atop a pole in Cairo, Illinois, in 1907. They sent postcards of burned torsos that looked like the petrified victims of Vesuvius, only these horrors had come at the hands of human beings in modern times. Some people framed the lynching photographs with locks of the victim's hair under glass if they had been able to secure any. One spectator wrote on the back of his postcard from Waco, Texas, in 1916: "This is the Barbecue we had last night my picture is to the left with the cross over it your son Joe."

This was singularly American. "Even the Nazis did not stoop to *selling souvenirs of Auschwitz,"* wrote Time *magazine many years later. Lynching postcards were so common a form of communication in turn-of-the-twentieth-century America that lynching scenes "became a burgeoning subdepartment of the postcard industry. By 1908, the trade had grown so large, and the practice of sending postcards featuring the victims of mob murderers had become so repugnant, that the U.S. postmaster general banned the cards from the mails." But the new edict did not stop Americans from sharing their lynching exploits. From then on, they merely put the postcards in an envelope.*

Part Three

The Eight Pillars of Caste

The Origins of Our Discontents

These are the historic origins, the pillars upholding a belief system, the piers beneath the surface of a caste hierarchy. As these tenets took root in the firmament, it did not matter so much whether the assumptions were true, as most were not. It mattered little that they were misperceptions or distortions of convenience, as long as people accepted them and gained a sense of order and means of justification for the cruelties to which they had grown accustomed, inequalities that they took to be the laws of nature.

These are the pillars of caste, the ancient principles that I researched and compiled as I examined the parallels, overlap, and commonalities of three major caste hierarchies. These are the principles upon which a caste system is constructed, whether in America, India, or Nazi Germany, beliefs that were at one time or another burrowed deep within the culture and collective subconscious of most every inhabitant, in order for a caste system to function.

———

Divine Will and the Laws of Nature

Before the age of human awareness, according to the ancient
Hindu text of India, Manu, the all-knowing, was seated in contemplation, when the great men approached him and asked
him, "Please, Lord, tell us precisely and in the proper order the
Laws of all the social classes as well as of those born in between."

Manu proceeded to tell of a time when the universe as
we know it was in a deep sleep, and the One "who is beyond
the range of senses," brought forth the waters and took birth
himself as Brahma, the "grandfather of all the worlds."

And then, to fill the land, he created the Brahmin, the highest caste, from his mouth, the Kshatriya from his arms, the
Vaishya from his thighs, and, from his feet, the Shudra, the lowest of the four *varnas,* or divisions of man, millennia ago and
into the fullness of time.

The fragment from which each caste was formed foretold
the position that each would fill and their placement, in order,
in the caste system. From lowest to highest, bottom to top: The
Shudra, the feet, the servant, the bearer of burdens. The Vaishya,
the thighs, the engine, the merchant, the trader. The Kshatriya,

the arms, the warrior, the protector, the ruler. And above them all, the Brahmin, the head, the mouth, the philosopher, the sage, the priest, the one nearest to the gods.

"The Brahmin is by Law the lord of this whole creation," according to the Laws of Manu. "It is by the kindness of the Brahmin that other people eat."

Unmentioned among the original four *varnas* were those deemed so low that they were beneath even the feet of the Shudra. They were living out the afflicted karma of the past, they were not to be touched and some not even to be seen. Their very shadow was a pollutant. They were outside of the caste system and thus outcastes. These were the Untouchables who would later come to be known as Dalits, the subordinate caste of India.

• • •

In the words of the sacred text of the Western world, the Old Testament, there had been a Great Flood. The windows of heaven had opened, along with the fountains of the deep, and all of humankind was said to have descended from the three sons of the patriarch Noah. By divine instruction, they survived the floodwaters in an ark, for more than forty days and forty nights, and thereafter, Noah became a man of the soil. His sons were Shem, Ham, and Japheth, who would become the progenitors of all humanity.

One season, Noah planted a vineyard, and he later drank of the wine of the fruit of the vineyard. The wine overtook him, and he lay uncovered inside his tent. Ham, who would become the father of a son, Canaan, happened into the tent and saw his father's nakedness and told his two brothers outside. Shem and Japheth took a garment and laid it across their shoulders. They walked backward into the tent and covered their father's nakedness. Their faces were turned in the other direction so that they would not see their father unclothed. When Noah awoke from his wine and found out what Ham had done, he cursed Ham's son, Canaan, and the generations to follow, saying, "Cursed be Canaan! The lowest of slaves will he be to his brothers."

The story of Ham's discovery of Noah's nakedness would pass down through the millennia. The sons of Shem, Ham, and Japheth spread across the continents, Shem to the east, Ham to the south, Japheth to the west, it was said. Those who decreed themselves the descendants of Japheth would hold fast to that story and translate it to their advantage. As the riches from the slave trade from Africa to the New World poured forth to the Spaniards, to the Portuguese, to the Dutch, and lastly to the English, the biblical passage would be summoned to condemn the children of Ham and to justify the kidnap and enslavement of millions of human beings, and the violence against them. From the time of the Middle Ages, some interpreters of the Old Testament described Ham as bearing black skin and translated Noah's curse against him as a curse against the descendants of Ham, against all humans with dark skin, the people who the Europeans told themselves had been condemned to enslavement by God's emissary, Noah himself.

And thus, a hierarchy evolved in the New World they created, one that set those with the lightest skin above those with the darkest. Those who were darkest, and those who descended from those who were darkest, would be assigned to the subordinate caste of America for centuries.

"The curse of Ham is now being executed upon his descendants," Thomas R. R. Cobb, a leading Confederate and defender of slavery, wrote, 240 years into the era of human bondage in America. Slavery officially ended in 1865, but the structure of caste remained intact, not only surviving but hardening. "Let the negro have the crumbs that fall from the white man's table," Thomas Pearce Bailey, a twentieth-century author, recorded in his list of the caste codes of the American South, echoing the Indian Laws of Manu.

The United States and India would become, respectively, the oldest and the largest democracies in human history, both built on caste systems undergirded by their reading of the sacred texts of their respective cultures. In both countries, the subordinate castes were consigned to the bottom, seen as deserving of their debasement, owing to the sins of the past.

These tenets, as interpreted by those who put themselves on high, would become the divine and spiritual foundation for the belief in a human pyramid willed by God, a Great Chain of Being, that the founders would further sculpt in the centuries to follow, as circumstances required. And so we have what could be called the first pillar of caste, Divine Will and the Laws of Nature, the first of the organizing principles inherent in any caste system.

———

Heritability

To work, each caste society relied on clear lines of demarcation in which everyone was ascribed a rank at birth, and a role to perform. You were born to a certain caste and remained in that caste, subject to the high status or low stigma it conferred, for the rest of your days and into the lives of your descendants. Thus, heritability became the second pillar of caste.

In India, it was generally the father who passed his rank to his children. In America, dating back to colonial Virginia, children inherited the caste of their mother both by law and by custom. And in disputes beyond these parameters, a child was generally to take the status of the lower-ranking parent.

The Virginia General Assembly declared the status of all people born in the colony. "Whereas some doubts have arisen whether children got by any Englishman upon a negro woman should be slave or free," the Assembly decreed in 1662, "be it therefore enacted and declared by this present Grand Assembly, that all children borne in this country shall be held bond or free only according to the condition of the mother."

With this decree, the colonists were breaking from English

legal precedent, the only precepts they had ever known, the ancient order that gave children the status of the father. This new law allowed enslavers to claim the children of black women, the vast majority of whom were enslaved, as their property for life and for ensuing generations. It invited them to impregnate the women themselves if so inclined, the richer it would make them. It converted the black womb into a profit center and drew sharper lines around the subordinate caste, as neither mother nor child could make a claim against an upper-caste man, and no child springing from a black womb could escape condemnation to the lowest rung. It moved the colonies toward a bipolar hierarchy of whites and nonwhites, and specifically a conjoined caste of whites at one end of the ladder and, at the other end, those deemed black, due to any physical manifestation of African ancestry.

Tied conveniently as it was to what one looked like, membership in either the upper or the lowest caste was deemed immutable, primordial, fixed from birth to death, and thus regarded as inescapable. "He may neither earn nor wed his way out," wrote the scholars Allison Davis and Burleigh and Mary Gardner in *Deep South,* their seminal 1941 study of caste in America.

It is the fixed nature of *caste* that distinguishes it from *class,* a term to which it is often compared. Class is an altogether separate measure of one's standing in a society, marked by level of education, income, and occupation, as well as the attendant characteristics, such as accent, taste, and manners, that flow from socioeconomic status. These can be acquired through hard work and ingenuity or lost through poor decisions or calamity. If you can act your way out of it, then it is class, not caste. Through the years, wealth and class may have insulated some people born to the subordinate caste in America but not protected them from humiliating attempts to put them in their place or to remind them of their caste position.

"Like the Hindu caste system, the black-white distinction in the United States has supplied a social hierarchy determined at birth, and arguably immutable, even by achievement," wrote the legal scholars Raymond T. Diamond and Robert J. Cottrol. "Blacks became like a group of American untouchables, ritually separated from the rest of the population."

In the winter of 2013, the Academy Award–winning actor Forest Whitaker, a distinguished, middle-aged, African-American man, walked into a gourmet delicatessen on the West Side of Manhattan for a bite to eat. Seeing it crowded or not finding what he wanted, he turned to leave without making a purchase, as many customers might. An employee thought it suspicious and blocked him at the door. That level of intervention was uncharacteristic at an establishment frequented by celebrities and college students. The employee frisked him up and down in front of other customers. Finding nothing, he allowed Whitaker, visibly shaken, to leave. The delicatessen owners later apologized for the incident and fired the employee. But the degradation of that moment stayed with the actor. "It's a humiliating thing for someone to come and do that," Whitaker said afterward. "It's attempted disempowerment."

Neither wealth nor celebrity has insulated those born to the subordinate caste from the police brutality that seems disproportionately trained on those at the bottom of the hierarchy. In 2015, New York City police officers broke an NBA player's leg outside of a nightclub in Manhattan. The injury left the player, a forward for the Atlanta Hawks, disabled for the rest of the season. It resulted in a $4 million settlement, the proceeds of which the player promptly said he would donate to a foundation for public defenders.

In 2018, police officers slammed a former NFL player to the ground after a disagreement he had with another motorist who had thrown coffee at his car, according to news reports. The video that surfaced that spring shows officers twisting Desmond Marrow's arms and legs and shoving him facedown onto the pavement. Then they turn him over and hold him down by the throat. He passes out under their weight. After the video went viral, an internal investigation was conducted and an officer was fired.

"No matter how great you become in life, no matter how wealthy you become, how people worship you, or what you do," NBA star LeBron James told reporters just the year before, "if you are an African-American man or African-American woman, you will always be that."

———

Endogamy and the Control of Marriage and Mating

The framers of the American caste system took steps, early in its founding, to keep the castes separate and to seal off the bloodlines of those assigned to the upper rung. This desire led to the third pillar of caste—endogamy, which means restricting marriage to people within the same caste. This is an ironclad foundation of any caste system, from ancient India, to the early American colonies, to the Nazi regime in Germany. Endogamy was brutally enforced in the United States for the vast majority of its history and did the spade work for current ethnic divisions.

Endogamy enforces caste boundaries by forbidding marriage outside of one's group and going so far as to prohibit sexual relations, or even the appearance of romantic interest, across caste lines. It builds a firewall between castes and becomes the primary means of keeping resources and affinity within each tier of the caste system. Endogamy, by closing off legal family connection, blocks the chance for empathy or a sense of shared destiny between the castes. It makes it less likely that someone in the dominant caste will have a personal stake in the happiness, fulfillment, or well-being of anyone deemed beneath them or personally identify with them or their plight. Endogamy, in fact, makes it more likely that those in the dominant caste will see those deemed beneath them as not only less than human but as an enemy, as not of their kind, and as a threat that must be held in check at all costs.

"Caste," wrote Bhimrao Ambedkar, the father of the anti-caste movement in India, "means an artificial chopping off of the population into fixed and definite units, each one prevented from fusing into another through the custom of endogamy." Thus, "in showing how endogamy is maintained," he added, "we shall practically have proved the genesis and also the mechanism of Caste."

In 1691, Virginia became the first colony to outlaw marriage between blacks and whites, a ban that the majority of states would take up for the next three centuries. Some states forbade the marriage of whites to Asians or Native Americans in addition to African-Americans, who were uniformly excluded. While there was never a single nationwide ban on intermarriage, despite several attempts to enact one, forty-one of the fifty states passed laws making intermarriage a crime punishable by fines of up to $5,000 and up to ten years in prison. Some states went so far as to forbid the passage of any *future* law permitting intermarriage. Outside of the law, particularly in the South, African-Americans faced penalty of death for even the appearance of breaching this pillar of caste.

The Supreme Court did not overturn these prohibitions until 1967. Still, some states were slow to officially repeal their endogamy laws. Alabama, the last state to do so, did not throw out its law against intermarriage until the year 2000. Even then,

40 percent of the electorate in that referendum voted in favor of keeping the marriage ban on the books.

It was the caste system, through the practice of endogamy—essentially state regulation of people's romantic choices over the course of centuries—that created and reinforced "races," by permitting only those with similar physical traits to legally mate. Combined with bans on immigrants who were not from Europe for much of American history, endogamy laws had the effect of controlled breeding, of curating the population of the United States. This form of social engineering served to maintain the superficial differences upon which the hierarchy was based, "race" ultimately becoming the result of who was officially allowed to procreate with whom. Endogamy ensures the very difference that a caste system relies on to justify inequality.

"What we look like," wrote the legal scholar Ian Haney López, "the literal and 'racial' features we in this country exhibit, is to a large extent the product of legal rules and decisions."

This pillar of caste was well enough understood and accepted that, as late as 1958, a Gallup poll found that 94 percent of white Americans disapproved of marriage across racial lines. "You know the Negro race is inferior mentally," a southern physician told researchers back in 1940, expressing a commonly held view. "Everyone knows that, and I don't think God meant for a superior race like the whites to blend with an inferior race."

The protocol was strictly enforced against lower-caste men and upper-caste women, while upper-caste men, the people who wrote the laws, kept full and flagrant access to lower-caste women, whatever their age or marital status. In this way, the dominant gender of the dominant caste, in addition to controlling the livelihood and life chances of everyone beneath them, eliminated the competition for its own women and in fact for all women.

In the mid-1830s in Grand Gulf, Mississippi, white men burned a black man alive and stuck his head on a pole at the edge of town for all to see, as a lesson to men in the subordinate caste. The black man had been tortured and beheaded after he stood up and killed the dominant-caste man "who owned his wife and was in the habit of sleeping with her," according to a contemporaneous account. As he faced death for taking an extreme and assuredly suicidal step to protect his wife in that world, the doomed husband said that "he believed he should be rewarded in heaven for it."

More than a century later, in December 1943, an earnest fifteen-year-old boy named Willie James Howard was working during the holiday school break at a dime store in Live Oak, Florida. He was an only child and, having made it to the tenth grade, was expected to exceed what anyone else in the family had been able to accomplish. That December, he made a fateful gesture, unknowing or unmindful of a central pillar of caste. He was hopeful and excited about his new job and wanted so badly to do well that he sent Christmas cards to everyone at work. In one Christmas card, the one to a girl his age named Cynthia, who worked there and whom he had a crush on, he signed, "with L" (for love).

It would seem an ordinary gesture for that time of the year, sweet even, but this was the Jim Crow South; the boy was black, and the girl was white. She showed the card to her father. Word got back to Willie James that his card had somehow disturbed her. So, on New Year's Day 1944, he hand-delivered an apologetic note trying to explain himself: "I know you don't think much of our kind of people but we don't hate you, all we want [is] to be your friends but you [won't] let us please don't let anybody else see this I hope I haven't made you mad. . . ." He added a rhyme: "I love your name, I love your voice, for a S.H. (sweetheart) you are my choice."

The next day, the girl's father and two other white men dragged Willie James and his father to the banks of the Suwannee River. They hog-tied Willie James and held a gun to his head. They forced him to jump and forced his father at gunpoint to watch him drown. Held captive and outnumbered as the father was, he was helpless to save his only child.

The men admitted to authorities that they had abducted the boy and bound his hands and feet. They said he just jumped and drowned on his own. Within days, the boy's parents fled for their lives. A young Thurgood Marshall of the NAACP alerted the Florida governor, to no avail. The NAACP field secretary, Harry T. Moore, managed to convince the boy's parents to overcome their terror and to sign affidavits about what had happened the day their son was killed. A local grand jury refused to indict the boy's abductors, and federal prosecutors would not intervene.

No one was ever held to account or spent a day in jail for the death of Willie James. His abduction and death were seen as upholding the caste order. Thus the terrors of the southern caste system continued, carried forth without penalty. Sanctioned as it was by the U.S. government, the caste system had become not simply southern, but American.

Purity versus Pollution

The fourth pillar of caste rests upon the fundamental belief in the purity of the dominant caste and the fear of pollution from the castes deemed beneath it. Over the centuries, the dominant caste has taken extreme measures to protect its sanctity from the perceived taint of the lower castes. Both India and the United States at the zenith of their respective caste systems, and the short-lived but heinous regime of the Nazis, raised the obsession with purity to a high, if absurdist, art.

In some parts of India, the lowest-caste people were to remain a certain number of paces from any dominant-caste person while walking out in public—somewhere between twelve and ninety-six steps away, depending on the castes in question. They had to wear bells to alert those deemed above them so as not to pollute them with their presence. A person in the lowest subcastes in the Maratha region had to "drag a thorny branch with him to wipe out his footprints" and prostrate himself on the ground if a Brahmin passed, so that his "foul shadow might not defile the holy Brahmin."

Touching or drawing near to anything that had been touched

by an Untouchable was considered polluting to the upper castes and required rituals of purification for the high-caste person following this misfortune. This they might do by bathing at once in flowing water or performing Pranayama breaths along with meditation to cleanse themselves of the pollutants.

In Germany, the Nazis banned Jewish residents from stepping onto the beaches at the Jews' own summer homes, as at Wannsee, a resort suburb of Berlin, and at public pools in the Reich. "They believed the entire pool would be polluted by immersion in it of a Jewish body," Jean-Paul Sartre once observed.

In the United States, the subordinate caste was quarantined in every sphere of life, made untouchable on American terms, for most of the country's history and well into the twentieth century. In the South, where most people in the subordinate caste were long consigned, black children and white children studied from separate sets of textbooks. In Florida, the books for black children and white children could not even be stored together. African-Americans were prohibited from using white water fountains and had to drink from horse troughs in the southern swelter before the era of separate fountains. In southern jails, the bedsheets for the black prisoners were kept separate from the bedsheets for the white prisoners. All private and public human activities were segregated from birth to death, from hospital wards to railroad platforms to ambulances, hearses, and cemeteries. In stores, black people were prohibited from trying on clothing, shoes, hats, or gloves, assuming they were permitted in the store at all. If a black person happened to die in a public hospital, "the body will be placed in a corner of the 'dead house' away from the white corpses," wrote the historian Bertram Doyle in 1937.

This pillar of caste was enshrined into law in the United States in 1896, after a New Orleans man challenged an 1890 Louisiana law that separated "the white and colored races" in railroad cars. Louisiana had passed the law after the collapse of Reconstruction and the return to power of the former Confederates. A committee of concerned citizens of color came together and raised money to fight the law in court. On the appointed day, June 7, 1892, Homer A. Plessy, a shoemaker who looked white but was categorized as black under the American definition of race, bought a first-class ticket from New Orleans to Covington on the East Louisiana Railroad and took his seat in the whites-only car. In that era, a person of ambiguous racial origin was presumed not to be white, so the conductor ordered him to the colored car. Plessy refused and was arrested, as the committee had anticipated. His case went to the Supreme Court, which ruled seven to one in favor of Louisiana's "separate but equal" law. It set in motion nearly seven decades of formal, state-sanctioned isolation and exclusion of one caste from the other in the United States.

The Sanctity of Water

The waters and shorelines of nature were forbidden to the subordinate castes if the dominant caste so desired. Well into the twentieth century, African-Americans were banned from white beaches and lakes and pools, both north and south, lest they pollute them, just as Dalits were forbidden from the waters of the Brahmins, and Jews from Aryan waters in the Third Reich.

This was a sacred principle in the United States well into the second half of the twentieth century, and the dominant caste went to great lengths to enforce it. In the early 1950s, when Cincinnati agreed under pressure to allow black swimmers into some of its public pools, whites threw nails and broken glass into the water to keep them out. In the 1960s, a black civil rights activist tried to integrate a public pool by swimming a lap and then emerging to towel off. "The response was to drain the pool entirely," wrote the legal historian Mark S. Weiner, "and refill it with fresh water."

Decades before, in 1919, a black boy paid with his life and set off a riot in Chicago for inadvertently breaching this pillar of caste. Seventeen-year-old Eugene Williams was swimming in Lake Michigan, at a public beach on the city's South Side, and happened to wade past the imaginary line that separated the races. He unknowingly passed into the white water, which flowed into and looked no different from the black water. He was stoned and drowned to death for doing so. The tensions over the breaching of boundaries that summer incited the dominant caste and set off one of the worst race riots in U.S. history.

In the decades after, people in the upper caste rose up in hysterics at the sight of a subordinate-caste person approaching their water. In August 1931, a new public park opened in Pittsburgh, with pools the size of a football field and big enough for ten thousand swimmers. But soon afterward, as the *Pittsburgh Post-Gazette* reported, "each Negro who entered the pool yesterday was immediately surrounded by whites and slugged or held beneath the water until he gave up his attempts to swim and left."

A white woman in Marion, Indiana, seemed to be speaking for many in the dominant caste across America when she said

that white people wouldn't swim with colored people because they "didn't want to be polluted by their blackness." Far
from her, in Elizabeth, New Jersey, whites blocked African-
Americans at the stairwells and entrances the week the city
first allowed black swimmers to its public pool. There, and
elsewhere, "every black swimmer that entered the water quite
literally risked his or her life," historian Jeff Wiltse wrote.

It was in this atmosphere, in 1951, that a Little League baseball team in Youngstown, Ohio, won the city championship.
The coaches, unthinkingly, decided to celebrate with a team
picnic at a municipal pool. When the team arrived at the gate,
a lifeguard stopped one of the Little Leaguers from entering. It
was Al Bright, the only black player on the team. His parents
had not been able to attend the picnic, and the coaches and
some of the other parents tried to persuade the pool officials
to let the little boy in, to no avail. The only thing the lifeguards
were willing to do was to let them set a blanket for him outside
the fence and to let people bring him food. He was given little
choice and had to watch his teammates splash in the water and
chase each other on the pool deck while he sat alone on the
outside.

"From time to time, one or another of the players or adults
came out and sat with him before returning to join the others,"
his childhood friend, the author Mel Watkins, would write
years later.

It took an hour or so for a team official to finally convince
the lifeguards "that they should at least allow the child into
the pool for a few minutes." The supervisor agreed to let the
Little Leaguer in, but only if everyone else got out of the water,
and only if Al followed the rules they set for him.

First, everyone—meaning his teammates, the parents, all the white people—had to get out of the water. Once everyone cleared out, "Al was led to the pool and placed in a small rubber raft," Watkins wrote. A lifeguard got into the water and pushed the raft with Al in it for a single turn around the pool, as a hundred or so teammates, coaches, parents, and onlookers watched from the sidelines.

After the "agonizing few minutes" that it took to complete the circle, Al was then "escorted to his assigned spot" on the other side of the fence. During his short time in the raft, as it glided on the surface, the lifeguard warned him over and over again of one important thing. "Just don't touch the water," the lifeguard said, as he pushed the rubber float. "Whatever you do, don't touch the water."

The lifeguard managed to keep the water pure that day, but a part of that little boy died that afternoon. When one of the coaches offered him a ride home, he declined. "With champion trophy in hand," Watkins wrote, Al walked the mile or so back home by himself. He was never the same after that.

The Hierarchy of Trace Amounts:
Griffes, Marabons, and Sangmelees

The American caste system was an accelerated one, compressed into a fraction of the time that India's caste system has been in existence. Its founders used the story of Noah and his sons to justify the bottom of the hierarchy but, without further biblical instruction, as in the Laws of Manu, they shaped the upper caste as they went along. This policing of purity in the United

States began with the task of defining the dominant caste itself.

From the start, the founders labored over who should be allowed into the dominant caste. The vast majority of human beings, including many who are now considered white, would not have fit their definition. Twenty-five years before the American Revolution, Benjamin Franklin worried that, with its growing German population, Pennsylvania would "become a Colony of Aliens, who will shortly be so numerous as to Germanize us, instead of our Anglifying them, and will never adopt our Language or Customs any more than they can acquire our Complexion."

At first, Congress, in 1790, restricted American citizenship to white immigrants, "free white persons," according to the statute. But "whiteness" had yet to be settled, and by the mid-nineteenth century, with millions of people immigrating from Germany and fleeing famine in Ireland, supremacists on both sides of the Atlantic fretted over what was to become of a country flooded by "the most degenerate races of olden day Europe," in the words of Arthur de Gobineau, a widely read nineteenth-century advocate of Aryan supremacy. "They are the human flotsam of all ages: Irish, cross-bred Germans and French, and Italians of even more doubtful stock."

For most of American history, anyone not Anglo-Saxon fell somewhere on a descending scale of human "pollution." Like a field marshal defending his flanks in multiple theaters, the dominant caste fought the "tainted" influx of new immigrants with two of the most stringent immigration bans ever enacted, just before and after the turn of the twentieth century.

The country tried to block the flow of Chinese immigrants

into the western states with the Chinese Exclusion Act of 1882. Then it turned to the immigrants arriving from southern and eastern Europe, the "scum and offscouring," as a former Virginia governor put it, newcomers who purportedly brought crime and disease and polluted the bloodlines of America's original white stock. Congress commissioned an analysis of the crisis, an influential document known as the Dillingham Report, and the House Committee on Immigration and Naturalization called hearings as the United States tried to further curate its population.

"The moral fiber of the nation has been weakened and its very life-blood vitiated by the influx of this tide of oriental scum," Rev. M. D. Lichliter, a minister from Harrisburg, Pennsylvania, said in his testimony before the committee in 1910. "Our grand Anglo-Saxon character must be preserved, and the pure unmixed blood flowing down from our Aryan progenitors must not be mixed with the Iberic race," a term applied to southern Italians in the era of eugenics.

The findings set the stage for the 1924 Immigration Act, which restricted immigration to quotas based on the demographics of 1890—that is, before Poles, Jews, Greeks, Italians, and others outside of western Europe had arrived in great numbers.

Their status contested, these groups were not always extended the protections accorded to unassailably "white" people, not then anyway. There was an attempt to exclude Italian voters from "white" primaries in Louisiana in 1903. The decade before, in 1891, eleven Italian immigrants in New Orleans lost their lives in one of the largest mass lynchings in American history, after the police chief was assassinated and the immigrants were seen as the prime suspects. After the lynching, hundreds more were rounded up and arrested. One of the organizers of the lynch mob, John M. Parker, later described Italians as "just a little worse than the Negro, being if anything filthier in [their] habits, lawless, and treacherous." He went on to be elected governor of Louisiana.

Later, in 1922, a black man in Alabama named Jim Rollins was convicted of miscegenation for living as the husband of a white woman named Edith Labue. But when the court learned that the woman was Sicilian and saw "no competent evidence" that she was white, the judge reversed the conviction. The uncertainty surrounding whether she was "conclusively" white led the court to take the extraordinary step of freeing a black man who in other circumstances might have faced a lynching had she been seen as a white woman.

By then, a majority of the states had devised, or were in the process of devising, ever more tortured definitions of *white* and *black*.

Arkansas first defined *Negro* as "one in whom there is a visible and distinct admixture of African blood." Then in 1911, the state changed it to anyone "who has . . . any negro blood whatever," as it made interracial sex a felony. The state of Alabama defined a black person as anyone with "a drop of negro blood," in its intermarriage ban. Oregon defined as nonwhite any person "with ¼ Negro, Chinese or any person having ¼ Negro, Chinese or Kanaka blood or more than ½ Indian blood." North Carolina forbade marriage between whites and any person "of Negro or Indian descent to 3rd generation inclusive." The state of Georgia defined *white* to mean "no ascertainable trace of Negro, African, West Indian, Asiatic blood."

Louisiana had a law on the books as recently as 1983 setting the boundary at "one-thirty-second Negro blood." Louisiana culture went to great specificity, not so unlike the Indian Laws of Manu, in delineating the various subcastes, based on the estimated percentage of African "blood." There was griffe (three-fourths black), marabon (five-eighths black), mulatto (one-half), quadroon (one-fourth), octaroon (one-eighth), sextaroon (one-sixteenth), demi-meamelouc (one-thirty-second), and sangmelee (one-sixty-fourth). The latter categories, as twenty-first-century genetic testing has now shown, would encompass millions of Americans now classified as Caucasian. All of these categories bear witness to a historic American, dominant-caste preoccupation with race and caste purity.

Virginia went all in and passed what it called the Racial Integrity Act of 1924, which, besides prohibiting interracial marriage, defined a white person as one "who has no trace whatsoever of any blood other than Caucasian."

"The 'traceable amount' was meant to ensure that even blacks who did not look black were kept in their place," wrote Diamond and Cottrol. "Tracing black ancestry as far back as possible became a prerequisite to the smooth functioning of the caste system."

The Trials of the Middle Castes:
The Race to Get Under the White Tent

By extending the dream of dominion over the land and all others in it to anyone who could meet the definition of *white,* the American caste system became an all-or-nothing gambit for the top rung. Which is why, when Ybor City, Florida, began segregating its streetcars in 1905, Cubans, who had been uncertain as to how they would be classified, were relieved and overjoyed "to discover that they were allowed to sit in the white section."

Those permitted under the white tent could reap the rewards of full citizenship, rise to positions of high status, or as far as their talents could take them, get access to the best the country had to offer, or, at the very least, be accorded respect in everyday interactions from subordinate groups who risked assault for any misstep. A two-tiered caste system raised the stakes for whiteness, leading to court dockets filled with people on the borderline seeking admission to the upper caste.

A Japanese immigrant named Takao Ozawa had lived in the United States for more than twenty years. He tried to make the case that he was worthy of citizenship and should qualify as white because his skin was lighter than that of many "white people." He argued, what really was the difference? How could he not be white if his skin was white? What did it mean to be white if someone with actual white skin was not white?

His case went all the way to the U.S. Supreme Court. In 1922, the Court held unanimously that *white* meant not skin color but "Caucasian," and that Japanese were not Caucasian, notwithstanding the fact that few white Americans had origins in the Caucasus Mountains of Russia either and that those who did were at that very moment being kept out, too.

After the ruling, a newspaper that catered to Japanese immigrants mocked the decision: "Since this newspaper did not believe whites are the 'superior race,' it is 'delighted' the high tribunal 'did not find the Japanese to be free white persons.'"

A few months later, an immigrant from the dominant caste

of India sought to make common cause with his upper-caste counterparts in America when his application for citizenship made it to the Supreme Court. Bhagat Singh Thind argued that he was Caucasian, Aryan in fact, descended from the same stock as Europeans, given that it was widely held that Aryans migrated south to India and formed that country's upper caste. It could be said that he had a more rightful claim to being Caucasian than the people judging him. After all, the Caucasus Mountains were next to Iran and closer to neighboring India than to western Europe.

The Court did not agree and rejected Thind's quest for citizenship in 1923. "It may be true that the blond Scandinavian and the brown Hindu have a common ancestor in the dim reaches of antiquity," wrote the Court, "but the average man knows perfectly well that there are unmistakable and profound differences between them today."

These decisions were a heartbreaking catastrophe for Asians seeking citizenship. With pro–western European sentiment running high, the government began rescinding the naturalized citizenship of people of Asian descent who were already here. This amounted to an abandonment of people who had lived legally in the United States for most of their adult lives, as would echo a century later with immigrants crossing the southern U.S. border with Mexico.

It could lead to tragic consequences. Vaishno Das Bagai, an Indian immigrant, had been in the United States for eight years by the time the Supreme Court ruled that Indians were not white and thus were ineligible for citizenship. He had a wife and three children and his own general store on Fillmore Street in San Francisco. He tended his store in three-piece suits and kept his hair cut short with a part on the side. Bagai lost his citizenship in the crackdown on nonwhite immigrants. He was then stripped of the business he had built, due to a California law restricting the economic rights of people who were not citizens. Shorn of a passport, he was then thwarted in his attempt to get back to India and was now a man without a country.

Far from his original home and rejected by his new one, he rented a room in San Jose, turned on the gas and took his life. He left a suicide note, in which he lamented the futility of all that he had sacrificed to come to America: "Obstacles this way, blockades that way, and bridges burnt behind."

No matter which route a borderline applicant took to gain acceptance, the caste system shape-shifted to keep the upper caste pure by its own terms. What a thin, frayed thread held the illusions together. A Japanese novelist once noted that, on paper anyway, it was a single apostrophe that stood between rejection and citizenship for a Japanese Ohara versus an Irish O'Hara. These cases laid bare not just the absurdity but the inaccuracy of these artificial labels and the perception of purity or pollution implied by them. At the same time, they exposed the unyielding rigidity of a caste system, defiant in the face of evidence contrary to its foundation, how it holds fast against the assault of logic.

Defining Purity and the Constancy of the Bottom Rung

As the middle castes pressed for admittance to the rungs above them, what was consistent was the absolute exclusion of the "polluting" lowest caste. African-Americans were not just *not* citizens, they were, like their Dalit counterparts in India, forced outside the social contract.

They and the Dalits bore the daily brunt of the taint ascribed to their very beings. The Dalits were not permitted to drink from the same cups as the dominant castes in India, live in the villages of the upper-caste people, walk through the front doors of upper-caste homes, and neither were African-Americans in much of the United States for most of its history. African-Americans in the South were required to walk through the side or back door of any white establishment they approached. Throughout the United States, sundown laws forbade them from being seen in white towns and neighborhoods after sunset, or risk assault or lynching. In bars and restaurants in the North, though they might be permitted to sit and eat, it was common for the bartender to make a show of smashing the glass that a black patron had just sipped from. Heads would turn as restaurant patrons looked to see where the crashing sound had come from and who had offended the sensibilities of caste pollution.

Untouchables were not allowed inside Hindu temples, and black Mormons in America, by way of example, were not allowed inside the temples of the religion they followed and could not become priests until 1978. Enslaved black people were prohibited from learning to read the Bible or any book for that matter, just as Untouchables were prohibited from learning Sanskrit and sacred texts. In churches in the South, black worshippers sat in the galleries or in the back rows, and, when such arrangements were inconvenient to the dominant caste, "the negroes must catch the gospel as it escapes through the windows and doors" from outside. To this day, Sunday morning has been called the most segregated hour in America.

Well into the civil rights era, the caste system excluded African-Americans from the daily activities of the general public in the South, the region where most of them lived. They knew to disregard any notice of a circus coming to town or of a political rally; those things were not intended for them. "They were driven from Independence Day parades," wrote the historian David Roediger, "as 'defilers' of the body politic."

What a British magistrate observed about the lowest castes in India could as well have been said of African-Americans. "They were not allowed to be present at the great national sacrifices, or at the feasts which followed them," wrote the colonial administrator and historian W. W. Hunter. "They could never rise out of their servile condition; and to them was assigned the severest toil in the fields."

Their exclusion was used to justify their exclusion. Their degraded station justified their degradation. They were consigned to the lowliest, dirtiest jobs and thus were seen as lowly and dirty, and everyone in the caste system absorbed the message of their degradation.

Well into the twentieth century, a panic could afflict people in the dominant caste if ever a breach occurred. A young dominant-caste man raised in the Depression-era South had been well taught the rules of the caste system and adhered to them as expected. When he went north in the mid-twentieth century and joined the military, he had to confront the mythologies of his upbringing.

"Strange things pop up at us like gargoyles when we are liberated from our delusions," the white southerner said.

Up north, on occasion, he found himself in situations where black people were permitted in the same work settings as whites.

"I thought I was entirely prepared, emotionally and intellectually," the man, an editor at *Look* magazine, recalled years later.

But he discovered that he was a captive of his own conditioning, which he called a certain madness.

Every time he reached the point where he had to shake hands with a black person, he felt an automatic revulsion that had been trained into him. He recoiled even though it had been black women who had bathed him as a child, had mixed the dough for his biscuits, and whose touch had not repulsed him when extended in servitude. But with presumed equals, "each time I shook hands with a Negro," he said, "I felt an urge to wash my hands. Every rational impulse, all that I considered best in myself struggled against this urge. But the hand that had touched the dark skin had a will of its own and would not be dissuaded from signaling it was unclean. That is what I mean by madness."

— —

Occupational Hierarchy: The Jatis and the Mudsill

When a house is being built, the single most important piece of the framework is the first wood beam hammered into place to anchor the foundation. That piece is called the mudsill, the sill plate that runs along the base of a house and bears the weight of the entire structure above it. The studs and subfloors, the ceilings and windows, the doors and roofing, all the components that make it a house, are built on top of the mudsill. In a caste system, the mudsill is the bottom caste that everything else rests upon.

A southern politician declared this central doctrine from the floor of the U.S. Senate in March 1858. "In all social systems, there must be a class to do the menial duties, to perform the drudgery of life," Sen. James Henry Hammond of South Carolina told his fellow senators. "That is a class requiring but a low order of intellect and but little skill. Its requisites are vigor, docility, fidelity. Such a class you must have. . . . It constitutes the very mud-sill of society."

He exulted in the cunning of the South, which, he said, had "found a race adapted to that purpose to her hand. . . . Our slaves are black, of another and inferior race. The status in which we have placed them is an elevation. They are elevated from the condition in which God first created them, by being made our slaves."

Hammond owned several plantations and more than three hundred souls, having acquired this fortune by marrying the plain and callow young daughter of a wealthy landowner in South Carolina. He rose to become governor of the state and a leading figure in the antebellum South. Well before making this speech, he had established himself as one of the more repugnant of men ever to rise to the Senate, one scholar calling him "nothing less than a monster." He is known to have repeatedly raped at least two of the women he enslaved, one of them believed to have been his daughter by another enslaved woman.

His political career was nearly derailed when it became public that he had sexually abused his four young nieces, their lives so ruined that none of them ever married after reaching adulthood. In his diary, he spoke blithely of the nieces, blaming them for the "intimacies." For these and other things, his wife left him, taking their children with her, only to later return. He rebounded from these malefactions to be elected to the U.S. Senate.

But he is best known for the speech that distilled the hierarchy of the South, which spread in spirit to the rest of the country, into a structure built on a mudsill. In so doing, he defined the fifth pillar of caste, the division of labor based on one's place in the hierarchy. Therein, he identified the economic purpose of a hierarchy to begin with, that is, to ensure that the tasks necessary for a society to function get handled whether or not people wish to do them, in this case, by being born to the disfavored sill plate.

In the Indian caste system, an infinitely more elaborate hierarchy, the subcaste, or *jati,* to which a person was born established the occupation their family fulfilled, from cleaners of latrines to priests in the temples. Those born to families who collected refuse or tanned the hides of animals or handled the dead were seen as the most polluted and lowest in the hierarchy, untouchable due to the dreaded and thankless though necessary task they were presumably born to fulfill.

Similarly, African-Americans, throughout most of their time in this land, were relegated to the dirtiest, most demeaning, and least desirable jobs by definition. After enslavement and well into the twentieth century, they were primarily restricted to the role of sharecroppers and servants—domestics, lawn boys, chauffeurs, and janitors. The most that those who managed to get an education could hope for was to teach, minister to, attend to the health needs of, or bury other subordinate-caste people.

"There is severe occupational deprivation in each country," wrote the scholars Sidney Verba, Bashiruddin Ahmed, and Anil Bhatt in a 1971 comparative study of India and the United States. "A deprivation—at least in terms of level—of roughly similar magnitude."

The state of South Carolina, right after the Civil War, explicitly prohibited black people from performing any labor other than farm or domestic work, setting their place in the caste system. The legislature decreed that "no person of color shall pursue or practice the art, trade or business of an artisan, mechanic or shop-keeper, or any other trade, employment or business (besides that of husbandry, or that of a servant under contract for labor) on his own account and for his own benefit until he shall have obtained a license from the judge of the district court, which license shall be good for one year only." The license was set at an intentionally prohibitive cost of $100 a year, the equivalent of $1,500 in 2018. This was a fee not required of the dominant caste, whose members, having not been enslaved for a quarter millennium, would have been in better position to afford.

The law went nominally out of effect during the decade known as Reconstruction, when the North took control of the former Confederacy, but it returned in spirit and custom after the North retreated and the former enslavers took power again, ready to avenge their defeat in the Civil War. In North Carolina, during slavery and into the era of sharecropping, people in the lowest caste were forbidden to sell or trade goods of any kind or be subject to thirty-nine lashes. This blocked the main route to earning money from their own farm labors and forced them into economic dependence on the dominant caste.

"The caste order that followed slavery defined the Negroes as workers and servants of the whites," wrote the scholar Edward Reuter. "The range of occupations was narrow, and many of those outside the orbit of common labor were closed to the Negroes."

The South foreclosed any route to a station higher than that assigned them. "Anything that causes the negro to aspire above the plow handle, the cook pot, in a word the functions of a servant," Gov. James K. Vardaman of Mississippi said, "will be the worst thing on earth for the negro. God Almighty designed him for a menial. He is fit for nothing else."

Those who managed to go north after the Civil War and in the bigger waves of the Great Migration, starting in World War I, found that they could escape the South but not their caste. They entered the North at the bottom, beneath southern and eastern Europeans who might not yet have learned English but who were permitted into unions and into better-served neighborhoods that barred black citizens whose labor had cleared the wilderness and built the country's wealth. While there was no federal law restricting people to certain occupations on the basis of race, statutes in the South and custom in the North kept lower-caste people in their place. Northern industries often hired African-Americans only as strikebreakers, and unions blocked them from entire trades reserved for whites, such as pipe fitters or plumbers. City inspectors would refuse to sign off on the work of black electricians. A factory in Milwaukee turned away black men seeking jobs as they walked toward the front gate. In New York and Philadelphia, black people were long denied licenses merely to drive carts.

"Every avenue for improvement was closed against him," wrote William A. Sinclair, author of a history of slavery and its aftermath, of the fate of the subordinate-caste man.

There were exceptions—those select enslaved people, often the children of slaveholders, who were permitted to serve as carpenters or blacksmiths or in other trades as would be required on large plantations like Thomas Jefferson's at Monticello.

In 1890, "85 percent of black men and 96 percent of black women were employed in just two occupational categories," wrote the sociologist Stephen Steinberg, "agriculture and domestic or personal service." Forty years later, as the Depression set in and as African-Americans moved to northern cities, the percentages of black people at the bottom of the labor hierarchy remained the same, though, by then, nearly half of black men were doing manual labor that called merely for a strong back. Only 5 percent were listed as white-collar workers—many of them ministers, teachers, and small business owners who catered to other black people.

North and south, the status of African-Americans was so well understood that people in the dominant caste were loath to perform duties they perceived as beneath their station. A British tourist in the 1810s noted that white Americans well knew which tasks were seen as befitting only black people. White paupers in Ohio "refused to carry water for their own use," wrote the historian David R. Roediger, "for fear of being considered 'like slaves.'"

The historic association between menial labor and blackness served to further entrap black people in a circle of subservience in the American mind. They were punished for being in the condition that they were forced to endure. And the image of servitude shadowed them into freedom.

As the caste system shape-shifted in the twentieth century, the dominant caste found ever more elaborate ways to enforce occupational hierarchy. "If white and colored persons are employed together," wrote the historian Bertram Doyle in the 1930s, "they do not engage in the same tasks, generally, and certainly not as equals. . . . Negroes are seldom, if ever, put into authority over white persons. Moreover, the Negro expects to remain in the lower ranks; rising, if at all, only over other Negroes." No matter how well he does his job, Doyle wrote, "he cannot often hope for promotion."

Your place was preordained before you were born. "A Negro

may become a locomotive fireman," Doyle wrote, "but never an engineer."

Thus, caste did not mean merely doing a certain kind of labor; it meant performing a dominant or subservient role. "There must be, then, a division of labor where the two races are employed, and menial labor is commonly supposed to be the division assigned to Negroes," Doyle wrote, "and he must look and act the part."

A black man in the 1930s was on his way to pay a visit to a young woman he fancied, which occasioned him to go into the town square. There, some white men approached him and "forced him to procure overalls, saying he was 'too dressed up for a weekday.'"

Slavery set the artificial parameters for the roles each caste was to perform, and the only job beyond the plow or the kitchen that the caste system openly encouraged of the lowest caste was that of entertainment, which was its own form of servitude in that world. It was in keeping with caste notions of their performing for the pleasure of the dominant caste. It affirmed the stereotypes of innate black physicality, of an earthiness based on animal instinct rather than human creativity and it presented no threat to dominant-caste supremacy in leadership and intellect.

Making enslaved people perform on command also reinforced their subjugation. They were made to sing despite their exhaustion or the agonies from a recent flogging or risk further punishment. Forced good cheer became a weapon of submission to assuage the guilt of the dominant caste and further humiliate the enslaved. If they were in chains and happy, how could anyone say that they were being mistreated? Merriment, even if extracted from a whip, was seen as essential to confirm that the caste structure was sound, that all was well, that everyone accepted, even embraced their station in the hierarchy. They were thus forced to cosign on their own degradation, to sing and dance even as they were being separated from spouses or children or parents at auction. "This was done to make them appear cheerful and happy," wrote William Wells Brown, a speculator's assistant before the Civil War, whose job it was to get the human merchandise into sellable condition. "I have often set them to dancing," he said, "when their cheeks were wet with tears."

African-Americans would later convert the performance role that they were forced to occupy—and the talent they built from it—into prominence in entertainment and in American culture disproportionate to their numbers. Since the early twentieth century, the wealthiest African-Americans—from Louis Armstrong to Muhammad Ali—have traditionally been entertainers and athletes. Even now, in a 2020 ranking of the richest African-Americans, seventeen of the top twenty—from Oprah Winfrey to Jay-Z to Michael Jordan—made their wealth as innovators, and then moguls, in the entertainment industry or in sports.

Historically, this group would come to dominate the realm carved out for them, often celebrated unless they went head to head against an upper-caste person, as did the black boxer Jack Johnson when he unexpectedly knocked out James Jeffries in 1910. The writer Jack London had coaxed Jeffries out of retirement to fight Johnson in an era of virulent race hatred, and the press stoked passions by calling Jeffries "the Great White Hope." Jeffries's loss on that Fourth of July was an affront to white supremacy, and triggered riots across the country, north and south, including eleven separate ones in New York City, where whites set fire to black neighborhoods and tried to lynch two black men over the defeat. The message was that, even in an arena into which the lowest caste had been permitted, they were to know and remain in their place.

For centuries, enslaved people had been ordered to perform at the whim of the master, either to be mocked in the master's parlor games or to play music for their balls, in addition to their hard labors in the field. "Menial and comic roles were the chief ones allotted to Negroes in their relationships with white people," wrote the anthropologists W. Lloyd Warner and Allison Davis of slavery-based caste relations that worked their way into American culture.

The caste system took comfort in black caricature as it upheld the mythology of a simple, court jester race whose jolly natures shielded them from any true suffering. The images soothed the conscience and justified atrocities. And thus minstrelsy, in which white actors put burnt cork on their faces and mocked the subordinate caste, became a popular entertainment as the Jim Crow regime hardened after slavery ended. Whites continued the practice at fraternity parties and talent shows and Halloween festivities well into the twenty-first century.

At the same time, black entertainers have long been rewarded and often restricted to roles that adhere to caste stereotype. The first African-American to win an Academy Award, Hattie McDaniel, was commended for her role as Mammy, a solicitous and obesely desexed counterpoint to Scarlett O'Hara, the feminine ideal, in the 1939 film *Gone with the Wind*. The Mammy character was more devoted to her white family than to her own, willing to fight black soldiers to protect her white enslaver.

That trope became a comforting staple in film portrayals of slavery, but it was an ahistorical figment of caste imagination. Under slavery, most black women were thin, gaunt even, due to the meager rations provided them, and few worked inside a house, as they were considered more valuable in the field. Yet the rotund and cheerful slave or maidservant was what the dominant caste preferred to see, and McDaniel and other black actresses of the era found that those were the only roles they could get. Because many of these women had been raised in the North or the West, they knew little of the southern Negro vernacular that scripts called for and had to learn how to speak in the exaggerated, at times farcical, way that Hollywood directors imagined that black people talked.

This mainstream derision belies the serious history of arbitrary abuse of African-Americans under slavery when their degradation was entertainment for the dominant caste. In one case, two planters in South Carolina were dining together at one of their plantations. The two were passing the time, discussing their slaves and debating whether the slaves had the capacity for genuine religious faith. The visiting planter said he didn't much believe they did.

The planter who was hosting begged to differ.

"I have a slave who I believe would rather die than deny his Saviour," he said.

The guest ridiculed the host and challenged him to prove it. So the host summoned an enslaved man of his and ordered him to deny his faith in the Lord Jesus Christ. The enslaved man affirmed his faith in Jesus and pleaded to be excused. The master, seeking to drive home his point to the fellow slaveowner, kept asking the man to deny Jesus, and the man, as expected, kept declaring his faith. The host then whipped the enslaved man, now for disobedience, and continued to whip him, the whip cord cutting to bone. The enslaved man of faith "died in consequence of this severe infliction."

Similarly, soldiers of the Third Reich used weakened and malnourished Jewish prisoners for entertainment. An SS squad leader, who oversaw the construction of the firing range at Sachsenhausen, forced prisoners to jump and turn like dancing bears around a shovel for his amusement. One of them refused to dance and, for this, the SS squad leader took the shovel and beat him to death with it.

Every act, every gesture, was calculated for the purpose of reminding the subordinate caste, in these otherwise unrelated caste systems, of the dominant caste's total reign over their very being. The upper caste, wrote the nineteenth-century author William Goodell, made "the claim of absolute proprietorship in the human soul itself."

Dehumanization and Stigma

Dehumanization is a standard component in the manufacture of an out-group against which to pit an in-group, and it is a monumental task. It is a war against truth, against what the eye can see and what the heart could feel if allowed to do so on its own.

To dehumanize another human being is not merely to declare that someone is not human, and it does not happen by accident. It is a process, a programming. It takes energy and reinforcement to deny what is self-evident in another member of one's own species.

It is harder to dehumanize a single person standing in front of you, wiping away tears at the loss of a loved one, just as you would, or wincing in pain from a fall as you would, laughing at an unexpected double entendre as you might. It is harder to dehumanize a single individual that you have gotten the chance to know. Which is why people and groups who seek power and division do not bother with dehumanizing an individual. Better to attach a stigma, a taint of pollution to an entire group.

Dehumanize the group, and you have completed the work

of dehumanizing any single person within it. Dehumanize the group, and you have quarantined them from the masses you choose to elevate and have programmed everyone, even some of the targets of dehumanization, to no longer believe what their eyes can see, to no longer trust their own thoughts. Dehumanization distances not only the out-group from the in-group, but those in the in-group from their own humanity. It makes slaves to groupthink of everyone in the hierarchy. A caste system relies on dehumanization to lock the marginalized outside of the norms of humanity so that any action against them is seen as reasonable.

Both Nazi Germany and the United States reduced their out-groups, Jews and African-Americans, respectively, to an undifferentiated mass of nameless, faceless scapegoats, the shock absorbers of the collective fears and setbacks of each nation. Germany blamed Jews for the loss of World War I, for the shame and economic straits that befell the country after its defeat, and the United States blamed African-Americans for many of its social ills. In both cases, individuals were lumped together for sharing a single, stigmatizing trait, made indistinct and indistinguishable in preparation for the exploitation and atrocities that would be inflicted upon them. Individuals were no longer individuals. Individuality, after all, is a luxury afforded the dominant caste. Individuality is the first distinction lost to the stigmatized.

We are sorrowfully aware of the monstrously swift murder of 6 million Jews and 5 million others during the Holocaust. What we may not be as familiar with are the circumstances leading up to that horror and the millions who suffered in the labor camps of the Third Reich, the process of dehumanization before any of those atrocities could be conducted and the inter-connectedness not just of humanity but of evil within it.

Held hostage in labor camps in different centuries and an ocean apart, both Jews and African-Americans were subjected to a program of purposeful dehumanization. Upon their arrival at the concentration camps, Jews were stripped of the clothing and accoutrements of their former lives, of everything they had owned. Their heads were shaved; their distinguishing features of sideburns or mustaches or the crowns of lush hair were deleted from them. They were no longer individuals, they were no longer personalities to consider, to engage with, to take into account.

During the morning and evening roll calls, they were forced to stand sometimes for hours into the night as the SS officers counted the thousands of them to check for any escapees. They stood in the freezing cold or summer heat in the same striped uniforms, with the same shorn heads, same sunken cheeks. They became a single mass of self-same bodies, purposely easier for SS officers to distance themselves from, to feel no human connection with. Loving fathers, headstrong nephews, beloved physicians, dedicated watchmakers, rabbis, and piano tuners all merged into a single mass of undifferentiated bodies that were no longer seen as humans deserving of empathy but as objects over whom they could exert total control and do whatever they wanted to. They were no longer people, they were numbers, a means to an end.

Upon their arrival at the auction blocks and labor camps of the American South, Africans were stripped of their given names and forced to respond to new ones, as would a dog to a new owner, often mocking names like Caesar or Samson or

Dred. They were stripped of their past lives and identities as Yoruba or Asante or Igbo, as the son of a fisherman, nephew of the village priest, or daughter of a midwife. Decades afterward, Jews were stripped of their given and surnames and forced to memorize the prison numbers assigned them in the concentration camps. Millennia ago, the Untouchables of India were assigned surnames that identified them by the lowly work they performed, forcing them to announce their degradation every time they introduced themselves, while the Brahmins, many quite literally, carried the names of the gods.

In the two more modern caste systems, at labor camps in central and eastern Europe and in the American South, well-fed captors forced their hostages to do the heaviest work of inhuman exertion, while withholding food from those whose labors enriched the captors, providing barely enough to sustain the human metabolism, the bare minimum for human subsistence. The Nazis approached human deprivation as a science. They calculated the number of calories required for a certain task, say, chopping down trees and digging up stumps, and fed those laborers one or two hundred calories fewer as a cost savings and to keep them too weak to fight back as they slowly starved to death.

Southern planters provided their African captives, who were doing the hardest labor in the hierarchy, the least nutrients of anyone on the plantation. Both groups were rarely allowed protein, restricted to feed rather than food, some taunted with the extravagance of their captors' multi-course feasts.

They were under the complete control and at the whim of their captors, who took every chance to reassert their debasement. Jews were given prison uniforms of coarse fabric in sizes that were purposely too big or too small. Enslaved African-Americans were allotted garments of coarse gray cloth, a cross between an "undergarment and an ordinary potato bag," that was made "without regard to the size of the particular individual to whom it was allotted, like penitentiary uniforms."

Beyond all of this, the point of a dehumanization campaign was the forced surrender of the target's own humanity, a karmic theft beyond accounting. Whatever was considered a natural human reaction was disallowed for the subordinate caste. During the era of enslavement, they were forbidden to cry as their children were carried off, forced to sing as a wife or husband was sold away, never again to look into their eyes or hear their voice for as long as the two might live.

They were punished for the very responses a human being would be expected to have in the circumstances forced upon them. Whatever humanity shone through them was an affront to what the dominant caste kept telling itself. They were punished for being the humans that they could not help but be.

In India, Dalits, suffering the deprivations of their lowly status, were nonetheless beaten to death if ever they stole food for the sustenance denied them. As with African-Americans during the time of enslavement, it was a crime for Dalits to learn to read and write, "punishable by cutting off their tongue or by pouring molten lead into the ear of the offender," wrote V. T. Rajshekar, editor of *Dalit Voice*.

In the United States, African-Americans, denied pay for their labors during slavery and barely paid afterward in the twentieth century, were whipped or lynched for stealing food, for the accusation of stealing seventy-five cents, for trying to stand up for themselves or appearing to question a person in the dominant caste. In Nazi labor camps, one of the many cruel details a prisoner could be assigned was to work in the bakery. There, day in and day out, starving captives, forced to subsist on rations of watery nettle or beet soup, kneaded and baked the breads and pastries for their SS tormenters. They were surrounded by the scent of fresh-rising dough but risked a beating or worse if caught taking a crust of bread.

In America, slave auctions became public showcases for the dehumanization project of caste-making. As the most valuable liquid assets in the land, combined, worth more than land itself, enslaved people were ordered to put on a cheery face to bring a higher profit to the dominant-caste sellers who were breaking up their families. Women were forced to disrobe before the crowd, to submit to hours of physical probing by roughhousing men who examined their teeth, their hands, or whatever other parts of their bodies the potential bidders decided to inspect. Their bodies did not belong to them but to the dominant caste to do whatever it wished and however it wished to do it. At auction, they were to answer any question put to them with "a smiling, cheerful countenance" or be given thirty lashes for not selling themselves well enough to the seller's satisfaction.

"When spoken to, they must reply quickly and with a smile on their lips," recalled John Brown, a survivor of slavery, who was sold away from his own mother and subjected to these scenes many times thereafter. "Here may be seen husbands separated from their wives, only by the width of the room, and children from their parents, one or both, witnessing the driving of the bargain that is to tear them asunder for ever, yet not a word of lamentation or anguish must escape from them; nor when the deed is consummated, dare they bid one another good-bye, or take one last embrace."

• • •

In the United States, there developed two parallel worlds existing on the same plane with flagrant double standards to emphasize the purposeful injustices built into the system. Presaging the disparities that led to mass incarceration in our era, the abolitionist minister William Goodell observed the quandary of black people in antebellum America. "He is accounted criminal for acts which are deemed innocent in others," Goodell wrote in 1853, "punished with a severity from which all others are exempted. He is under the control of the law, though unprotected by the law, and can know law only as an enemy."

In Virginia, there were seventy-one offenses that carried the death penalty for enslaved people but only imprisonment when committed by whites, such as stealing a horse or setting fire to bales of grain. Something as ordinary to most humans as a father helping a son with his lessons was prohibited. A black father in Georgia could "be flogged for teaching his own child" to read. Free black people were forbidden to carry firearms, testify against a white person, or raise a hand against one even in self-defense.

"Richmond required that Negroes and mulattoes must step aside when whites passed by, and barred them from riding in carriages except in the capacity of menials," the historian Kenneth Stampp wrote. "Charleston slaves could not swear, smoke, walk with a cane, assemble at military parades, or make joyful demonstrations."

Just as enslaved and malnourished Africans had to drain the swamps, chop down the trees, clear the land to build the plantations and infrastructure of the South, the starving captives of the Third Reich had to drain the swamps, chop down the trees, dig up the tree roots, carry the logs to build the infrastructure of their torment. They worked the clay pits and quarries to make bricks for the Reich. Under both regimes, the hostages built the walls that would imprison them and often died as they did so.

Each day during the early years of Nazi expansion, some two thousand prisoners were marched through the village of Oranienburg, north of Berlin, over the canal bridge, from the concentration camp to the clay pits, and would often return that evening with a cart filled with the people who had died of exhaustion or had been killed that day.

• • •

At the depths of their dehumanization, both Jews and African-Americans were subjected to gruesome medical experimentation at the hands of dominant-caste physicians. In addition to the horrifying torture of twins, German scientists and SS doctors conducted more than two dozen types of experiments on Jews and others they held captive, such as infecting their victims with mustard gas and testing the outer limits of hypothermia.

In the United States, from slavery well into the twentieth century, doctors used African-Americans as a supply chain for experimentation, as subjects deprived of either consent or anesthesia. Scientists injected plutonium into them, purposely let diseases like syphilis go untreated to observe the effects, perfected the typhoid vaccine on their bodies, and subjected them to whatever agonizing experiments came to the doctors' minds.

These amounted to unchecked assaults on human beings. One plantation doctor, according to the medical ethicist Harriet A. Washington in her groundbreaking book *Medical Apartheid,* made incisions into a black baby's head to test a theory for curing seizures. The doctor opened the baby's skull with cobbler's tools, puncturing the scalp, as he would later report, "with the point of a crooked awl."

That doctor, James Marion Sims, would later be heralded as the founding father of gynecology. He came to his discoveries by acquiring enslaved women in Alabama and conducting savage surgeries that often ended in disfigurement or death. He refused to administer anesthesia, saying vaginal surgery on them was "not painful enough to justify the trouble." Instead, he administered morphine only after surgery, noting that it "relieves the scalding of the urine," and, as Washington writes, "weakened the will to resist repeated procedures."

A Louisiana surgeon perfected the cesarean section by experimenting on the enslaved women he had access to in the 1830s. Others later learned how to remove ovaries and bladder stones. They performed these slave cabin experiments in search of breakthroughs for their white patients who would one day undergo surgery in hospitals and under the available anesthesia.

Their total control over black bodies gave them unfettered access to the anatomy of live subjects that would otherwise be closed to them. Sims, for example, would force a woman to disrobe and get on her knees on a table. He would then allow other doctors to take turns with the speculum to force her open, and invite leading men in town and apprentices in to see for themselves. He later wrote, "I saw everything as no man had seen before."

• • •

In America, a culture of cruelty crept into the minds, made violence and mockery seem mundane and amusing, built as it was into the games of chance at carnivals and county fairs well into the twentieth century. These things built up the immune system against empathy. There was an attraction called the "Coon Dip," in which fairgoers hurled "projectiles at live African Americans." There was the "Bean-em," in which children flung beanbags at grotesquely caricatured black faces, whose images alone taught the lesson of caste without a word needing to be spoken.

And enthusiasts lined up to try their luck at the "Son of Ham" shows at Coney Island or Kansas City or out in California, "in which white men paid for the pleasure of hurling baseballs at the head of a black man," Smith wrote.

A certain kind of violence was part of an unspoken curriculum for generations of children in the dominant caste. "White culture desensitized children to racial violence," wrote the historian Kristina DuRocher, "so they could perpetuate it themselves one day."

PILLAR NUMBER SEVEN

———

Terror as Enforcement, Cruelty as a Means of Control

The only way to keep an entire group of sentient beings in an artificially fixed place, beneath all others and beneath their own talents, is with violence and terror, psychological and physical, to preempt resistance before it can be imagined. Evil asks little of the dominant caste other than to sit back and do nothing. All that it needs from bystanders is their silent complicity in the evil committed on their behalf, though a caste system will protect, and perhaps even reward, those who deign to join in the terror.

Jews in Nazi-controlled Europe, African-Americans in the antebellum and Jim Crow South, and Dalits in India were all at the mercy of people who had been fed a diet of contempt and hate for them, and had incentive to try to prove their superiority by joining in or acquiescing to cruelties against their fellow humans.

Above all, the people in the subordinate caste were to be reminded of the absolute power the dominant caste held over them. In both America and in Germany, people in the dominant caste whipped and hanged their hostages for random and capricious breaches of caste, punished them for the natural human responses to the injustice they were being subjected to. In America, "the whip was the most common instrument of punishment," the historian Kenneth Stampp wrote. "Nearly every slaveholder used it, and few grown slaves escaped it entirely."

In Germany, the Nazis forced and strapped Jews and political prisoners onto a wooden board to be flogged for minor infractions like rolling cigarettes from leaves they gathered or killing rats to augment their bare rations. The captives were forced to count out each lash as it was inflicted upon them. The Nazis claimed a limit of twenty-five lashes, but would play mind games by claiming that the victim had not counted correctly, then extend the torture even longer. The Americans went to as many as four hundred lashes, torture that amounted to murder, with several men, growing exhausted from the physical exertion it required, taking turns with the whip.

In the New World, few living creatures were, as a class of beings, subjected to the level of brute physical assault as a feature of their daily lives for as many centuries as were the subjects of American slavery. It was so commonplace that some overseers, upon arriving at a new plantation, summarily chose "to whip every hand on the plantation to let them know who was in command," Stampp wrote. "Some used it as incentive by flogging the last slave out of the cabin in the morning. Many used it to 'break in' a young slave and to 'break the spirit' of an insubordinate older one."

A teenager endured a whipping that went on for so long, he passed out in the middle of it. "He woke up vomiting," the historian Edward Baptist recounted. "They were still beating him. He slipped into darkness again."

One enslaver remarked "that he was no better pleased than when he could hear . . . the sound of the driver's lash among the toiling slaves," for then, Baptist wrote, "he knew his system was working."

After slavery ended, the former Confederates took power again, but now without the least material investment in the lives of the people they once had owned. They pressed down even harder to keep the lowest caste in its place. African-Americans were mutilated and hanged from poplars and sycamores and burned at the courthouse square, a lynching every three or four days in the first four decades of the twentieth century.

A slaveholder in North Carolina seemed to speak for the enforcers of caste throughout the world. "Make them stand in fear," she said.

• • •

The dominant caste demonstrated its power by forcing captives to perform some of the more loathsome duties connected to the violence against their fellow captives. People in the upper caste did not often trouble themselves with the dirty work, unless specifically hired for the job of enforcement, as were the plantation overseers in the American South. It was caste privilege to order the lowest caste to do their bidding and dirty work.

It was part of the psychological degradation that reinforced one's own stigma and utter subjugation, so dominated that they were left with little choice but to cooperate if they were to save themselves for one more day. The Nazis in Germany and the planters in the authoritarian South sowed dissension among the subordinate caste by creating a hierarchy among the captives, rewarding those who identified more with the oppressor rather than the oppressed and who would report back to them any plots of escape or uprising. They would select a captive they felt they could control and elevate that person above the others.

In Nazi labor camps, it was the *kapo,* the head Jew in each hut of captives, whose job it was to get everyone up by five in the morning and to exact discipline. In exchange, he would get a bunk of his own or other meager privileges. In the American South, it was the slave driver, the head Negro, who served this role, setting the pace for the work at hand and elevated with the task of watching over the others and disciplining them when called to do so.

The dominant caste often forced its captives to exact punishment on one another or to dispose of the victims as their tormenters watched. In Nazi Germany, the SS guards were not the ones who put the prisoners into the ovens. The captives were forced into that grim detail. It was not the SS who collected the bodies of the people who had died the night before. That was left to the captives. In the American South, black men were made to whip their fellow slaves or to hold down the legs and arms of the man, woman, or child being flogged. Later, when lynchings were the primary means of terror, it was the people who had done the lynching who told the family of the victim or the black undertaker when they would be permitted to take down what was left of the body from the lynching tree.

• • •

One day in the mid-eighteenth century, an elder of the Presbyterian Church was passing through a piece of timbered land in a slaving province of the American South when he heard what he called "a sound as of murder." He rode in that direction and discovered "a naked black man, hung to the limb of a tree by his hands, his feet chained together and a pine rail laid with one end on the chain, between his legs, and the other upon the ground to steady him." The overseer had administered four hundred lashes on the man's body. "The miserably lacerated slave was then taken down and put to the care of a physician," the Presbyterian elder said.

The elder asked the overseer, one of the men who had inflicted this upon another human being, "the offence for which all this was done." He was told that the enslaved man had made a comment that was seen as beyond his station. It began when the owner said that the rows of corn the enslaved man had planted were uneven. The enslaved man offered his opinion. "Massa, much corn grow on a crooked row as a straight one," the enslaved man replied. For that, he was flogged to the brink of death.

"This was it, this was enough," the Presbyterian elder said. The overseer boasted of his skill in managing the master's property. The enslaved man "was submitted to him, and treated as above."

A century later, slavery was over, but the rules, and the consequences for breaking them, were little changed. A young white anthropologist from Yale University, John Dollard, went south to the Mississippi Delta in 1935 for his research into the Jim Crow caste system. He noticed how subservient the black people were, stepping aside for him, taking their hats off, and calling him "sir" even if they were decades older.

One day he was out riding with some other white men, southern white men, who were checking out some black share-croppers. The black people were reluctant to come out of their cabins when the car with the white men pulled up. The driver had some fun with it, told the sharecroppers he was not going to hang them. Later, Dollard mentioned to the man that "the Negroes seem to be very polite around here."

The man let out a laugh. "They have to be."

Inherent Superiority
versus Inherent Inferiority

The Hollywood still is from a 1930s movie released during the depths of the Jim Crow era. A black woman, ample in frame and plain of face, wears a headscarf and servant's uniform. Her arms are wrapped around a white woman, slender, cherubic, and childlike, her golden hair and porcelain, air-brushed skin pops against the purposely unadorned darkness of the black woman. When they begin to speak, the dark woman will utter backward syllables of servility and ignorance. The porcelain woman will speak with the mannered refinement of the upper caste. The fragile frame of Mary Pickford is in direct contrast to the heft of Louise Beavers in a set piece of caste played out in a thousand films and images in America, implanting into our minds the inherent superiority in beauty, deservedness, and intellect of one group over another.

As it happens, the black actress, Louise Beavers, was nothing like the image she was given little option but to play. She grew up in California and had to learn and to master the broken dialect of southern field hands and servants. She was frequently under stress in the narrow box she was confined to, which led her to lose weight on set. The filmmakers made her attach padding to her already full frame, to ensure that she contrasted all the more with the waifish white ingenues who were the stars of whatever film she was in.

Beneath each pillar of caste was the presumption and continual reminder of the inborn superiority of the dominant caste and the inherent inferiority of the subordinate. It was not enough that the designated groups be separated for reasons of "pollution" or that they not intermarry or that the lowest people suffer due to some religious curse, but that it must be understood in every interaction that one group was superior and inherently deserving of the best in a given society and that those who were deemed lowest were deserving of their plight.

For the lowest-caste person, "his unquestioned inferiority had to be established," wrote the anthropologists Audrey and Brian Smedley, and that alleged inferiority would become the "basis for his allocation to permanent servile status."

African-Americans during the century of the Jim Crow regime and Jews during the murderous twelve years of the Third Reich were often prohibited from sidewalks and were forced instead to give way to the dominant caste or to walk in the gutter as a reminder of their degraded station.

"If a Negro, man or woman, met a white person on the street in Richmond, Virginia," for example, wrote the historian Bertram Doyle, they were "required to 'give the wall,' and if necessary to get off the sidewalk into the street, on pain of punishment with stripes on the bare back."

During the height of the caste systems in America, in India, and in the Third Reich, the lowest caste was not permitted to bear the symbols of success and status reserved for the upper caste. They were not to be dressed better than the upper caste, not to drive better cars than the upper caste, not to have homes more extravagant than the upper caste should they manage to secure them.

In India, the caste system dictated the length and folds of a Dalit woman's saris. Dalits were not to wear the clothing or jewelry of upper-caste people but rather tattered, rougher clothing as the "marks of their inferiority."

In America, the South Carolina Negro Code of 1735 went so far as to specify the fabrics enslaved black people were permitted to wear, forbidding any that might be seen as above their station. They were banned from wearing "any sort of garment or apparel whatsoever, finer, other or of greater value than Negro cloth, duffels, coarse kerseys, osnabrigs, blue linen, check linen, or coarse garlix, or calicoes," the cheapest, roughest fabrics available to the colony. Two hundred years later, the spirit of that law was still in force as African-American soldiers were set upon and killed for wearing their army uniforms.

In Germany, one of the characteristics that enraged the Nazis was the wealth and success of German Jews and any public display of it. Late in the Second World War, a young Jewish woman in Berlin had on a fur coat when the Gestapo rounded her and others up and shoved them onto cattle cars to the concentration camps. Upon arrival, the SS were incensed to see a Jewish woman in fur that their wives could likely not afford, and, out of hatred, forced her into the camp's pigsty and rolled her in her fur coat, over and over, in the icy muck, leaving her to die in the bitter cold. But this was just days before the Allied forces reached them, and this was how she survived, eating the food scraps thrown into the sty. She huddled beside the pigs and stayed warm until liberation.

· · ·

From the beginning, the power of caste and the superior status of the dominant group was perhaps never clearer than when the person deemed superior was unquestionably not. Given that intelligence is distributed in relatively similar proportions among individuals in any subset, it was a special form of human abuse that everyone in a particular group, regardless of intellect, morality, ethics, or humaneness, was automatically accorded control over everyone in another group, regardless of their gifts.

The historian Kenneth Stampp described the arbitrary nature of life for enslaved people in the caste system, the terrifying forced submission to individuals who were unfit for absolute power over the life and death of another. "They were owned by a woman 'unable to read or write,'" Stampp wrote, "'scarcely able to count to ten,' legally incompetent to contract marriage," and yet had to submit to her sovereignty, depend upon her for their next breath. They were owned by "drunkards, such as Lilburne Lewis, of Livingston County, Kentucky, who once chopped a slave to bits with an ax," Stampp wrote; "and by sadists, such as Madame Lalaurie, of New Orleans, who tortured her slaves for her own amusement."

In order to survive, "they were to give way to the most wretched white man," observed *The Farmers' Register* of 1834. They had to adjust themselves to the shifting and arbitrary demands of whatever dominant person they happened to be encountering in that moment.

This created a nerve-jangling existence, given that "any number of acts," according to a North Carolina judge during the time of slavery, could be read as "insolence," whether it was "a look, the pointing of a finger, a refusal or neglect to step out of the way when a white person is seen to approach."

To these, the nineteenth-century orator Frederick Douglass added the following gestures that could incite white rage and violence. "In the tone of an answer," Douglass wrote, "in answering at all; in not answering; in the expression of countenance; in the motion of the head; in the gait, manner and bearing." Any one of these, "if tolerated, would destroy that subordination, upon which our social system rests," the North Carolina judge said.

This code extended for generations. Years after the Nazis were defeated across the Atlantic, African-Americans were still being brutalized for the least appearance of stepping out of their place. Planters routinely whipped their sharecroppers for "trivial offenses," wrote Allison Davis and Burleigh and Mary Gardner in 1941. A planter in Mississippi said that, if his tenant "didn't stop acting so big, the next time it would be the bullet or a rope. That is the way to manage them when they get too big." In 1948, a black tenant farmer in Louise, Mississippi, was severely beaten by two whites, wrote the historian James C. Cobb, "because he asked for a receipt after paying his water bill."

The most trivial interaction had to be managed with ranking in mind. Well into the 1960s in the American South, the mere boarding of a public bus was a tightly choreographed affair devised for maximum humiliation and stigma to the lowest caste. Unlike dominant-caste passengers who climbed aboard, paid their bus fare, and took a seat, black passengers had to climb up, pay their fare, then get off the bus so as not to pollute or disturb the white section by walking through it. Having been forced to disembark after paying, they then had to run to the back door of the bus to board in the colored section. It was not uncommon for the bus to drive off before they could make it to the back door. The passengers who had the least room for error, the least resources to lose the benefit of the ticket they had paid for, the least cushion to weather a setback, would now be humiliated as the bus pulled off without them, now likely to arrive late for work, thus putting already tenuous jobs at further risk.

"The Negro occupies a position of inferiority and servility, of which he is constantly reminded when traveling, by restriction and by the attitudes of his white neighbors," wrote the historian Bertram Doyle.

The laws and protocols kept them both apart and low. The greater the chasm, the easier to distance and degrade, the easier to justify any injustice or depravity.

"The human meaning of caste for those who live it is power and vulnerability, privilege and oppression, honor and denigration, plenty and want, reward and deprivation, security and anxiety," wrote the preeminent American scholar of caste, Gerald Berreman. "A description of caste which fails to convey this is a travesty."

In the slaveholding South, some in the dominant caste grew so accustomed to the embedded superiority built into their days, and the brutality that it took to maintain it, that they wondered how they might manage in the afterlife. "Is it possible that any of my slaves could go to Heaven," a dominant-caste woman in South Carolina asked her minister, "and I must see them there?"

· · ·

A century after the slaveholder spoke those words, the caste system had survived and mutated, its pillars intact. America was fighting in World War II, and the public school district in Columbus, Ohio, decided to hold an essay contest, challenging students to consider the question "What to do with Hitler after the War?"

It was the spring of 1944, the same year that a black boy was forced to jump to his death, in front of his stricken father, over the Christmas card the boy had sent to a white girl at work. In that atmosphere, a sixteen-year-old African-American girl thought about what should befall Hitler. She won the student essay contest with a single sentence: "Put him in a black skin and let him live the rest of his life in America."

Part Four

———

The Tentacles of Caste

Brown Eyes versus Blue Eyes

The third-graders fidgeted in their seats and rested their chins on their folded forearms as their teacher, Mrs. Elliott, told them the rules of a class experiment she wanted to try with them. This was in the farm town of Riceville, Iowa, in the late 1960s, and all of the children, the descendants of immigrants from Germany and Scotland and Ireland and Scandinavia, had roughly the same skin color as their teacher and, from afar, little by which to distinguish one from another. But after the assassination of Martin Luther King, Jr., and the turmoil that followed beyond the cornfields that surrounded them, Jane Elliott decided she needed to do something out of the ordinary to teach her dominant-caste students how it felt to be judged on the basis of an arbitrary physical trait—the color of their eyes.

She announced to the children that they would do things differently that day. She laid out arbitrary stereotypes for a neutral trait that, for now, in her classroom, would put a student with that trait in essentially the lowest caste. She told the children that brown-eyed people are not as good as blue-eyed people, that they are slower than blue-eyed people, not as smart as blue-eyed people, that, until she said otherwise, the brown-eyed students would not be allowed to drink from the water fountain, that they had to use paper cups instead. She told the children that the brown-eyed people could not play with the blue-eyed people on the playground and would have to come in early, but that the blue-eyed students would get to stay out longer for recess.

The students looked confused at first. Then, in a matter of minutes, a caste hierarchy formed. It started as soon as the teacher told the children to open their books to a certain page to begin their lesson.

"Everyone ready?" Mrs. Elliott asked the class. One little girl was still turning the pages in her book to get to the right one. The teacher looked at the girl, her eyes judging and impatient. "Everyone but Laurie," Mrs. Elliott said with exasperation. "Ready, Laurie?"

A blue-eyed boy interjected. "She's a brown-eyed," he said, having caught on instantly to the significance of what had never mattered for as long as he had known the girl.

When lunchtime approached, the teacher told the blue-eyed children they would get to eat first and would be permitted a second helping, but the brown-eyed children weren't allowed to.

"They might take too much," the teacher told them.

The brown-eyed children looked downcast and defeated. One boy got into a fight at recess because one of the blue-eyed boys had called him a name.

"What did he call you?" the teacher asked him.

"Brown eyes," the boy said, tears at the surface of those eyes.

An otherwise neutral trait had been converted into a disability. The teacher later switched roles, and the blue-eyed children became the scapegoat caste, with the same caste behavior that had arisen the day before between these artificially constructed upper and lower castes.

"Seems when we were down on the bottom, everything bad was happening to us," one girl said. "The way you're treated you felt like you didn't want to try to do anything," said another.

Classroom performance fell for both groups of students during the few hours that they were relegated to the subordinate caste. The brown-eyed students took twice as long to finish a phonics exercise the day that they were made to feel inferior.

"I watched my students become what I told them they were," she told NBC News decades later.

When the brown-eyed children were put on a pedestal and made dominant, Elliott told the network, she saw "little wonderful brown-eyed white people become vicious, ugly, nasty, discriminating, domineering people in the space of fifteen minutes."

With the blue-eyed children scapegoated and subordinated, "I watched brilliant, blue-eyed, white Christian children become timid and frightened and angry and unable to learn in the space of fifteen minutes," she said.

"If you do that with a whole group of people for a lifetime," she said, "you change them psychologically. You convince those who are analogous to the brown-eyed people that they are superior, that they are perfect, that they have the right to rule, and you convince those who take the place of the blue-eyed students that they are less than. If you do that for a lifetime, what do you suppose that does to them?"

CHAPTER TEN

Dominant Group Status Threat
and the Precarity of the Highest Rung

In late 2015, two economists at Princeton University announced the startling revelation that the death rates of middle-aged white Americans, especially less-educated white Americans at midlife, had risen for the first time since 1950. The perplexing results of this study on mortality rates in the United States sounded alarms on the front pages of newspapers and at the top of news feeds across the nation.

The surge in early deaths among middle-aged white people went counter to the trends of every other ethnic group in America. Even historically marginalized black and Latino Americans had seen their mortality rates fall during the time period studied, from 1998 to 2013. The rise in the white death rate was at odds with prevailing trends in the rest of the Western world.

Americans had enjoyed increasing longevity the previous century, with each succeeding generation, due to healthier lifestyles and advancements in medicine. But starting just before the turn of the twenty-first century, the death rates among middle-aged white Americans, ages forty-five to fifty-four, began to rise, as the least educated, in particular, succumbed to suicide, drug overdoses, and liver disease from alcohol abuse, according to the authors of the seminal study, Anne Case and the Nobel laureate Angus Deaton. These "deaths of despair," as the economists called them, accounted for the loss of some half a million white Americans during that period, more than the number of American soldiers who died during World War II. These are people who might still be alive had this group kept to previous generational trends.

"These are deaths that do not have to happen," Case said at a conference on inequality. "These are people who are taking their lives, either slowly or quickly."

What could account for the worsening prospects of this group of Americans, unique in the Western world and singular even in the United States?

The authors noted that, since the 1970s, real wages had stagnated for blue-collar workers, leading to economic insecurity and to a generation less well off than previous ones. But they acknowledged that similar stagnation had occurred in other Western countries. They noted that comparable Western countries had a more generous safety net that could offer protections not available in the United States. Yet white Americans would not be the only group affected by wage stagnation and a thin safety net. Blue-collar workers of other backgrounds would be equally at risk from the uncertainties of the economy, if not more so. Black death rates have been historically higher than those of other groups, but even their mortality rates were falling, year by year. It was white Americans at midlife who were dying of despair in rising numbers.

In caste terms, these are the least well off, most precariously situated members of the dominant caste in America. For generations, they could take for granted their inherited rank in the hierarchy and the benefits that accrued from it.

We may underestimate, though, the aftershocks of a shift in demographics, the erosion of labor unions, the perceived loss of status, the fears about their place in the world, and resentment that the kind of security their fathers could rely upon might now be waning in what were supposed to be the best years of their lives. Rising immigration from across the Pacific and the Rio Grande and the ascendance of a black man as president made for an inversion of the world as many had known it, and some of them might have been more susceptible to the calls to "take our country back" after 2008 and to "make America great again" in 2016.

In America, political scientists have given this malaise of insecurities a name: dominant group status threat. This phenomenon "is not the usual form of prejudice or stereotyping that involves looking down on outgroups who are perceived to be inferior," writes Diana Mutz, a political scientist at the University of Pennsylvania. "Instead, it is born of a sense that the outgroup is doing too well and thus, is a viable threat to one's own dominant group status."

Working-class whites, the preeminent social economist Gunnar Myrdal wrote, "need the demarcations of caste more than upper class whites. They are the people likely to stress aggressively that no Negro can ever attain the status of even the lowest white."

The American caste system, which co-opted this class of white workers nearly from the start, "drove such a wedge between black and white workers that there probably are not today in the world two groups of workers with practically identical interests" who are "kept so far apart that neither sees anything of common interests," the scholar W.E.B. Du Bois wrote.

These insecurities extend back for centuries. A Virginia slaveholder remarked in 1832 that poor whites had "little but their complexion to console them for being born into a higher caste." When a hierarchy is built around the needs of the group to which one happens to have been born, it can distort the perceptions of one's place in the world. It can create an illusion that one is innately superior to others if only because it has been reinforced so often that it becomes accepted as subconscious truth.

"Nobody could take away from you this whiteness that made you and your way of life 'superior,'" wrote the white southern author Lillian Smith. "They could take your house, your job, your fun; they could steal your wages, keep you from acquiring knowledge; they could tax your vote or cheat you out of it; they could by arousing your anxieties make you impotent; but they could not strip your white skin off of you. It became the poor white's most precious possession, a 'charm' staving off utter dissolution."

Things began to change in the 1960s when civil rights legislation opened labor markets to women of all races, to immigrants from beyond Europe, and to African-Americans whose life-and-death protests helped unlock doors for all of these groups. New people flooded the labor pool at the precise moment that manufacturing was on the decline, and every worker now faced greater competition.

"In the span of a few cruel years," wrote the *New York Times* columnist Russell Baker in the 1960s, of the white Anglo-Saxon Protestant, "he has seen his comfortable position as the 'in' man of American society become a social liability as the outcasts and the exploited have presented their due bills on their conscience."

Some people from the groups that were said to be inherently inferior managed to make it into the mainstream, a few rising to the level of people in the dominant caste, one of them, in 2008, rising to the highest station in the land. This left some white working-class Americans in particular, those with the least education and the material security that it can confer, to face the question of whether the commodity that they could take for granted—their skin and ascribed race—might be losing value.

If the lower-caste person manages actually to rise above an upper-caste person, the natural human response from someone weaned on their caste's inherent superiority is to perceive a threat to their existence, a heightened sense of unease, of displacement, of fear for their very survival. *If the things that I have believed are not true, then might I not be who I thought I was?*" The disaffection is more than economic. The malaise is spiritual, psychological, emotional. Who are you if there is no one to be better than?

"It's a great lie on which their identity has been built," said Dr. Sushrut Jadhav, a prominent Indian psychiatrist, based in London, who specializes in the effects of caste on mental health.

Thus, a caste system makes a captive of everyone within it. Just as the assumptions of inferiority weigh on those assigned to the bottom of the caste system, the assumptions of superiority can burden those at the top with unsustainable expectations of needing to be several rungs above, in charge at all times, at the center of things, to police those who might cut ahead of them, to resent the idea of undeserving lower castes jumping the line and getting in front of those born to lead.

Custom and law segregated the white working and middle classes for so long that most would not have been in a position to see firsthand the headwinds confronting disfavored Americans. The hand of government in the lives of white citizens has often been made invisible and has left distortions as to how each group got to where they are, allowing resentments and rivalries to fester. Many may not have realized that the New Deal reforms of the 1930s, like the Social Security Act of 1935 (providing old age insurance) and the Wagner Act (protecting workers from labor abuse), excluded the vast majority of black workers—farm laborers and domestics—at the urging of southern white politicians.

Further tipping the scales, the Federal Housing Administration was created to make homeownership easier for white families by guaranteeing mortgages in white neighborhoods while specifically excluding African-Americans who wished to buy homes. It did so by refusing to back mortgages in any neighborhood where black people lived, a practice known as redlining, and by encouraging or even requiring restrictive covenants that barred black citizens from buying homes in white neighborhoods.

Together, these and other government programs extended a safety net and a leg-up to the parents, grandparents, and great-grandparents of white Americans of today, while shutting out the foreparents of African-Americans from those same job protections and those same chances to earn or build wealth.

These government programs for the dominant caste were in force during the lifetimes of many current-day Americans.

These programs did not open to African-Americans until the late 1960s, and then only after the protests for civil rights. The more recent forms of state-sanctioned discrimination, along with denying pay to enslaved people over the course of generations, has led to a wealth gap in which white families currently have ten times the wealth of their black counterparts. If you are not black and "if you or your parents were alive in the 1960s and got a mortgage," wrote Ben Mathis-Lilley in *Slate*, "you benefited directly and materially from discrimination."

The very machinery upon which many white Americans had the chance to build their lives and assets was forbidden to African-Americans who were still just a generation or two out of enslavement and the apartheid of Jim Crow, burdens so heavy and borne for so long that if they were to rise, they would have to work and save that much harder than their fellow Americans.

Rather than encouraging a greater understanding of how these disparities came to be or a framework for compassion for fellow Americans, political discourse has usually reinforced prevailing stereotypes of a lazy, inferior group getting undeserved handouts, a scapegoating that makes the formal barriers all the more unjust and the resentments of white working-class citizens all the more tragic. The subordinate caste was shut out of "the trillions of dollars of wealth accumulated through the appreciation of housing assets secured by federally insured loans between 1932 and 1962," a major source of current-day wealth, wrote the sociologist George Lipsitz. "Yet they find themselves portrayed as privileged beneficiaries of special preferences by the very people who profit from their exploitation and oppression."

Once labor, housing, and schools finally began to open up to the subordinate caste, many working- and middle-class whites began to perceive themselves to be worse off, by comparison, and to report that they experienced more racism than African-Americans, unable to see the inequities that persist, often in their favor.

Unconscious Bias: A Mutation in the Software

Toward the end of the twentieth century, social scientists found new ways to measure what had transformed from overt racism to a slow boil of unspoken antagonisms that social scientists called unconscious bias.

By adulthood, researchers have found, most Americans have been exposed to a culture with enough negative messages about African-Americans and other marginalized groups that as much as 80 percent of white Americans hold unconscious bias against black Americans, bias so automatic that it kicks in before a person can process it, according to the Harvard sociologist David R. Williams. The messaging is so pervasive in American society that a third of black Americans hold anti-black bias against themselves.

"All racial ethnic minority groups are stereotyped more negatively than whites," Williams said. "Blacks are viewed the worst, then Latinos, who are viewed twice as negatively as Asians. There is a hierarchy of rank."

What kind of person is likely to carry this kind of unconscious bias? "This is a wonderful person," Williams said, "who has sympathy for the bad things that have happened in the past. But that person is still an American and has been fed the larger stereotypes of blacks that are deeply embedded in the culture of this society. So, despite holding no explicit racial prejudices, they nonetheless hold implicit bias that's deep in their subconscious. They have all these negative images of African-Americans so that when they meet an African-American, although self-consciously they are not prejudiced, the implicit biases nonetheless operate to shape their behavior. This discriminatory behavior is activated more quickly and effortlessly than conscious discrimination, more quickly than saying, 'I've decided to discriminate against this person.'

"This is the frightening point," he said. "Because it's an automatic process, and it's an unconscious process, people who engage in this unthinking discrimination are not aware of it. They are not lying to you when they say, 'I didn't treat this person differently, and I treat everyone the same.' They mean it because, consciously, that is the way they see themselves. These implicit biases shape their behavior in ways they are not even aware of. The research suggests that about 70 to 80 percent of whites fall into this category."

These autonomic responses contribute to disparities in hiring, in housing, in education, and in medical treatment for the lowest-caste people compared to their dominant-caste counterparts and, as with other aspects of the caste system, often go against logic. For example, a pioneering study by the sociologist Devah Pager found that white felons applying for a job were more likely to get hired than African-Americans with no criminal record.

CHAPTER ELEVEN

A Scapegoat to Bear the Sins of the World

Every year, on the day of atonement, the ancient Hebrews took two male goats and presented them before the Lord at the entrance to the tent of meeting. Then the high priest cast lots to determine the fate of each goat.

One they would kill as a sacrifice to the Lord to cleanse and make sacred the sanctuary. The other, the scapegoat, they would present to the Lord alive.

The high priest would lay both hands on the head of the live goat and confess upon its head all the guilt and misdeeds of the Israelites. All of their sins he would transpose to the goat, and the goat was then banished to the wilderness, carrying on its back the weight of the faults of the Israelites, and thus freeing the Israelites to flourish in peace.

The goat was cast out to suffer for the sins of others and was called the scapegoat.

This was the ritual according to Leviticus that was passed down through the ages, adopted by the ancient Greeks. It survives not only in individual interactions but within nations and castes. For the ancients, the scapegoat served as the healing agent for the larger whole. In modern times, the concept of the scapegoat has mutated from merely the bearer of misfortune to the person or group blamed for bringing misfortune.

In a caste system, whether in the United States or in India or in World War II Germany, the lowest caste performed the unwitting role of diverting society's attention from its structural ills and taking the blame for collective misfortune. It was seen, in fact, as misfortune itself.

A scapegoat caste has become necessary for the collective well-being of the castes above it and the smooth functioning of the caste system. The dominant groups can look to those cast out as the cause of any fate or misfortune, as representing the worst aspects of society. "The scapegoater feels a relief in being lighter," wrote the Jungian psychologist Sylvia Brinton Perera, "without the burden of carrying what is unacceptable to his or her ego ideal, without shadow." The ones above the scapegoat can "stand purified and united with each other, feeling blessed by their God."

In the American South, the designated scapegoat was expelled not to the wilderness but to the margins of society, an attempted near banishment from the human race. Many men and women in the dominant caste blamed the people they enslaved for poor harvests or for meager returns, called the people who worked as many as eighteen hours a day for the enrichment of others lazy, and took out their frustrations on the bodies of those they held captive.

The caste system spared no one in the scapegoat caste. When pregnant women were to be whipped, "before binding them to the stakes, a hole is made in the ground to accommodate the enlarged form of the victim," a Mr. C. Robin of Louisiana wrote in describing what he had witnessed.

After the Civil War, Confederates blamed the people they had once owned for the loss of the war. Well into the twentieth century, into the lifetimes of people among us today, lynchings served as a form of ritual human sacrifice before audiences sometimes in the thousands. People drove in from neighboring states, schools let out early so that white children could join their parents to watch men in the dominant caste perform acts of sadism on people from the subordinate caste before hanging them from the limb of a sycamore. Lynchings almost always occurred "at the hands of persons unknown," performed "in a collective way so that no one person could be blamed."

"Whites were unified in seeing the Negro as a scapegoat and proper object for exploitation and hatred," wrote Gunnar Myrdal, a leading social economist in the 1940s. "White solidarity is upheld and the caste order protected."

As scapegoats, they are seen as the reason for societal ills. The scapegoats are blamed for a crime rate that they alone do not cause and for drugs that they are no more likely to use than the dominant caste, but for which they are incarcerated at six times the rate as whites accused of similar offenses. Thousands of African-Americans are behind bars for having been in possession of a substance that businessmen in the dominant caste are now converting to wealth in the marijuana and CBD industry.

In the United States and in India, people in the dominant caste have blamed stagnant careers or rejections in college admissions on marginalized people in the lower caste, even though African-Americans in the United States and Dalits in

India are rarely in positions to decide who will get hired at corporations or admitted to universities. In the United States, it is a numerical impossibility for African-Americans to wreak such havoc in employment and higher education: there are simply not enough African-Americans to take the positions that every member of the dominant caste dreams of holding.

Notably, while affirmative action grew out of the civil rights movement fought by lowest-caste people and their white allies, decades of analysis show that it is white women, and thus white families, rather than African-Americans, who became the prime beneficiaries of a plan intended to redress centuries of injustice against the lowest-caste people. Scapegoating nimbly obscures the structural forces that make life harder than it has to be for many Americans for the benefit of a few, primarily in the dominant caste. It blames societal ills on the groups with the least power and the least say in how the country operates while allowing the larger framework and those who control and reap the dividends of these divisions to go unchecked. It worsens during times of economic tensions when the least secure in the dominant group attacks a group in the minority "for structural economic problems that actually harmed both," one social scientist observed, "and that neither caused."

• • •

The human impulse to blame a disfavored outsider group puts the lives of both the favored and disfavored in peril.

On an autumn evening in October 1989, a suburban Boston couple, expecting their first child that December, were driving home from a childbirth class. The husband, twenty-nine-year-old

Charles Stuart, was the reserved and ambitious store manager at a luxury furrier downtown. His wife, thirty-year-old Carol DiMaiti Stuart, was a petite and gregarious attorney. They had bought a split-level house in the suburbs and had already decided that if that baby was a boy, they would name him Christopher. They were both children of the dominant caste, who had risen from modest, blue-collar backgrounds. They had just celebrated their fourth wedding anniversary.

That evening, they were driving home through the neighborhood of Roxbury, which had been the landing place for waves of European immigrants and, after World War II, became mostly black, poor and working class, ravaged by the war on drugs. The husband was behind the wheel of their Toyota and had taken a somewhat circuitous route. At a traffic light in the Mission Hill section, shots were fired, hitting the wife in the head and the husband in the abdomen, both at close range. The husband was in better shape than the wife, and he called police dispatch from his car phone. His wife died at the hospital of the massive wounds she sustained. Their baby was delivered in the wife's final hours, two months premature, and named Christopher as his parents had wished. He lived for only seventeen days.

The night of the shooting, Charles Stuart told police that a black man with a raspy voice and wearing a jogging suit had forced his way into the car and had mugged and shot them. The tragedy triggered every deep-seated fear and horror in Boston and across the nation. The husband's desperate call to police dispatch aired repeatedly on television, as did video footage of paramedics pulling the mortally wounded wife from the Toyota.

Outraged over an incomprehensible tragedy, the city went into action and began a massive manhunt. Mayor Raymond

Flynn vowed to "get the animals responsible" and ordered every available detective diverted to the case. Officers combed Roxbury and stopped and strip-searched every man who fit the description, which meant almost any black man on the streets, hundreds of them. The hunt for a suspect became the near singular fixation for weeks. The dragnet yielded a thirty-nine-year-old unemployed black man with a criminal record whom Charles picked out in a police lineup. People began calling for the death penalty.

For months, officials had paid little notice to inconsistencies in the husband's behavior, distracted as they were by a storyline tailored to their expectations. The night of the shooting, Charles had driven around aimlessly for thirteen minutes while talking to dispatch, rather than heading back to the hospital that the couple had just left, claiming not to recognize any landmarks in the city he had lived in all his life. "He never tried to comfort his wife, never called her name," according to *Time* magazine. "In the ambulance to the hospital, he only asked about the seriousness of his own wound, and never about his wife's condition."

Not long before, he had taken out several insurance policies on his young and healthy wife. After his release from the hospital, he collected on one of them and promptly bought a new car, a Nissan Maxima, and a thousand-dollar pair of women's diamond earrings. It turned out that he had been staying out late on Friday evenings and into the early morning hours to the consternation of his wife in the months before her death. He had been seen with a young blond woman who worked summers at the furrier and whom he had arranged to phone him at the hospital, though she vehemently denied a relationship as the story broke. He had told friends he did not want the baby, that it would disrupt his climb up the social ladder.

Those contradictory details were not powerful enough to dislodge the fixed assumptions about the case. But there had been a third person involved on the night of the shooting, and as Christmas approached, that person began to crack. It was the husband's brother, Matthew. Charles had planned ahead for Matthew to meet the car at a rendezvous site the night of the shooting. Before the brother arrived, Charles had stopped the car and shot his wife in the head, after which Charles pointed the gun at himself, intending to shoot his foot but misfiring into his torso instead. Charles told his brother to take and dispose of Carol's jewelry and purse and the gun that Charles had used to kill her. This would make it look like the robbery he would later report to the police.

But afterward, the brother's conscience began to plague him, and he told other members of the family. He said he thought he was helping his brother in an insurance scam when he got the purse and gun, not in a murder plot. Word got back to Charles Stuart that his brother was planning to go to the police and testify against him in exchange for immunity. With the investigation closing in on him, the husband jumped to his death from the Tobin Bridge into the Mystic River that January. His brother, Matthew, later pleaded guilty to conspiracy and possession of a firearm, among other charges, and served three years in prison.

In the end, the husband alone was responsible for the death of his wife, but the caste system was his unwitting accomplice. He knew that he could count on the caste system to spring into action as it is programmed to do, that people would readily accept his account if the perpetrator were black, believe the dominant-caste man over subordinate people, focus on them rather than him, see the scapegoat caste as singularly capable of any depravity, and would deflect any suspicion away from him. The story didn't even have to be airtight to be believed. It needed only to be plausible. Any sympathy would accrue to him and not the scapegoat caste, which bears the burdens of someone else's sins, no matter the protestations.

The caste system had given Charles Stuart cover and endangered the life of Carol DiMaiti Stuart, as it had for white women in the Jim Crow South, where husbands and lovers knew that a black man could be blamed for anything that befell a white woman if the dominant caste chose to accuse him. This is not to say that any group is more prone to criminality or subterfuge than another. It is to say that one of the more disturbing aspects of a caste system, and of the unequal justice it produces, is that it makes for a less safe society, allowing the guilty to shift blame and often to go free. A caste system gives us false comfort, makes us feel that the world is in order, that we automatically know the good guys from the bad guys.

It is possible that nothing could have saved Carol Stuart's life, given the man she was married to. We will never know. Had the husband not been able to depend upon the universal decoy of black criminality, had he not been able to count on the instinctive reviling of the lowest caste and the corresponding presumption of virtue of the dominant caste, had he not been able to correctly assume that the caste system would act on his behalf, perhaps he might not have been as brazen, perhaps he might have tried something else, divorce, for instance. Perhaps he might not have felt as free to attempt something so heinous.

Perhaps the wife might not have been killed, their son not been lost, at least not that night and not in that way, if he thought the suspicion would rightly be trained on the actual perpetrator from the start.

• • •

Decades later, in the years of anxiety after the 2016 election, Anthony Stephan House, a thirty-nine-year-old project manager in Austin, Texas, was getting ready to take his eight-year-old daughter to school. It was just before seven in the morning on March 2, 2018. Something prompted him to go to his front door, and when he stepped over the threshold, he noticed a package on the porch. As he picked it up, it exploded. He died shortly after his arrival at the hospital.

His death was ruled a homicide for obvious reasons at first, but the investigation quickly pivoted away. House was African-American, living on the working-class black and Latino east side of Austin with its aging ranch houses and ramblers. The police figured that the bombing might be drug-related. Maybe it was intended as retribution for a drug dealer but left at the wrong house. They considered another possibility, that maybe he had detonated the bomb himself, a theory that blamed the victim for his own death.

"We can't rule out that Mr. House didn't construct this himself and accidentally detonate it, in which case it would be an accidental death," Assistant Police Chief Joseph Chacon said.

"Based on what we know right now," Brian Manley, then interim police chief, told reporters the day of House's death, "we have no reason to believe this is anything beyond an isolated incident that took place at this residence and in no way this is linked to a terroristic attack."

Those assumptions would prove to be tragically misdirected. Ten days later, seventeen-year-old Draylen Mason, a high school senior who was a beloved bass violinist with the Austin Youth Orchestra, discovered a package outside his family's door. When he brought it inside, it exploded in the kitchen, killing him, and leaving his mother critically wounded. They, too, were African-American. Later that morning, a few miles away, a seventy-five-year-old Latina, Esperanza Herrera, was critically injured when a package left at her mother's house detonated when she picked it up.

It was only then, ten days after the first bombing, that the Austin police began warning citizens to take precautions with unknown packages. A serial bomber was at large in Austin, had been at large from the first bomb attack. The bombings were now being considered a possible hate crime. The fact that the victims were black and Latina meant that some people could distance themselves from the bombings if they chose. Until the bomber expanded his reach. Less than a week later, on the other side of Austin, two white men in their twenties were walking in a well-to-do white neighborhood when a bomb triggered by a trip wire detonated in the street and seriously injured them.

Two days after that, a bomb exploded on a conveyor belt at a FedEx warehouse, and another was discovered at a FedEx before it could detonate. The police now raced at warp speed. Surveillance cameras caught images of the man who had dropped off the last package bombs and recorded the license plate on his car. The police began tracking him by the location of his cellphone. They discovered that the suspect was a twenty-three-year-old unemployed white man named Mark Conditt, who was from a conservative Christian family. The day after the explosion at the FedEx warehouse, a SWAT team closed in on him. Cornered by officers, Conditt detonated a bomb inside his car and blew himself up.

Spectacular police work had brought the bomber down within twenty-four hours, aided in no small part by the suspect's own change in tactics but also by their taking swift action once the caste blinders were removed. The police chief apologized to black citizens and to the family of the first victim, who had been portrayed as a suspect in his own death. But African-American residents, the scapegoat caste, were left with lingering questions, questions whose answers they lived with every day: Why had the police paid little heed when the first bombs killed or harmed people of color? Why had they disregarded the potential threat? Why did authorities wait ten days to warn the public? Why did they let precious time pass, blaming the first victim for his own death?

"How messed up is it that police can make it seem like the person did it themself?" Fatima Mann, an advocate for poor families in Austin, told *The Washington Post*. "It's insulting and offensive and tiring."

A scapegoat, like the man who was the first to die in Austin, is seen by definition as expendable. People can come to disregard the predicaments facing people deemed beneath them, seeing their misfortunes as having no bearing on their own lives, seeing whatever is happening to them as, say, a black problem, rather than a human problem, unwittingly endangering everyone.

CHAPTER TWELVE

―――

The Intrusion of Caste in Everyday Life

Every day across America, wherever two or more are gathered, caste can infect the most ordinary of interchanges, catching us off guard, disrupting and confusing and potentially causing mayhem for anyone in the hierarchy.

These are scenes of caste in action:

> *The doorbell rang at the home of an accountant from the dominant caste in a wealthy suburb of a midwestern city. The accountant and his family had only recently moved into the neighborhood. Through the glass sidelights of his front door, he could see a woman, an African-American woman, there on his landing.*
>
> *He knew exactly what this meant. The dry cleaner in town offered its customers pickup and drop-off, so he went to get the clothes that needed cleaning and then opened the door to hand the armload of tousled clothes to the woman waiting out front.*
>
> *The woman stepped back. "Oh, I'm not the dry cleaner,"the woman said. "I'm your next-door neighbor. I came over to introduce myself and welcome you to the neighborhood."*

The woman was the fashionable wife of a prominent car-diologist, exceedingly upper class, yet labeled subordinate caste on sight, still, to someone who had just moved next door to her. They would both have to recover from that one.

• • •

A college professor in Chicago had just returned from a bike ride and picked up his mail in the lobby of his apartment build-ing off Michigan Avenue. He was African-American, in his thirties, patrician of face, still in his helmet and cycling gear. He stepped onto the elevator en route to his floor and, barely noticing the other man on the elevator with him, began going through his mail. He saw something of interest and unsealed one of his envelopes.

The other man was horrified.

"You're supposed to be delivering the mail, not opening it."

This seemed to have come out of nowhere, and the college professor looked up and saw that the other man was white, but didn't fully register the accusation, was just going about his day, and gave an honest reply.

"Oh, I want to see what's inside," the professor said.

The other man looked even more stricken now, shaking his head in disgust, mistakenly believing he was witnessing a crime in progress.

The professor got off on his floor and only later did it occur to him that he had been taken for a delivery boy in his own building, an assumption so ludicrous he hadn't bothered to consider it in the moment, which left the dominant-caste man convinced that he had just seen a black messenger brazenly break open an "actual" resident's mail in full view of another resident. This is the self-perpetuating mischief of caste.

• • •

The phone kept ringing at the civil engineer's desk. He had deadlines to meet and projects bearing down on him. But, over and over, the phone broke his concentration and wasted his limited time. The engineer was from the dominant caste, and so, too, was the man pestering him. On the face of it, the intrusion would seem to have nothing to do with caste. Here was a white contractor calling a white engineer for answers about a project under way.

The engineer was a supervisor with a general idea of the project, but the project was not his. It belonged to another engineer on the team, as the contractor well knew, one who happened to be African-American and a woman.

The white contractor had been told to go to her with any questions he had. But the contractor had ignored her, ignored protocol, and had gone to the dominant-caste engineer instead. The white engineer answered the contractor's questions at first, to be polite and move things along. But the phone kept ringing, and it was disrupting his own work, and it was hindering the project in question.

The black engineer could hear this unfold in front of her from her cubicle next to the white engineer's. From her desk, she could hear it every time his phone rang, while hers sat mute and silent. She could hear the white engineer's impatient replies to questions that both of them knew should have come to her.

The white engineer grew agitated with disbelief. When the

contractor called the next time, the white engineer let him have it. "I indicated to you from the beginning that you need to talk to D. about day-to-day matters," the white engineer said. "If you have a problem with that, we'll have to find another contractor for the job."

The minute the white engineer hung up, the black engineer's phone rang.

On an ordinary workday, the caste system had pulled a dominant-caste man into its undertow. It had drained him of time and disrupted the operation. He found himself in an unexpected fight against an invisible foe, forced to take a stand for his colleague and against, perhaps unbeknownst to him on a conscious level, the caste system itself.

• • •

If there is anything that distinguishes caste, however, it is, first, the policing of roles expected of people based on what they look like, and, second, the monitoring of boundaries—the disregard for the boundaries of subordinate castes or the passionate construction of them by those in the dominant caste—to keep the hierarchy in place.

After the 2016 election, the surveillance of black citizens by white strangers became so common a feature of American life that these episodes have inspired memes of their own, videos gone viral, followed by apologies from management or an announcement of company-wide diversity training. People in the dominant caste have been caught on video inserting themselves into the everyday lives of black people they do not know and calling the police on them. It is a distant echo of an earlier time when anyone in the dominant caste was deputized, obligated even, to apprehend any black person during the era of slavery.

In New Haven, Connecticut, a woman called campus police on a graduate student at Yale University who had fallen asleep while studying in the common area of her dormitory. Officers demanded her identification even after she unlocked the door to her dorm room. "You're in a Yale building," an officer said, "and we need to make sure that you belong here."

A woman walking her dog stood and blocked a marketing consultant from getting into his own condo building in St. Louis. She demanded that he show proof that he lived there before she would step aside. When he walked past her, she followed him into the elevator and onto his floor to see if he in fact lived there. In the video that the man took as a precaution, she can be seen tracking him all the way to his apartment, checking whether he was a resident even after he unlocked his door to go inside.

And a woman began to stalk a black man in Georgia when she saw him out with two white children. From her car, the woman trailed Corey Lewis, their babysitter, as he drove from a Walmart to a gas station and to his home after he did not permit the woman, a complete stranger, to talk with the children alone to see if they were all right. Lewis, a youth pastor who runs an after-school program, started recording the situation on his cellphone. In it, the children can be seen calm and unfazed, buckled in their seatbelts in the back of his car.

His voice is strained and disbelieving. "This lady is following me," he says in the video, "all because I got two kids in the back seat that do not look like me."

The woman called 911 and asked if she should keep

following him. She continued to trail him even though she was told not to. By the time Lewis got home, a patrol car had pulled up behind him, an officer heading toward him.

"Jesus have mercy—what is wrong with this country?" a woman outside of the camera frame cried. The officer told the children, a six-year-old boy and a ten-year-old girl, to step out of the car, and Lewis's voice grew tense. The outcome of this police encounter and his very safety depended on what those children said, and he asked them to please tell the officer who he was.

"Please," he said to them.

Satisfied that Lewis was, in fact, their babysitter and that the children were okay, the officer, just to be safe, called the parents, who were out at dinner.

"It just knocked us out of our chair," the children's father, David Parker, told *The New York Times*.

Afterward, a reporter asked one of the children, ten-year-old Addison, what she would tell the woman who followed them that day. Her father told the *Times* her response: "I would just ask her to, next time, try to see us as three people rather than three skin colors, because we might've been Mr. Lewis's adopted children."

• • •

These intrusions of caste would seem to harm the targets more than anyone. Given the widely publicized attacks and shootings of black citizens at the hands of police, most Americans know by now that calling the police on a black person can carry life-and-death consequences. Frivolous calls squander public resources and distract police from actual, serious crime to the detriment of us all.

Beyond that, when any citizen is disrupted in the midst of everyday life and responsibilities, it is, in fact, a societal disruption, a tear in the daily workings of human interaction. These people are part of the American economy, and when they are interrupted, schools and business and institutions suffer an invisible loss in output as their workers get blindsided from their tasks.

These intrusions serve to reinforce caste by derailing lower-caste people, subverting their work lives in an already competitive society, imposing additional burdens not borne by their dominant-caste colleagues as they go about their work, as occurred to me in Michigan some years ago.

I could hear footsteps behind me but paid little attention. This was an airport, and there were footfalls and roller bags all around. I had just landed in Detroit on an early-morning flight from Chicago for interviews I needed to conduct as a national correspondent for *The New York Times*.

I'd already lost an hour going from Central to Eastern time, and I was thinking of all I'd have to do in the space of the next eight hours. If the first interview was at ten-thirty, and if it took me forty minutes to get downtown, maybe more since this was rush hour, I needed to get straight to the rental car to make this work.

Any delays in the day's interviews and I might not make the flight back to Chicago that evening. I thought to myself that I'd worry about that later and just get to the Avis bus as soon as I could. I thought about how it always seems that the shuttle you're looking for is the one that has just pulled off, and no matter what company you've booked, the one you need is always the last to show up.

I was walking fast, because I always walk fast, and I was heading to the sliding-glass doors in the direction of the shuttle stop when I heard them. The footsteps were closer and faster and heading toward me. Why would anybody be heading toward me? It was a man and a woman. It happened to be a white man and a white woman, the woman's light brown hair swinging just above her shoulders as she ran. They had a parka-and-corduroy look about them, and both were out of breath as they reached me.

"We need to talk to you," they said, walking alongside me.

I could see the shuttle bus lane through the sliding-glass doors, and buses pulling up, and was not fully registering whatever it was they were saying.

"Why are you in Detroit? What are you here for?"

"I'm on business. I'm here for work."

I was thinking that I did not have time for whatever travel survey they were conducting. And now I could see that Avis was on schedule. The shuttle bus was pulling to the curb. People were queuing up to board.

"I have to catch my shuttle bus," I told them as I walked out of the terminal doors.

"Where are you coming from?" they asked, one on each side of me now.

"I just flew in from Chicago," I said, nearing the clot of people in suits and overcoats boarding the shuttle bus.

"Is that where you live?"

"Why are you asking me this? I need to get on the bus."

"We need to know if you live in Chicago, and what you're doing in Detroit."

The last of the passengers were climbing on board. The doors of the bus were wide open. The driver was looking down at me and at them. The man and the woman stood there holding up the bus, holding up the passengers, holding up me.

"What is this for?"

"We're DEA. We need to know where you live, how long you will be in Detroit, and exactly what you're doing here."

This was too preposterous to comprehend. The Drug Enforcement Administration? Why in the world were they stopping me, out of all the travelers at the airport? This was a day trip, so I didn't have luggage, like a lot of business travelers between cities close to each other. I was in a suit like everyone else, Coach bag slung over my shoulder. Covering the Midwest as I was at the time, I used to tell people that I catch planes like other people catch the subway. Airports were a second home to me. How could they not see that I was like every other business traveler boarding the shuttle?

The people on the bus were checking their watches and glaring down at me through the windows as I stood at the steps. The driver shifted in his seat, and I could hear the shake of the engine, the snort of the brakes, transmission about to shift, the driver's impatient hand on the door pull.

I blurted out what they wanted to know so that they would leave me alone.

"I live in Chicago. I'm here for the day. I'm a reporter for *The New York Times*. I need to get on this bus."

"We will allow you to board. We will have to ride with you."

I was shaking now as I climbed onto the shuttle, its air thick with the scorn of fellow travelers. I looked for an empty seat, people pulling away as I sat down. This whole exchange had delayed everyone on the bus, and for all that anyone could see, it was because of a woman, a black woman who probably didn't even belong with real business travelers and might be a criminal to boot.

The two agents took seats directly in front of me, staring and assessing, their eyes never leaving me. Twitter did not exist, and there were no cameras on cellphones to go into video mode. The bus was filled with business people, white people, or, I should say, white business people. I was the only African-American on the bus and one of the few women, and there were two agents surveilling me and my every move.

The other passengers glared at me and at the two agents and back again at me. I was in utter disbelief, too shocked even to register fear. It was a psychic assault to sit there, accused and condemned, not just by the agents but by everyone on the bus who looked with contempt and disdain, seeing me as not like them, when I was exactly like them—a frequent flyer on business like anyone else on the bus, early on a weekday morning, having just flown into a major American city and needing to focus on the work that I, like them, was there to do. I wanted to proclaim my innocence of whatever it was that all of them were thinking.

When you are raised middle class and born to a subordinated caste in general, and African-American in particular, you are keenly aware of the burden you carry and you know that working twice as hard is a given. But more important, you know there will be no latitude for a misstep, so you must try to be virtually perfect at all times merely to tread water. You live with the double standard even though you do not like it. You know growing up that you cannot get away with the things that your white friends might skate by with—adolescent pranks or shoplifting on a dare or cursing out a teacher. You knew better, even if you were so inclined, which I wasn't and never have been.

I needed to regain my composure and clear myself of the accusation of their presence. They hadn't believed I was a reporter, so I decided to be conspicuously what I was. I fished my pen and notebook out of my bag. I figured nobody could stop me from taking notes. It was a natural and protective reflex for me, like breathing. I had a captive audience bearing witness to my performance of emergency journalism.

In silence, I looked across at the agents and, with my quaking right hand, made notes of what they were wearing, what they looked like, how they were looking at me. They hadn't expected this, and they turned to look out of a window and down at the floor.

It was a long ride to the car rental lot. Now they felt the sting of inspection as I jotted down everything I could about them, and, in that moment, I took back some fraction of the power they had taken from me, proved who and what I was to anyone watching, or at least that was how it felt to me at the time.

Soon the bus pulled into the Avis lot, and I took a deep breath. They had ridden all the way from the airport, trailing me, and I had no idea what the next step would be. When the bus came to a stop, I stood up like the other passengers. The agents looked up from their seats.

"Have a nice day," they said. And it was over just like that.

Except it wasn't. I somehow made it to the rental counter and somehow got the keys to a car, but I don't remember any of it. What I recall is getting turned around in a parking lot that

I had been to dozens of times, going in circles, not able to get out, not registering the signs to the exit, not seeing how to get to Interstate 94, when I knew full well how to get to I-94 after all the times I'd driven it.

Now, in the car, away from the agents, I was beginning to comprehend the seriousness of that encounter, only now able to admit my terror. The other business travelers were likely well on their way to their appointments, perhaps annoyed at the delay but able to make preparations in their heads for their meetings, maybe get a coffee on the way.

This was the thievery of caste, stealing the time and psychic resources of the marginalized, draining energy in an already uphill competition. They were not, like me, frozen and disoriented, trying to make sense of a public violation that seemed all the more menacing now that I could see it in full. The quiet mundanity of that terror has never left me, the scars outliving the cut.

We are told over and over again in our society not to judge a book by its cover, not to assume what is inside before we have had a chance to read it. Yet humans size up and make assumptions about other humans based upon what they look like many times a day. We prejudge complicated breathing beings in ways we are told never to judge inanimate objects.

———

CHAPTER THIRTEEN

The Urgent Necessity
of a Bottom Rung

It turns out that the greatest threat to a caste system is not lower-caste failure, which, in a caste system, is expected and perhaps even counted upon, but lower-caste success, which is not. Achievement by those in the lowest caste goes against the script handed down to us all. It undermines the core assumptions upon which a caste system is constructed and to which the identities of people on all rungs of the hierarchy are linked. Achievement by marginalized people who step outside the roles expected of them puts things out of order and triggers primeval and often violent backlash.

The scholar W.E.B. Du Bois recognized this phenomenon in his research into what happened after the end of the Civil War: "The masters feared their former slaves' success," he wrote, "far more than their anticipated failure."

Decades after the Civil War, the entire world was at war and well into a fourth year of trench combat that was tearing Europe apart. The year was 1918, after the Americans had finally sent in their troops. The French welcomed the reinforcement during World War I, had badly needed it. The French began commanding some of the American troops, and it was then that the problems began. The French were treating the soldiers according to their military rank rather than their rank in the American caste system. They were treating black soldiers as they would white soldiers, as they would treat other human beings, having drinks with them, patting their shoulders for a job well done. This rankled the white soldiers in an era of total segregation back home, and this breach had to be put to a stop.

American military command informed the French of how they were to treat the black soldiers, clarified for them that these men were "inferior beings," no matter how well they performed on the front lines, that it was "of the utmost importance" that they be treated as inferior.

The fact that military command would take the time in the middle of one of the most vicious wars in human history to instruct foreigners on the necessity of demeaning their own countrymen suggests that they considered adherence to caste protocols to be as important as conducting the war itself. As it was, the white soldiers were refusing to fight in the same trenches as black soldiers and refusing to salute black superiors.

The American military communicated its position, and French commanders, in turn, had to convey the rules to their soldiers and officers who had come to admire the black soldiers and had developed a camaraderie with them. "This indulgence and this familiarity," read the announcement, "are matters of grievous concern to the Americans. They consider them an affront to their national policy."

In apprising their officers of the new protocols, French command noted the contradictions given that "the (black American) soldiers sent us have been the choicest with respect to physique and morals." Still, in trying to translate the rules of the American caste system, the French command gave this directive: "We cannot deal with them on the same plane as with the white American officers without deeply wounding the latter. We must not eat with them, must not shake hands or seek to talk or meet with them outside of the requirements of military service."

More pointedly, the French officers were told: "We must not commend too highly the black American troops, particularly in the presence of (white) Americans. It is all right to recognize their good qualities and their services, but only in moderate terms."

Later, in the final months of the war, an African-American soldier, Pvt. Burton Holmes, was grievously wounded in a hail of machine gun fire and heavy German artillery in an ambush of his unit in September 1918. He managed to make his way back to the command post to exchange rifles because the one he had been given was malfunctioning.

Commanders wanted to get him to the hospital for treatment, but he refused and rejoined the fight with a backup rifle. He continued to fire upon the enemy until his last breath. Another African-American in Company C, Freddie Stowers, crawled into enemy shelling and led the assault on German trenches. He, too, died on the front lines defending France and America.

White officers who had witnessed their bravery broke with caste and nominated both men for the Medal of Honor. But this was the height of the eugenics era, when black inferiority was near universal convention in American culture. The government refused to grant the medal to either soldier. The award intended for Holmes was downgraded to a lesser citation, and the recommendation for Stowers was lost for half a century.

These actions were in keeping with societal norms that people in the lowest caste were not to be commended even in death, lest the living begin to think themselves equal, get uppity, out of their place, and threaten the myths that the upper caste kept telling itself and the world.

"Imagine," Dr. Jeff Gusky, a physician who, decades later, took an interest in the case, told the *Army Times* in 2018, "how powerful this would have been in the American press . . . if word got out that there were two black soldiers who died in this ambush and were both nominated for the Medal of Honor."

A generation later, during the Second World War, there was continued resistance to the lowest caste rising from its assigned place even in the most mundane of endeavors. One day in the spring of 1942, white army officers happened to assign black soldiers to direct traffic in Lincolnton, Georgia, as an army convoy passed through. It caused an uproar in town. The sight of black men in uniform, standing at an intersection, "halting white motorists, apparently sent some residents over the edge," wrote the historian Jason Morgan Ward.

After the war ended, in February 1946, Sgt. Isaac Woodard, Jr., was riding a Greyhound bus home to North Carolina from Augusta, Georgia, where he had been honorably discharged, having served in the Pacific theater. At a stop along the way, Woodard asked the bus driver if he could step off the bus to relieve himself. The driver told him to sit down, that he didn't have time to wait. Woodard stood up to the driver and told him, "I am a man just like you." Woodard had been out of the country and away from Jim Crow for three years, had served his country and taken on "a degree of assertiveness and self-confidence that most southern whites were not accustomed to nor prepared to accept," in the words of the southern author and judge Richard Gergel.

The driver backed down for the time being, told him to "go ahead then and hurry back." But at the next stop, outside Aiken, South Carolina, the bus driver notified the police.

There the police chief arrested Woodard on charges of disorderly conduct. At the bus stop and later in jail, the police chief beat him and jabbed his eyes with a billy club, blinding him. The next day a local judge found him guilty as charged, and, though he asked to see a doctor, the authorities did not get him one for several more days. By the time he was finally transferred to an army hospital, it was too late to save his eyesight. He was blind for the rest of his life.

The NAACP brought the case to the attention of President Harry S. Truman, a midwestern moderate who was incensed to learn that authorities in South Carolina had taken no action in the maiming of an American soldier. He ordered the Justice Department to investigate based on the fact that Woodard was in uniform at the time he was beaten and that the initial assault occurred at a bus stop on federal property.

But the federal trial ran into caste obstructions in South Carolina. The local prosecutor relied solely on the testimony of the bus driver who had called the police, the defense attorney hurled racial epithets in open court at the blinded sergeant, and, when the all-white jury returned a not-guilty verdict for the police chief, the courtroom broke out in cheers.

It had been revealed during the trial that Woodard had apparently said "yes" instead of "yes, sir" to the police chief during the arrest. This, combined with the elevated position his uniform conveyed, was seen as reason enough for punishment in the caste system. After the trial, the police chief who had admitted to jabbing Woodard in the eyes went free. Woodard went north to New York as part of the Great Migration. The northern white judge assigned to the case lamented, "I was shocked by the hypocrisy of my government."

The message was clear to those whose lives depended on staying in their place, or appearing to. "If a Negro rises, he will be careful not to become conspicuous, lest he be accused of putting on airs and thus arouse resentment," wrote the ethnographer Bertram Schrieke. "Experience or example has taught him that competition and jealousy from the lower classes of whites often form an almost unsurpassable obstacle to his progress."

• • •

It was largely black efforts to rise beyond their station that set off the backlash of lynchings and massacres after Reconstruction following the Civil War, that sparked the founding of the Ku Klux Klan and the imposition of Jim Crow laws to keep the lowest caste in its place. A white mob massacred some sixty black people in Ocoee, Florida, on Election Day in 1920, burning black homes and businesses to the ground, lynching and castrating black men, and driving the remaining black population out of town, after a black man tried to vote. The historian Paul Ortiz has called the Ocoee riot the "single bloodiest election day in modern American history."

It occurred amid a wave of anti-black pogroms in more than a dozen American cities, from East St. Louis to Chicago to Baltimore, as black southerners arrived north during the Great Migration and many tried to make their claims to citizenship after risking their lives in the Great War. One thing these rampages had in common: the mobs tended to go after the most prosperous in the lowest caste, those who might have managed to surpass even some people in the dominant caste. In the 1921 riot in Tulsa, Oklahoma, a mob leveled the section of town that was called black Wall Street, owing to the black banking, insurance, and other businesses clustered together and surrounded by well-kept brick homes that signaled prosperity. These were burned to the ground and never recovered.

• • •

The lowest caste was to remain in its place like an ill-fitting suit that must constantly be altered, seams and darts re-sewn to fit the requirements of the upper caste, going back to the enslavers who resented displays of industriousness and intellect in the people they saw themselves as owning. "When slaves earned money they became 'vain and arrogant,'" wrote the historian Kenneth Stampp, "and felt 'more independent.'"

They were not to be credited for their ideas or innovations, even at the risk of progress for everyone. Crediting them would undermine the pretext for their enslavement, meaning their presumed inferiority in anything other than servitude. In the summer of 1721, an epidemic of smallpox, one of the deadliest afflictions of the era, besieged the city of Boston. It sent stricken people into quarantine, red flags signaling to all who might pass, "God have mercy on this house."

Cotton Mather was a Puritan minister and lay scientist in Boston and had come into possession of an African man named Onesimus. The enslaved African told of a procedure he had undergone back in his homeland that protected him from this illness. People in West Africa had discovered that they could fend off contagions by inoculating themselves with a specimen of fluid from an infected person. Mather was intrigued by the idea Onesimus described. He researched it, and decided to call it "variolation." It would become the precursor to immunization and "the Holy Grail of smallpox prevention for Western doctors and scientists," wrote the medical ethicist and author Harriet A. Washington.

During the 1721 outbreak, Mather tried to persuade Bostonians to protect themselves with this revolutionary method, but did not anticipate the resistance and rage, the "horrid Clamour," that arose from Bostonians. The idea sounded outlandish to them. They feared it could spread smallpox all the more, and they also wanted nothing to do with a practice that had come from Africa and had been suggested by an African slave. Physicians dismissed the procedure out of hand and "resented being told by a gaggle of ministers that Africans had devised the panacea they had long sought," Washington wrote. Rage turned to violence when someone hurled a lighted grenade into Mather's house. Mather escaped serious injury, but wrote that he could see no difference between adopting the African solution for smallpox and using the Native Americans' antidote for snake venom, which the colonists had readily taken up.

Only one physician, Zabdiel Boylston, was willing to try the new method. He inoculated his son and the enslaved people he owned. In the end, the epidemic would wipe out more than 14 percent of Boston's population. But of the 240 people that Boylston had inoculated, only six died—one in forty, as against one in seven people who forwent inoculation.

By 1750, vaccinations, based on the method introduced by Onesimus, would be standard practice in Massachusetts and later in the rest of the country. "What is clear is that the knowledge he passed on saved hundreds of lives—and led to the eventual eradication of smallpox," wrote the author Erin Blakemore. "It remains the only infectious disease to have been entirely wiped out."

For his contribution to science, Onesimus does not appear even to have fully won his freedom. What little that is known is that Mather grew sour on him, and Onesimus managed to buy partial freedom by paying Mather money toward the purchase of another slave. He had gone well beyond what would have been expected of a man of the lowest caste, and, as often happens, does not appear to have reaped the rewards for a role that was beyond his station.

• • •

Instead, the rewards and privileges flowed from upholding the caste order. Doing so could boost the prospects of those who knew to stay in their place, the more conspicuous, the better. Two centuries after Onesimus's day, the Jim Crow regime would make a single exception to its iron law of segregation between blacks and whites. It was for black maids who had shown themselves sufficiently faithful to be entrusted with the care of white children. These women alone could ride in the whites-only section of a train or bus if they were out taking care of a white child. This exception served several purposes: It enshrined the white child as the ticket to a first-class seat for a black person. It reinforced the servile role, the natural place, of the subordinate caste. It elevated the black nursemaid by fiat of the dominant caste. It made domestics superior to even the likes of the great orator Frederick Douglass, who was once reduced to sitting on top of cargo on a train journey. It protected the children of the dominant caste from enduring for a single trip the taint and discomforts of the colored car. And it reminded everyone in the subordinated caste that they would only rise with the permission of the dominant caste, and on its terms, and only as long as they kept to the role assigned them.

They were to be given no quarter, no latitude to imagine themselves in any place other than the bottom rung. From Reconstruction to the civil rights era, southern school boards spent as little as one-tenth the money on black schools as for white schools, openly starving them of resources that might afford them a chance to compete on level ground. School terms for black students were made shorter by months, giving them less time in class and more time in the field for the enrichment of the ruling caste.

In hiring black teachers for segregated schools during Jim Crow, a leading southern official, Hoke Smith, made a deliberate decision: "When two Negro teachers applied to a school, to 'take the less competent.'" It was a nakedly creative way to cripple black prospects for achievement. It put black children under the instruction of the least qualified teachers. It passed over the brightest, most accomplished applicants—in fact, punished excellence—while elevating the mediocre in a purposeful distortion of meritocracy. All of this created dissension in the lowest caste over the patent unfairness and worked to crush the ambitions of those with the most talent. In these and other ways, the caste system trained the people in the lowest caste that the only way to survive was to play the comforting role of servile incompetent. The caste system all but ensured black failure by preempting success.

In a caste system, there can be little allowance for the disfavored caste to appear equal, much less superior, at some human endeavor.

In the early years of the Third Reich, the Nazis made a point of excluding Jews from any position or circumstance in which they might outshine Aryans. This extended to classrooms in which the Berlin Gestapo went to the trouble of ordering that "everything must be done to put an end to the appearance that Aryan students are receiving assistance from Jews in preparing their exams." These were the ways that, irrespective of the natural range of intelligence and talent arising in any human subset, the people in the dominant caste were artificially propped up as superior in all things, a setup for disillusionment not of their own making.

• • •

The investment in the established hierarchy runs sufficiently deep that people in the dominant caste have historically been willing to forgo conveniences to themselves to keep the fruits of citizenship within their own caste.

After the Supreme Court outlawed segregation in public schools in *Brown v. Board of Education* in 1954, the white-run school board in Prince Edward County, Virginia, delayed integrating as long as it could and then shut down the school system entirely rather than allow black students into classrooms with white students. The county had no public schools for five years, from 1959 to 1964, forcing parents of both races to find alternatives for their children. Local whites diverted government funds to private academies for white students, while black parents, whose tax dollars were now going to the white students, had to make do on their own.

Around the same time, civil rights legislation outlawed segregation in public facilities, and, in response, cities in the South closed, auctioned off, or poured concrete into their whites-only pools so that nobody could swim, rather than sharing the water with black people. But those in the dominant caste had the means and resources, acquired over generations of collective income and wealth disparities, to build private pools behind gated communities for themselves and their children, leaving the lowest caste locked out again.

It is in these ways that a caste system shape-shifts and protects its beneficiaries, a workaround emerges, provisions are made, and the hierarchy remains intact, even in the face of challenges from the highest authority in the land. This is how a caste system, it seems, manages always to prevail.

In-group–out-group tensions remain a feature of American life. When black teenagers attended a pool party in a predominantly white, gated community in McKinney, Texas, in 2015, white residents called the police on them for trespassing.

Afterward, as shown in a video that drew international attention, an officer who responded to the call yanked a fifteen-year-old girl from the sidewalk, slammed her to the ground facedown, and pinned her with his full weight. Here was a grown man with his knees bearing down on her slight, bikini-clad frame, as she sobbed, helpless, beneath him. When black boys instinctively rushed to help her, the officer pointed his gun at them and they backed away, the full power of the state treating them not as children but as threats to society.

It was a scene that would be hard to imagine occurring with a young girl from the same caste—the dominant caste—as the officer. Within days, the officer resigned, but the incident demonstrated the depth of assumptions about who belongs where in a caste society, and the instantaneous walls erected and punishments meted out for breaching those boundaries even in our era.

——————

CHAPTER FOURTEEN

Last Place Anxiety:
Packed in a Flooding Basement

Caste puts the richest and most powerful of the dominant caste at a remove, in the penthouse of a mythical high-rise, and everyone else, in descending order, on the floors beneath them. It consigns people in the subordinate caste to the basement, amid the flaws in the foundation and the cracks in the stonework that it appears others choose not to see.

When those in the basement begin rising to the floors above them, surveillance begins, the whole building is threatened. Thus caste can pit the basement-dwellers against themselves in a flooding basement, creating an illusion, a panic even, that their only competition is one another.

It can lead those down under to absorb into their identities the conditions of their entrapment and to do whatever it takes to distinguish themselves as superior to others in their group, to be first among the lowest.

"The stigmatized stratify their own," wrote the anthropologist J. Lorand Matory, "because no one wants to be in last place."

Over the generations, they learn to rank themselves by their proximity to the random traits associated with the dominant caste. Historically, the caste system has granted privileges to some in the subordinated group with the use of a toxic tool of caste known as colorism.

Among marginalized Americans, the closer they have been to the dominant caste in skin color and in hair and facial features, the higher on the scale they have generally ranked, the women in particular, and the more value attached to them even by those whose appearance is further from the caste-driven ideal. This distortion in human value is especially insidious in America, owing to the historic means by which most African-Americans acquired their range in color and facial features—the rape and sexual abuse of enslaved African women at the hands of their masters and of other men in the dominant caste over the centuries.

With few other outlets for control and power, people on the bottom rung may put down others of their own caste to lift themselves up in the eyes of the dominant. The caste system has historically rewarded snitches and sellouts among the lowest caste, as with the enforcers in the concentration camps of the Third Reich and the slave drivers on southern plantations. This was such a common device that, in America, there are several names for such a person, among them Uncle Tom or HNIC, short for Head Negro in Charge. People in the lowest caste came to resent these stooges of the caste system as much as, if not more than, they resented the dominant caste itself.

Even as others in the lowest caste try to escape the basement, those left behind can tug at the ones trying to rise. Marginalized people across the world, including African-Americans, call this phenomenon "crabs in a barrel." Many of the slave rebellions or the later attempts at unionizing African-American laborers in the South were thwarted because of this phenomenon, people subverting those who tried to get out, the spies paid with an extra peck of privilege for forewarning the dominant caste of unrest. These behaviors unwittingly work to maintain the hierarchy that those betraying their brethren are seeking to escape.

But this universal impulse may not always be caused by rank envy. A group already under siege may feel that "the team just cannot afford losing any member," wrote Sudipta Sarangi, an Indian specialist in organizational management. "If a certain member of the group starts climbing up—by doing better in life—the sheer fear of that individual's exit pushes everyone to pull him down."

• • •

Success in the American caste system requires some level of skill at decoding the preexisting order and responding to its dictates. Upon entry to the American caste system, immigrants learn to distance themselves from those in the basement, lest they land there themselves.

Though it was the protest movements of the subordinated caste that helped open the door to nonwhite immigrants in 1965, immigrants of color, like immigrants throughout American history, face the dilemma of adhering to the unwritten rules of caste. They face the painful dilemma of either rejecting the lowest caste of indigenous African-Americans or making common cause with those who fought so that they could enter the country to begin with.

But caste inverts the path to acceptance in America for people of African descent. Immigrants from Europe in the previous century were often quick to shed their names and drop the accents and folkways of the old country. They played down their ethnicity to gain admission to the dominant caste. Black immigrants discover that because they look like the people consigned to the lowest caste, the caste system rewards them for doing the opposite of the Europeans. "While white immigrants stand to gain status by becoming 'Americans,'" wrote the sociologist Philip Kasinitz, "by assimilating into the higher status group—black immigrants may actually lose social status if they lose their cultural distinctiveness."

Many recent African immigrants are better educated, better traveled than many Americans, may be fluent in multiple languages, and do not wish to be demoted to the lowest caste in their adopted homeland. The caste system encourages black immigrants to do everything they can to build distance between themselves and the subordinated caste they might be taken for. Like everyone else, they are exposed to the corrosive stereotypes of African-Americans and may work to make sure that people know that they are not of that group but are Jamaican or Grenadian or Ghanaian.

A Caribbean immigrant told Kasinitz: "Since I have been here, I have always recognized that this is a racist country, and I have made every effort not to lose my accent."

It is a clever, self-perpetuating tool of the caste system to keep those at the bottom divided in a manufactured fight to avoid last place. This has led to occasional friction between people descended from Africans who arrived in America at different points in our history. Some immigrants from the Caribbean and Africa, like their predecessors from other parts of the world, may show a wariness of African-Americans, warn their children not to "act like African-Americans" or not to bring one home to date or marry. In so doing, they may fall into the trap of trying to prove, not that the stereotype is false, but that they do not fit the lie.

Up and down the hierarchy, Ambedkar noted, "each caste takes its pride and its consolation in the fact that in the scale of castes it is above some other caste."

Try as it may to entice newcomers to take sides in upholding the hierarchy, the caste system fails to reach some people. Some children of immigrants from the Caribbean, people like Eric Holder, Colin Powell, Malcolm X, Shirley Chisholm, and Stokely Carmichael, among many others, have shared in the common plight of those in the lowest caste, become advocates for justice, and transcended these divisions for the greater good.

• • •

Caste helps explain the otherwise illogical phenomenon of African-Americans or women or other marginalized people who manage to rise to authority only to reject or diminish their own. Caught in a system that grants them little true power or authority, they may bend to the will of caste and put down their own if they wish to rise or to be accepted or merely to survive in the hierarchy. They learn that they may not be held accountable because of the low status of those they betray or neglect.

Many cases of mistreatment of people in the lowest caste occur at the hands of those of their same caste, as in the case of Freddie Gray, who died of spinal injuries at the hands of police officers in Baltimore. Gray was handcuffed in the back of a police van but not secured with safety belts, according to court testimony. The van swerved and curved, knocking Gray around the cargo area, handcuffed and unable to keep himself from crashing into the interior walls of the van. Three of the officers involved were black, including the driver of the van. This combination of factors allowed society to explain away Gray's death as surely having nothing to do with race, when in fact it was likely caste at work. All of these officers were either acquitted or had their charges dropped.

It is in keeping with caste protocols that, of the few officers who have been prosecuted for police brutality in recent high-profile cases, a notable number of them were men of color—a Japanese-American officer in Oklahoma, a Chinese-American officer in New York City, and a Muslim-American officer in Minneapolis. These are cases in which men of color pay the price for what upper-caste men often have gotten away with.

This phenomenon runs across levels of marginalization. The supervisor of the officers at the chokehold death of Eric Garner was a black woman. The people hardest on women employees can sometimes be women supervisors under pressure from and vying for the approval of male bosses in a male-dominated hierarchy in which fewer women are allowed to rise. Each of these cases presents a complicated story that presumably dismisses race or sex as a factor, but one that makes perfect sense, and maybe only makes sense, when seen through the lens of a caste system.

The enforcers of caste come in every color, creed, and gender. One does not have to be in the dominant caste to do its bidding. In fact, the most potent instrument of the caste system is a sentinel at every rung, whose identity forswears any accusation of discrimination and helps keep the caste system humming.

CHAPTER FIFTEEN

———

Satchel Paige and the Illogic of Caste

His fastball, shot toward home plate like a pistol bullet, once was clocked at 103 miles an hour, fast enough to "tear the glove off the catcher," in the words of the sportswriter Robert Smith. LeRoy "Satchel" Paige was one of the greatest baseball pitchers ever to step onto a mound. Yet, coming of age in the early twentieth century, when Jim Crow was at its cruelest, he never had the chance to become all that he could have been. And the world of baseball forwent a talent that surely would have changed the fate of matchups and pennant races, perhaps entire teams, and the sport itself.

Here was a man who threw so hard and so fast that "catchers had to cushion their gloves with beefsteak so that their hands wouldn't be burning after the game," his biographer Larry Tye told National Public Radio.

Here was a man so confident that he told whoever was paying him that he would strike out the first nine batters with a money-back guarantee and told the outfielders to just take a seat.

It happened that Paige was not only fast but threw with

such precision that teammates let him practice knocking lit cigarettes out of their mouths with his fastballs. "That we know of, he never knocked out a ballplayer," Tye told NPR. "He knocked out one cigarette after another, and that was extraordinary faith."

The beloved Yankee center fielder Joe DiMaggio, who went to bat against Paige at exhibition games before Paige was hired by the majors, called him the best pitcher he had ever faced. In his day, Paige "may well have been the fastest pitcher in the nation," wrote Smith in *Pioneers of Baseball,* "or even in history."

He didn't get the chance to make the most of it.

For more than half a century, America's pastime was rigidly segregated, the very best players of either caste rarely getting to meet on the field and never in an official game. Paige got into baseball in the late 1920s and thus spent most of his career playing on all-black teams that were every bit as talented but lacking in the resources and infrastructure of the all-white majors. The full measure of his and his teammates' talents cannot truly be known because of the incomplete record-keeping and scant media coverage in the devalued world of the Negro Leagues.

Paige was widely considered superior not solely because of his innate talent and ingenuity but because he worked so long and hard at it—a work ethic that had him barnstorming the country, pitching for the Negro Leagues and then for whoever else was willing to pay him. He pitched nearly every day, all year long, not just during the traditional baseball season and without the luxury of the relief pitchers in the majors. He gave his pitches names like the bat dodger and the midnight crawler and the hesitation pitch, where he would pause after planting his left foot, psyching the batter into swinging prematurely.

Though he was one of the greatest pitchers in baseball history, the limits of the caste system reduced him at one point to picking up spare change by pitching batting practice for white players in the minor leagues. By the time major league baseball opened up to African-Americans in 1946, when Jackie Robinson signed with the Brooklyn Dodgers, Satchel Paige was already forty and considered too old for the game.

But two years later, the Cleveland Indians were in the midst of one of the tightest pennant races in American League history, and the owner thought Paige might put them over the top now that the color bar had been lifted. The owner, Bill Veeck, approached Paige in the middle of the 1948 season and signed him as a free agent.

Paige was well past his peak when he finally got his shot at the majors. At forty-two, he was the oldest rookie in baseball, old enough to be his teammates' father. Still, at one of his first starting games in the big league, fans stormed the turnstiles to see him play at Comiskey Park. There, he pitched a 5–0 shutout for Cleveland over the Chicago White Sox, helping Cleveland make it to the playoff, and ultimately to the World Series, just as the team owner had hoped.

That year, Paige would become the first African-American to pitch in the World Series, though given the assumptions about his age and the politics of a championship season, he was assigned as a relief pitcher. When it was his turn at the mound, he pitched for two-thirds of an inning while the Indians were trailing the Boston Braves and did not allow a hit. The Cleveland Indians won the World Series that year.

He would go on to pitch in the majors for a few more seasons, but his best years were behind him, the career he should have had in a fairer world deprived of him, and there was nothing that anyone could do to make up for what had been withheld. The majors turned to him one more time, in the fall of 1965, to pitch at the age of fifty-nine. By then he was older than most of the managers. The Kansas City Athletics were last in the standings, and attendance had plummeted. The owner got the idea to recruit Paige, who had always been a showman, to pitch for the A's to fill the stands as a publicity stunt.

The fans turned out. They loaded onto the stands for the spectacle. But Paige came to play. The oldest pitcher in baseball history threw three scoreless innings that day against the Red Sox. Paige left the field with his team in the lead, a lead that the Athletics blew after he returned to the dugout, losing the game in the end. He had salvaged the team momentarily and was serenaded by the audience, who had come out mostly to see him pitch one last time.

Afterward, reporters asked him how it felt to pitch at nearly sixty years old to batters who could be his grandsons. "It was no big deal for me to come back up here," he said, "because I had no business being out. Now folks can see that I must have had a lot more going for me, and I deserved to be in the big leagues when I was in my prime."

Satchel Paige was cheated by a caste system at the height of its injustice and absurdity. But he was not the only loser to the illogic of caste. "Many critics agree that it was actually American baseball that was the loser in the Paige saga," wrote the sportswriter Mark Kram. "Any number of major league teams would have done better with Paige in their ranks when he was in his prime. Marginal teams might have won pennants; championship teams might have extended their domination."

Under the spell of caste, the majors, like society itself, were willing to forgo their own advancement and glory, and resulting profits, if these came at the hands of someone seen as subordinate.

Part Five

———

The Consequences of Caste

CHAPTER SIXTEEN

The Euphoria of Hate

The film footage, black and white, rough against the wall onto which it is projected, unfolds in a continuing loop in a cave of a viewing room at a Berlin museum. It shoves/heaves/spits you back in time to Saturday, July 6, 1940, at precisely three p.m. There is no commentary explaining the footage. You are forced to absorb the horror of it, in all of its banal pageantry, on your own.

Hitler is returning to Berlin after the Germans have seized Paris in the Battle of France. The camera captures his arrival at Anhalter Station and follows the flower-strewn Strassen along the parade route to the Reich Chancellery. Hitler's motorcade winds past people who are not just hurling confetti but are so tightly packed together that they themselves look like mounds of confetti thrown by the wind. Soldiers have to hold back the smiling, crying women, as would happen at Beatles concerts a generation from this moment. The roar of the crowd is not recognizably human but the rolling crash of ocean waves that recede and then batter the shore again. Church bells ring in the distance. The children and the men and the women flutter their own Nazi flags like bird wings.

The camera closes in, and you can begin to make out the individual

Heils—the male Heils from the high-pitched female Heils. A boy is hoisted on a street sign waving and heiling. A little girl is on a parent's shoulder heiling. Soldiers' heels press against the soil to keep their footing against the crowd, their jackboots braced against women's pumps, the women swooning and pushing, the soldiers grinning at the futility of holding back Hitler's screaming fans in a lighthearted tussle between pant cuffs and stockinged calves.

The camera cuts to the balcony and to the object of the throng's uncontained rapture. You see him first from behind, the silhouette of Hitler set against a million dots that are his jubilant fans. He stands like a statue, arms rigidly forward. He leans over the balcony and lets escape a smile of satisfaction. You recall that you have never seen an image of evil smiling, a quarter second of human emotion. He surveys the waving, cheering base of his power, and nods. "This is good," the look on his face is saying.

People laugh in reverie, jubilation all around, from the balcony and along the parade route and on the packed Platz where it appears that every German alive has managed to squeeze themselves in. So many that they are fairly holding one another up and jumping and waving their Nazi flags, a million Nazi flags. The motorcade had only minutes ago wound beneath Nazi banners a story high, blowing from above on both sides of the street, every few feet a Nazi banner, rows and rows for miles. This is the worship service of the true believers, looking now like mounds of pebbles on a beach, a million indistinguishable bees in a hive.

The film played in a loop on the wall without comment. None was necessary. I sat mesmerized and repulsed, sickened but unable to get up. Perhaps if I stayed long enough, I might begin to comprehend it. In that moment, you are face-to-face with the force of willing susceptibility to evil. The Nazis could not have risen to power and done what they did *without the support of the masses of people who were open to his spell. I could not stop watching it. The smiling, shining faces in this carpet of exuberant humanity—this massive number of people could not all be what we would consider evil. They are husbands, wives, mothers, fathers, children, uncles, nephews, all gathered at a ticker-tape parade on a brilliant, sunny day celebrating what we know to be a horror.*

I thought to myself, Did the German people know the carnage they were celebrating? Yes, it turns out, clips of bombing raids were shown during news reels before the feature film at the cinema. They knew that the French had been violently defeated. It was two years past Kristallnacht. They knew that Jewish friends and neighbors had been rounded up, publicly humiliated, taken away, never seen again. And the people in the crowd were smiling and happy. Everything that happened to the Jews of Europe, to African-Americans during the lynching terrors of Jim Crow, to Native Americans as their land was plundered and their numbers decimated, to Dalits considered so low that their very shadow polluted those deemed above them—happened because a big enough majority had been persuaded and had been open to being persuaded, centuries ago or in the recent past, that these groups were ordained by God as beneath them, subhuman, deserving of their fate. Those gathered on that day in Berlin were neither good nor bad. They were human, insecure and susceptible to the propaganda that gave them an identity to believe in, to feel chosen and important.

What would any of us have done had we been in their places? How many people actually go up against so great a tide of seeming inevitability? How many can see the evil for what it is, as it is occurring? Who has the courage to stand up to the multitudes in the face of a charismatic demigod who makes you feel better about yourself, part of something bigger than yourself, that you have been primed to believe?

Every last one of us would now say to ourselves, I would never have attended such an event, I would never have attended a lynching. I would never have stood by, much less cheered, as a fellow human was dismembered and then set on fire here in America. And yet tens of thousands of everyday humans did just that in the lifetime of the oldest among us in Germany, in India, in the American South. This level of cold-hearted disconnection did not happen overnight. It built up over generations of insecurities and resentments.

Some of the witnesses and participants who heiled Hitler and laughed at humans being tortured in the Jim Crow South are still alive, cradling grandchildren to their bosom. The camera in Berlin panned the crowd and fixed its lens on the children, a little girl with a blond pageboy and a barrette in her hair, heiling Hitler, hoisted on her parent's shoulders. She would be about eighty now, and this could be one of the earliest memories she carries inside her as a human being.

Germany bears witness to an uncomfortable truth—that evil is not one person but can be easily activated in more people than we would like to believe when the right conditions congeal. It is easy to say, *If we could just root out the despots before they take power or intercept their rise. If we could just wait until the bigots die away.* . . . It is much harder to look into the darkness in the hearts of ordinary people with unquiet minds, needing someone to feel better than, whose cheers and votes allow despots anywhere in the world to rise to power in the first place. It is harder to focus on the danger of common will, the weaknesses of the human immune system, the ease with which the toxins can infect succeeding generations. Because it means the enemy, the threat, is not one man, it is us, all of us, lurking in humanity itself.

CHAPTER SEVENTEEN

The Inevitable Narcissism of Caste

We are accustomed to the concept of narcissism—a complex condition of self-aggrandizing entitlement and disregard of others, growing out of a hollow insecurity—as it applies to individuals. But some scholars apply it to the behavior of nations, tribes, and subgroups. Freud was among the earliest psychoanalysts to connect a psychiatric diagnosis to Narcissus of Greek mythology, the son of the river god who fell in love with his own image in a pool of water and, not realizing that it was he who was "spurning" his affection, died in despair. "Narcissus could not conceive that he was in love with his own reflection," wrote the psychologist Elsa Ronningstam. "He was caught in an illusion."

So, too, with groups trained to believe in their inherent sovereignty. "The essence of this overestimation of one's own position and the hate for all who differ from it is narcissism," wrote the psychologist and social theorist Erich Fromm. "He is nothing," Fromm wrote, "but if he can identify with his nation, or can transfer his personal narcissism to the nation, then he is everything."

History has shown that nations and groups will conquer, colonize, enslave, and kill to maintain the illusion of their primacy. Their investment in this illusion gives them as much of a stake in the inferiority of those deemed beneath them as in their own presumed superiority. "The survival of the group," Fromm wrote, "depends to some extent on the fact that its members consider its importance as great or greater than that of their own lives, and furthermore that they believe in the righteousness, or even superiority, of their group as compared to others."

Thus, when under threat, they are willing to sacrifice themselves and their ideals for the survival of the group from which they draw their self-esteem. The social theorist Takamichi Sakurai wrote bluntly: "Group narcissism leads people to fascism. An extreme form of group narcissism means malignant narcissism, which gives rise to a fanatical fascist politics, an extreme racialism."

In modern times, this kind of group narcissism has gripped two nations in particular, according to Fromm: "the racial narcissism which existed in Hitler's Germany, and which is found in the American South," he wrote in 1964, at the height of the civil rights movement.

Fromm well knew the perils of group narcissism from both his training in psychoanalysis and his personal experience. He was a German Jew who fled to Switzerland after the Nazis took power in Germany, and then to the United States in 1934. He saw firsthand the Nazi appeals to the fears and insecurities of everyday Germans in the lead-up to the Nazi takeover.

"If one examines the judgment of the poor whites regarding blacks, or of the Nazis in regard to Jews," Fromm wrote, "one can easily recognize the distorted character of their respective judgments. Little straws of truth are put together, but the whole which is thus formed consists of falsehoods and fabrications. If the political actions are based on narcissistic self-glorifications, the lack of objectivity often leads to disastrous consequences."

In both instances, Fromm found the working class to be among the most susceptible, harboring an "inflated image of itself as the most admirable group in the world, and of being superior to another racial group that is singled out as inferior," he wrote. A person in this group "feels: 'even though I am poor and uncultured I am somebody important because I belong to the most admirable group in the world—I am white'; or 'I am Aryan.'"

A group whipped into narcissistic fervor "is eager to have a leader with whom it can identify," Fromm wrote. "The leader is then admired by the group which projects its narcissism onto him."

The right kind of leader can inspire a symbiotic connection that supplants logic. The susceptible group sees itself in the narcissistic leader, becomes one with the leader, sees his fortunes and his fate as their own. "The greater the leader," Fromm wrote, "the greater the follower. . . . The narcissism of the leader who is convinced of his greatness, and who has no doubts, is precisely what attracts the narcissism of those who submit to him."

• • •

Caste behavior is essentially a response to one's assigned place in the hierarchy. According to the script that the culture hands us all, the dominant caste (whether man over woman, rich over

poor, white over black, Brahmin over Dalit) is not to take instructions or even suggestions from the lower caste. The script
decrees that the dominant caste must be right, more informed,
more competent, first in all things.

The dominant caste tends to resist comparison to lower-
caste people, even the suggestion that they have anything in
common or share basic human experiences, as this diminishes
the dominant-caste person and forces the contemplation of
equality with someone deemed lower.

Years ago, a colleague fretted to me about his and his wife's
worries about his father-in-law, who had recently had a health
setback. The father-in-law lived in another state and was not
as sharp as he once had been, might have fallen recently or
suffered some other worrisome though not life-threatening
development. My colleague lamented to me that his wife was
going to have to make a trip many miles away to check on him,
and she would perhaps have to look into assisted living. It was
weighing on her, and him.

He was speaking directly to me, but his words seemed a general lament to the universe. He was facing an existential disruption that I could identify with. In the past, I had mentioned to
him the challenges I had had managing the care of my mother,
who had been disabled years before. He had listened at the time
with the detachment of those who have not yet faced the inevi-
table, who tell themselves, as we all do, that somehow we will
escape what we know is coming.

I told him I was sorry to hear that his family was going
through this. I can understand, I told him. As you know, I said,
I have been having to take care of my mother while being on
the road, and I, too, had to look into assisted living for her. He

seemed taken aback at the very suggestion that the situations might have anything whatsoever in common, as if this were tantamount to equating a giraffe with a kangaroo. The statement was seen as an insult to him and activated a deep-seated programming. "Why, you can't compare my father-in-law," he said of the preposterousness of the idea, "to *your mother*."

• • •

In the unspoken rules of caste, the people in the dominant caste are expected to be first or in the superior station. Historically, their job is to correct, direct, discipline, and police the people in the lowest caste. They are to be ever vigilant to any rise or breach on the part of those beneath them.

I had borne witness to this in the American caste system, but the more time I spent among Indians, the more these caste rules became apparent to me, predictive even, in my interactions with people from the world's original caste system. I learned to recognize almost immediately the differences between dominant-caste Indians and Dalits, even without the starker physical cues of dominant and subordinated castes in America.

I noticed, first, upper-caste people tended to be lighter in complexion and sharper in features, though that is not an iron-clad indicator. Secondly, I noticed that they were more likely to speak English with British diction, although that could be a sign of education and class as much as caste hierarchy. More revealingly and more consistently, I began to be able to distinguish people from their bearing and demeanor, in accord with the universal script of caste. It was no accident that my caste radar worked more efficiently when there was a group of people interacting among themselves. Caste is, in a way, a performance, and I could detect the caste positions of people in a group but not necessarily a single Indian by himself or herself. "There is never caste," the Dalit leader Ambedkar once said. "Only castes."

At a panel or seminar, upper-caste people were often the ones leading the discussion or doing most of the talking. They tended to speak more formally, giving direction, heads held high. On the other hand, the Dalits, as if trained not to bring attention to themselves, sat in the shadows, on the periphery at a conference seminar, asking few questions, daring not, it seemed, to intrude upon an upper-caste domain or conversation even if the discussion was about them, which in fact it was.

Even in the rarefied space of a scholarly presentation, when an upper-caste person was correcting a lower-caste person, the Dalit listened and took their admonishment without questioning, head often down or nodding that, *yes, you are correct, I will go back now and do what you have said.* I winced as I watched people talk down to scholars from the subordinate caste in an open forum.

In India, it was Dalits who gravitated toward me like long-lost relatives, surrounding me and propping themselves on a sofa near me for an impromptu subordinate-caste tête-à-tête. I discovered that they wanted to hear from me, or, I should say, commune with someone they recognized as a kindred spirit who shared a common condition. "We read James Baldwin and Toni Morrison because they speak to our experiences," a Dalit scholar said to me. "They help us in our plight."

I was standing during a lunch break at a conference in Delhi. A Dalit scholar and I were communing about our kindred perspectives when an upper-caste woman walked up and broke into the conversation to tell the Dalit woman what she should have included in her presentation, a point that she missed and which she would do well to include the next time.

When the upper-caste woman left after making her points, it was hard to get our footing again. She had jarred us from our parallel caste communing. I asked the Dalit woman if she knew the woman who had just interrupted us, because she had spoken with such familiarity and comfort. "No," the Dalit scholar said. "You see, that is what happens. She just let me know that she was upper caste and above me."

• • •

Though they may not recognize it on a conscious level, dominant-caste Americans often show nearly as much curiosity about the ethnic, and thus caste, origins of their fellow Americans as do people in India. When Americans seek to locate themselves in the hierarchy, the line of inquiry may be more subtle and may not have the same life-or-death consequences as in India. But it is there.

They will question a person whose race is ambiguous until they are satisfied of an origin. If descended from western Europe, they might query an Italian-American about their roots—what part of Italy, north or south, countryside or city—out of genuine interest or because they have visited or wish to, but also perhaps to locate them in the southern European hierarchy. If a person is part Irish and part Czech, they might emphasize, upon meeting someone, the Irish grandfather rather than the Czech grandmother. A white person might describe him- or herself as a mutt or as a "Heinz 57," which handily obscures lineage outside of northwestern Europe.

The old eugenics hierarchy of presumed value still lurks beneath the surface. A woman whose grandparents immigrated from Poland might say to an Irish-American—whose status is perceived as higher than hers—that they came from Austria (justifying it to herself by recalling the shifting borders in the twentieth century). But the same woman might "admit" that they came from Poland to an African-American of presumed lower rank, whom she had no need to impress, her higher status secure and understood.

Not long ago, in Boston and Chicago and Cleveland, people spoke of "white ethnics" from southern and eastern Europe as political voting blocs. They distinguished the "lace-curtain Irish" from the "shanty Irish." Once, at the end of a meeting in the Northeast a few years ago, a young white assistant in a room with black professionals was asked the routine question of how her name was spelled, which could have been Kathryn, Catherine, Katherine, or maybe Katharine. She straightened her back and answered pertly, "The English spelling," which seemed no answer at all and a curious bid to set herself apart from everyone else in the room, to pull rank with Anglo-Saxony, which no actual Anglo-Saxon would need to do. I thought to myself, *And exactly what spelling would that be?*

Three white women were once catching up over dinner about people they had known for years, their conversation flowing along caste lines beyond conscious awareness. One woman, of Irish descent, brought up someone whose family, she pointed out, had arrived from Germany in the first half of the twentieth century. This prompted a second woman to chime in that her family had come from Germany earlier. They arrived in the 1860s. The third woman brought up someone who had an unusual last name. The other two immediately asked its origin. "Is it German?" "No, Danish," came the answer. They moved on to another acquaintance. "Isn't his wife Spanish?" one woman asked another. "Oh, she's from a country in South America," another said, "like Colombia or Venezuela."

The conversation turned to the third woman and the strawberry-colored hair of some of her relatives. The German-American woman said they looked Irish.

"No," the third woman said. "We're Nordic."

The other two, the Irish-American and the German-American, fell silent. The conversation paused. Somehow everyone in the room realized the power of the word *Nordic* in all of its ambiguous specificity, ambiguous because it's not a country, specific in that it is language inherited from early twentieth-century eugenics, passed down through culture and lore. No one asked which country her family had come from—Sweden? Norway? Finland? Iceland?—or when they had arrived. If one was Nordic, it did not matter.

The word shut down conversation momentarily. Nordic has long been at the top of the hierarchy. And after all these decades, it still trumped everyone in the room.

CHAPTER EIGHTEEN

The German Girl with the Dark, Wavy Hair

There came a time during World War II when most every Jewish resident had vanished from German life. They were abducted or forced underground, and their absence left a vacuum and a paranoia among the Aryans who remained. Without a scapegoat to look down upon, the people had only themselves to regard and to distinguish, one from the other, and they scanned their countrymen for someone else to be better than.

The fixation on purity had put everyone on high alert, and, in the north of the country, in a village near Hanover, someone made a passing remark to a young German girl, raising suspicions about her appearance and, by extension, her lineage, and thus her worth.

The air was dense with nervous surveillance, a hunting hyperawareness of the least sign of difference. People had noticed that the girl's hair was darker than most, closer to that of Iberians to the south of them than to many Germans. Of course, the *Führer* himself had pitch-dark hair, and, for this, dark-haired Germans could console themselves if they happened to have this trait in common with their leader. But his hair was bristle straight, and on this score, too, the German girl near Hanover strayed from Aryan convention.

People thought it curious that this girl from a solid German family looked, to them, as if she could be from the Middle East, that she looked, as best they could tell from their limited knowledge, Persian. It was not clear that villagers had actually known any Persians, but the idea somehow got embedded in their minds. Did the family have any Persian blood or the blood of people from that part of the world in their background? More ominously, and implied if not said outright, any Jewish blood?

People noticed, and took the time to comment, that her hair curved in waves, fell in dark ripples rather than the flaxen silk that flowed straight down the backs of many Aryan girls. Not only that, people noticed that her skin was perceptibly if ever so slightly darker than that of many Germans, leaning golden and olive, one might say, rather than ivory and alabaster like the people around her, even those in her own family, as if a buried trait had somehow surfaced in her.

These are the minute distinctions that can take on greater significance when there are fewer distinctions to make. Under the Nazis, these distinctions carried graver consequences than idle chatter. This was an explosive observation at a time when Reich citizens were under threat to live up to Aryan ideals in order to survive.

The comments, or rather, in that era, accusations, rattled the German teenager. And so she went to a mirror with a measuring tape and measured the width and length of her eyes, her forehead and nose to see if they were within some standard that people spoke of in the era of eugenics and Aryan conformity.

She had pictures taken of herself gauging the features of her face to find some reassurance beyond her hair and skin.

The mere mention of perceived deviations from the Aryan standard brought unwanted, potentially dangerous scrutiny. As it was, Germans knew to have a "racial passport" on hand in the event that their Aryan status came into question. Even priests and nuns were arrested after a Jewish ancestor was uncovered.

The family grew concerned enough to make a discreet search into their family tree. Genealogists did brisk business in the Third Reich. Germans combed family Bibles and church records and government offices in case they were called upon to defend their origins. So, before they could be further accused, the family went back three generations to see for themselves if something other than Aryan blood had somehow slipped into their veins, some unwelcome intruder that a forebear might have adored but whose presence was now cause for shame.

The family happened to have found themselves in the clear and maintained their status as good Germans. The girl with the dark, wavy hair survived the war. She married and had children and grandchildren but spoke little of the Reich or the war that had defined her adolescence.

Decades later, a granddaughter would find a photograph of her. It shows a teenage girl holding a measuring tape to her face, a relic of the paranoia of the dominant caste. Even the favored ones were diminished and driven to fear in the shadow of supposed perfection.

CHAPTER NINETEEN

Shock Troops on the Borders of Hierarchy

At the dinner hour on a nineteenth-century steamboat in the antebellum South, the caste ritual went as follows: At the first bell, the white passengers were seated with the captain for their meal. After they finished, the second bell rang for the white crewmen—the engineers, the pilot, the servants. Only after all of the white people on board, of every class and status, completed their meals would the third bell ring, and the black crewmen, slave or free, be permitted to eat.

A problem arose, however, if there happened to be free black passengers in their midst. Free blacks paid their fare and were on paper in the same category as the white passengers. They were likely middle-class, but what mattered was that they were lowest caste. And historically, caste trumps class.

It was taboo for blacks and whites to sit, stand, or eat in the same space at the same time or even to use the same utensils. So they were not going to eat with their white counterparts or with the white crewmen who were presumably lower in class than they.

But there was more to it than that. Free blacks were an

affront to the caste system, always brushing against its borders. By their very existence, moving about as equals to the dominant caste, having the means to enter spaces considered the preserve of their betters, and having had the ingenuity to gain their freedom and to walk around in it, they threw the entire caste belief system into question. If people in the lowest caste had the capacity to be equal, why were they being enslaved? If they were smart enough to do something other than pick cotton or scrub floors, why then were they picking cotton and scrubbing floors? It was too mind-twisting to contemplate.

After the dinner service was cleared away and everyone else aboard had eaten and retired to their cabins or posts, the small group of black passengers, all women in this case, were permitted to eat in the pantry, "standing at the butler's table."

From the start of the caste system in America, people who were lowest caste but who had managed somehow to rise above their station have been the shock troops on the front lines of hierarchy. People who appear in places or positions where they are not expected can become foot soldiers in an ongoing quest for respect and legitimacy in a fight they had hoped was long over.

• • •

Public conveyances and recreational spaces have been the soundstage for caste confrontation precisely because they bring together in a confined space, for a limited time and purpose, groups that have historically been kept apart. They become test tubes of caste interaction, with its written and unwritten codes, its unspoken but understood rules of engagement.

In 2015, the members of a black women's book club were traveling by train on a wine tour of Napa Valley. They were laughing and chatting as were other tourists, given the nature of the outing and what all the passengers had been imbibing. But they alone seemed to attract the notice of the maître d'. "When you laugh," the maître d' told them, "I see it on the [other] passengers' faces." Soon the train stopped, and the black women, some of them senior citizens, were ejected and met by police, "as if we were criminals," they later said.

In 2018, the owner of a Pennsylvania golf club ordered black women club members to leave and called the police on them after white golfers complained that they were not moving fast enough. The women described themselves as experienced players aware of the game's protocols and said they had paced themselves according to the groups behind and in front of them. They said they noted that the men behind them were on break and were not ready to tee up. After arriving on the scene, the police determined that no charges were warranted. But the women said the confrontation had put them on edge, and they left to avoid further humiliation.

My work has required me to spend many, many hours in settings where I am often the only person of my ethnicity and gender, most often on planes. A flight attendant once commented on the miles I log year in and year out, "You fly more than we do." Because I fly so often, I frequently have cause to be seated in first or business class, which can turn me into a living, breathing social experiment without wanting to be. The things that have happened to me are far from the most grievous a person might suffer when traveling in a domain that can bring out the worst in most anyone. But some have stood out as a commentary on caste in action and can be demoralizing in the unexpected moment of intrusion.

For a flight out of Denver, I happened to be one of the first to board the plane, along with others in the front cabin. I could see the lead flight attendant greeting passengers at the boarding door. He was a man in his late twenties or early thirties, short blondish hair, and behind him was a second flight attendant, her brunette hair in a French twist.

The tendinitis in my wrist had been flaring up, and, as I stepped onto the plane with a splint on my forearm, I looked over to the lead flight attendant for help with my carry-on.

"Sir," I said, "I'm having a problem with my wrist, and I wondered if you would help me get my bag in the bin."

He looked past me to the men behind me at the boarding door, the kind of men who would come to mind when you think of first class. He waved me along as if I were holding up the line, though no one was moving at the moment. He seemed insulted even to have been asked, as if I was not aware of how the boarding process worked.

"There are two flight attendants in the back," he said. "They can help you when you get back there."

With those curt instructions, it was as if he had pulled me out of a lineup, singled me out from the other business travelers as the one who, on sight, did not belong, the one trespassing and now seeking special treatment to which I was not entitled. Marginalized people have a hard enough time moving about in a world built for others. Now it was as if I were taking up space that belonged to its rightful passengers. It came as a shock to me, perhaps because this clipped dismissal came from a man whose generation would not be expected to hold such retrograde assumptions. Somehow the air had turned confrontational. I had asked for something he did not believe I deserved.

"But I'm in first," I said.

That seemed only to make things worse. He had been caught in his moment of stereotyping and in front of others. He had disregarded all information inputs to the contrary, that I was boarding early, that luggage tags dangling from the bag I was seeking help with proclaimed that I had reached the highest possible level of loyalty to his airline. He could only have come to the conclusion he made on the basis of one thing alone: what I looked like.

He tried to recover from the faux pas of an openly dismissive caste assumption, for what is caste if not where one belongs in a hierarchy? He had to find a way to retain his own caste position, now that a flight attendant under him in the airline's hierarchy had heard him speak so brusquely to a passenger, wherever she happened to be seated.

"Well, leave it here, and we'll have to see what to do with it," he said, sighing as if it were a bass violin instead of a rolling bag.

The woman flight attendant who stood there during the exchange stepped forward and tried to set things right, cover for him, her superior.

"Here," she said, "let me help you with it. What seat are you in?"

She walked me to the seat and helped me hoist the bag into the bin. I thanked her for her kindness.

It was uncomfortable the rest of the flight. He was the only attendant in that cabin, and each time he passed through the aisle, the tension rose. I could feel the edge of it. He had been outed, and he punished me with a curt hostility until we landed.

• • •

It was a late-night flight from Portland, Oregon, to the East Coast. I had just boarded, and the flight attendant and I were looking for space to fit my roller bag into the haphazardly filled overhead compartments. Every time the flight attendant and I touched a bag to turn it on its side or to move it to the next bin, someone said, "No, you can't touch that one, that's my bag."

The man in the aisle seat behind me had two carry-ons overhead, taking up more space than allowed. I was anxious to get seated and out of this uncomfortable testing of wills. I offered to let him put his bag under my seat so that it would not take up space in front of him, anything to get the bag stored and get on our way.

"I'd be glad to do it," I told him and the flight attendant.

He let out a heavy breath.

"I put my bag where I wanted it. I don't want it under another seat."

He took the bag from the flight attendant and shoved it under his own seat. He then began complaining to the man in the window seat beside him, a man, like him, from the dominant caste, seated directly behind me.

"That's what happens when they let just anybody in first class," the owner of the bag said to the man next to him, loud enough for anyone around us to hear. "They should know better how to treat paying customers. I paid for my first-class ticket, and this is how they treat you."

The two men commiserated the whole flight, having found common cause and united by a shared resentment. It was a night flight, and I was exhausted from a long day of lectures. I needed to sleep. I let down the seat back. What did I do that for?

The man in the window seat behind me, who had been grousing about the unfairness of it all with the man whose bag had been moved, let out a howl.

"What do you think you're doing!" he yelled. "I'm trying to work here! Look what you've done. I've got my laptop out and you've shoved it into me!"

He slammed the back of my seat and pounded the tray forward, jostling me as he continued to hit from behind.

"I had no control over the seat back," I told him, looking back. "I'm just trying to get some rest." I looked over at the white man next to me, who had seen all of this, who would have felt the shudder of my seat being pushed from behind. He would not return a glance, isolating me further.

The men behind me continued to talk about the intrusions into first class. The air was thick with venom and made it impossible to sleep. I got up to tell the flight attendant to see if she might be able to help.

"I am desperately tired, and I need to sleep," I told her. "The man behind me is shoving my seat and making it impossible to get rest. Is there anything you could do? Could you explain the rules to him to defuse the situation?"

"Frankly, I don't know if it would help," she said. "Why don't you stay up here the rest of the flight?"

"I need to rest," I told her. "I can't sleep standing up here, and besides, I have a seat, and I should be able to sit in it."

"I know," she said. "I don't know what to tell you. It's up to you if you want to stay up here or go back."

I went back and sat up straight, across the length of the country. The caste system had put me in my place.

Part Six

———

Backlash

CHAPTER TWENTY

———

A Change in the Script

The greatest departure from the script of the American caste system was the election of an African-American to the highest office in the land. History has shown that there would be consequences to this disruption of the social order, and there were. What follows is not an analysis of the presidency of Barack Obama, but rather a look into the caste system's response to his ascension and the challenges it would place in his path.

First, to break more than two centuries of tradition and birthright, it would take the human equivalent of a supernova—a Harvard-trained lawyer, a U.S. senator from the land of Lincoln, whose expertise was the Constitution itself, whose charisma and oratory matched or exceeded that of most any man who had ever risen to the Oval Office, whose unusual upbringing inclined him toward conciliation of the racial divide, who famously saw the country as not blue states or red states but as the United States, whose wife, if it could be imagined, was also a Harvard-trained lawyer with as much star power as her husband, who, together with their two young daughters, made for a telegenic American dream family, and who, beyond all this, ran a scrupulous, near-flawless campaign, a movement really. It would take an idealist, who believed what most Americans would have sworn was impossible, for a black man to make it to the White House.

Secondly, his opponent, a beloved and aging war hero from Arizona, a wise and measured moderate Republican in a party that had grown more conservative, ran a less-than-energetic campaign and made several misjudgments, the most significant of which was choosing an unpredictable former governor of Alaska, a woman prone to gaffes and to quirky, word-salad misstatements, as his running mate.

Then, in the months leading up the election, a once-in-a-generation financial catastrophe descended on a country that seemed on the brink of financial ruin under the Republican administration then in power. Wall Street firms collapsed before our eyes, and the value of American homes, the primary source of many citizens' wealth, plunged in value, leaving millions of voters underwater.

In October 2008, a few weeks before the election, envelopes arrived in the mailboxes of millions of American households, mailings that became inadvertent leaflets in favor of the Democrat: the quarterly 401(k) statements that showed losses of as much as 40 percent of people's savings in the last year under the Republican president. By that November, some 12 million homeowners owed more on their mortgages than their houses were worth in what was now being called the Great Recession, among the worst economic downturns since the Great Depression.

People in the dominant caste who might have been on the

fence about taking a chance on an African-American candidate were looking at massive losses with no end in sight. *Hope* had been Obama's mantra during times that badly needed it. A record tide of people from the lower and middle castes, people who swelled with pride and whose votes now felt like a mission, came out for him, and, along with just enough dominant-caste voters who believed in him, too, swept Obama into the White House. The world was so joyous that a committee in Norway awarded him the Nobel Peace Prize within months of his inauguration. "Only very rarely has a person to the same extent as Obama captured the world's attention," the Nobel committee said, "and given its people hope for a better future."

• • •

Over the course of American history, the idea of a black man in the Oval Office was virtually unthinkable. But from a caste perspective, and beyond his own personal gifts, his singular origin story was one that the caste system would be more willing to accept, if any. His growing up in Hawaii, the son of an immigrant from Kenya and of a white woman from Kansas, was free from the heaviness of slavery and Jim Crow and the hard histories of regular African-Americans. His story did not trigger the immediate discomfort in the dominant caste, unlike those of everyday black people, who, if you scratch their family trees long enough, you run into a sharecropper cheated at settlement or an ancestor shut out of a neighborhood because of redlining, people for whom these injustices were not history, but their own or their foreparents' actual *lives.*

Rather, his origin story freed people in the dominant caste from having to think about the unsavory corners of American history. They could regard him with curiosity and wonderment and even claim him as part of themselves, if they chose. They could perhaps feel a connection to his mother and to his mother's mother, who tragically died just before Election Day. Both women were from the dominant caste and would not get to see how very far he would go in this world. The Delaware senator who would become his running mate, though, seemed to be speaking, however awkwardly, for some others in the ruling majority. "You've got the first sort of mainstream African-American who is articulate and bright and clean and a nice-looking guy," said Joe Biden. "I mean, that's a storybook, man."

After the election, white Americans in both parties extolled the progress the country had made in the past generation, relieved to be able to say that racism was a thing of the past. "We have a black president, for heaven's sakes," they would say, by way of example. The fact is, though, this was a development that the majority of the dominant caste was not truly in a position to claim. The majority of white voters did not support him in either of his presidential bids. He had star power and a way with babies and pensioners, but no matter how refined and inspirational, well-spoken and conciliatory he was, Obama's victory did not occur because most voters in the dominant caste had become more open-minded and enamored of him. As with other recent Democrats running for president, he won despite the bulk of the white electorate.

Even as they proclaimed a new post-racial world, the majority of white Americans did not vote for the country's first black president. An estimated 43 percent went for him in 2008. Thus, a solid majority of white Americans—nearly three out of every five white voters—did not back him in his first election, and fewer still—39 percent—voted for him in 2012. In the former Confederate state of Mississippi, only one in ten white voters pulled the lever for Obama. For much of his presidency, he was trying to win over people who did not want him in the Oval Office and some who resented his very existence.

As a measure of the enduring role of caste interests in American politics, the shadow of the Civil War seemed to hang over the 2008 election. It turned out that Obama carried every state that Abraham Lincoln had won in 1860, an election with an almost entirely white electorate but one that became a proxy for egalitarian sentiment and for the future of slavery and of the Republic. "The cultural divides of the Civil War on racial grounds," wrote the political scientist Patrick Fisher of Seton Hall University, "can thus still be considered to be influencing American political culture a century and a half later."

Lyndon B. Johnson, after signing the 1964 Civil Rights Act, is said to have predicted that the Democrats would lose the South for a generation for having stood up for the citizenship rights of African-Americans. That prophecy would prove to be correct but also an understatement. The Democrats would lose more than just the South and for well longer than a generation. From that moment forward, white Americans overall moved rightward toward the Republicans as the country enacted more egalitarian policies.

In the more than half century since that prophecy of 1964, no Democrat running for president has ever won a majority of the white vote. Lyndon Johnson was the last Democrat to win the presidency with a majority of the white electorate. Since that time, the Democrat who came closest, who attracted the largest percentage of white voters—at 48 percent—was fellow southerner Jimmy Carter in 1976. Only three Democrats have made it to the Oval Office since the Johnson and the civil rights era—Carter, Obama, and Bill Clinton, who won with 39 percent of the white vote in 1992 and 44 percent in 1996.

With whites pulling away from the Democrats and accustomed to prevailing in presidential elections through their sheer numbers, the outcome of the 2008 election was seen not merely as the defeat of John McCain, but perhaps a defeat of the historic ruling majority itself, "a challenge to the absoluteness of whites' dominance," wrote the political scientist Ashley Jardina of Duke University, who specializes in the behavior of the white electorate.

Combined with the 2008 U.S. Census Bureau projections of an end of the white majority by 2042, Obama's victory signaled that the dominant caste could undergo a not altogether certain but still unthinkable wane in power over the destiny of the United States and over the future of themselves and their children, and their sovereign place in the world. "The symbolism of Obama's election was a profound loss to whites' status," Jardina wrote.

This was something that no one in the dominant caste, or any other group in the country, for that matter, had ever had to contemplate. It meant that people who had always been first now had to consider the potential loss of their centrality. For many, "the ability of a black person to supplant the racial caste system," wrote the political scientist Andra Gillespie of Emory University, was "the manifestation of a nightmare which would need to be resisted."

That sense of fear and loss, however remote, "brought to the fore, for many whites," Jardina wrote, "a sense of commonality, attachment, and solidarity with their racial group," a sense of needing to band together to protect their place in the hierarchy.

The caste system sprang into action against this threat to the preexisting order. "The single most important thing we want to achieve," said Senate Majority Leader Mitch McConnell, Republican of Kentucky, on the eve of the midterm elections in 2010, "is for President Obama to be a one-term president."

• • •

An entire machinery had moved into place upon the arrival of the first head of state from the subordinate caste. A new party of right-wing detractors arose in his wake, the Tea Party, vowing to "take our country back." A separate movement of skeptics, who would come to be known as birthers, challenged the legitimacy of his citizenship and required him to produce an original birth certificate that they still chose to disbelieve. His opponents called him the "food stamp" president and depicted the president and the First Lady as simians. At opposition rallies, people brandished guns and bore signs calling for "Death to Obama."

In response to his election, Republicans began changing election laws, making it harder to vote. They did so even more vigorously after the Supreme Court overturned a section of the Voting Rights Act, removing federal election oversight that the states, each with a history of obstructing the minority vote, said was no longer needed.

Between 2014 and 2016, states deleted almost 16 million

people from voter registration lists, purges that accelerated in the last years of the Obama administration, according to the Brennan Center for Justice. States enacted new voter ID laws even as they created more barriers to obtaining this newly required ID. Together, these actions had the cumulative effect of reducing voter participation of marginalized people and immigrants, both of whom were seen as more likely to vote Democrat. "A paper found that states were far more likely to enact restrictive voting laws," wrote the commentator Jonathan Chait, "if minority turnout in their state had recently increased."

Contrary to the wistful predictions of post-racial harmony, the number of hate groups in the United States surged from 602 to more than 1,000 between 2000 and 2010, the middle of Obama's first term in office, according to the Southern Poverty Law Center. A 2012 study found that anti-black attitudes and racial stereotyping rose, rather than fell, as some might have hoped, in Obama's first term. The percentage of Americans who expressed explicit anti-black attitudes ticked upward from 48 percent in 2008 to 51 percent in 2012, but the percentage expressing implicit bias rose from 49 percent to 56 percent. The study found that higher percentages of white respondents now saw African-Americans as violent, irresponsible, and, most especially, lazy, after his victory, despite, or perhaps because of, the studiously wholesome black family in the White House headed by two Ivy League–educated parents.

With rising resentments, it would not be surprising that attacks on African-Americans might not only not have abated but would worsen under the unprecedented reversal of the social hierarchy. By the second term of the administration, in 2015, police were killing unarmed African-Americans at five times the rate of white Americans. It was a trend that would make police killings a leading cause of death for young African-American men and boys, these deaths occurring at a rate of 1 in 1,000 young black men and boys.

Early on, Obama had taken symbolic steps to bridge the racial divide. He held a "beer summit" with Henry Louis Gates, Jr., and the officer who had arrested Gates as he tried to enter his home near Harvard, having called the summit after the uproar over his comments that the police had "acted stupidly" in arresting the Harvard professor. When Trayvon Martin was killed, Obama observed that if he had had a son, the son would have looked like Trayvon. But the caste system rose up and his approval ratings fell after even these benign gestures. The opposition party stood firm against many of his ambitions and nominees, shutting down the government time and again, refusing to confirm or even consider his Supreme Court nominee Merrick Garland.

The caste system had handcuffed the president as it had handcuffed the African-Americans facedown on the pavement in the videos that had become part of the landscape. It was as if the caste system was reminding everyone of their place, and the subordinate caste, in particular, that no matter how the cast of the play was reshuffled, the hierarchy would remain as it always had been.

In a paradox of caste, many whites seemed to have known this, studies show, seemed to have trusted on some unconscious level that the caste system would hold the first black president, and the subordinate caste with which he had come to be associated, in check. As deeply as some people resented a black man presiding in the Oval Office, "most whites in the United States were not overwhelmingly concerned," Jardina writes, "that Obama would favor blacks over their own group."

Thus, within the parameters in which he was forced to maneuver, he made more headway with race-neutral goals. In so doing, he managed to reshape the country's healthcare system and lead on such issues as climate change, clean energy, gay marriage, sentencing reform, and investigations into police brutality that other administrations might have ignored altogether, while guiding the country out of recession.

But accomplishments from those considered to have stepped out of their place often only breed more resentment, in this case inciting the tremors of discontent among those feeling eclipsed by his very existence.

"Any upheaval in the universe is terrifying," James Baldwin once wrote, "because it so profoundly attacks one's sense of one's own reality."

Which is why Obama's presidency and his high approval ratings "masked an undercurrent of anxiety about our changing nation," according to Jardina. "It hid a swell of resistance to multiculturalism, and a growing backlash to immigration."

In November 2012, on the day after the first black president won reelection to a second term, Rush Limbaugh, the conservative radio talk show host, went on the air and lamented to his listeners. "I went to bed last night thinking we're outnumbered," Limbaugh said. "I went to bed last night thinking we've lost the country. I don't know how else you look at this."

That same day, a troubled sixty-four-year-old man in South Florida took the most extreme action imaginable. In the time leading up to the election, according to police, Henry Hamilton, owner of a tanning salon in Key West, told friends, "If Barack gets reelected, I'm not going to be around." He kept his word. His body was found in his condominium a day and a half after the returns came in. Two prescription bottles sat empty in his dining room. Beside him was a handwritten note demanding that he not be revived and cursing the newly reelected president.

CHAPTER TWENTY-ONE

———

Turning Point and the Resurgence of Caste

Caste does not explain everything in American life, but no aspect of American life can be fully understood without considering caste and embedded hierarchy. Many political analysts and left-leaning observers did not believe that a Trump win was possible and were blindsided by the outcome in 2016 in part because they had not figured into their expectations the degree of reliable consistency of caste as an enduring variable in American life and politics.

Trump channeled insecurities and disaffection that went deeper than economics, researchers have found. "White voters' preference for Donald Trump," wrote the political scientists John Sides, Michael Tesler, and Lynn Vavreck, ". . . was weakly related to their own job security but strongly related to concerns that minorities were taking jobs away from whites."

The tremors within the dominant caste had been building long before Trump announced his candidacy. "Defections accelerated over the course of Obama's presidency," Sides, Tesler, and Vavreck wrote. "This is why racial attitudes appear the more likely culprit."

In fact, "no other factor predicted changes in white partisanship during Obama's presidency as powerfully and consistently as racial attitudes," they said.

The researchers consider this kind of group hypervigilance to be what they call "'racialized economics': the belief that undeserving groups are getting ahead while your group is left behind."

The precarity of their lives and the changing demographics of the country induced a greater need to maintain whatever advantages they had come to expect and to shore up the one immutable characteristic that has held the most weight in the American caste system.

"Whites' racial attitudes are not merely defined by prejudice," writes Ashley Jardina of Duke University. "Many whites also possess a sense of racial identity and are motivated to protect their group's collective interests and to maintain its status. . . . Whiteness is now a salient and central component of American politics. White racial solidarity influences many whites' worldview and guides their political attitudes and behavior."

Consciously or not, many white voters "are seeking to reassert a racial order in which their group is firmly at the top."

The 2016 election thus became a cracked mirror held up to a country that had not been forced in this way to search its origins in more than a generation and was now seeing itself perhaps for the first time as it truly was. It was the culmination of forces that had been building for decades.

Democrat Hillary Clinton, the former secretary of state, was widely viewed as having won the presidential debates, despite her opponent's stalking of her at the podium and calling her a "nasty woman." She was seen as having carried herself with dignity and exhibiting a polished, if stiff, mastery of domestic and foreign affairs. Yet in polling she rarely managed to pull much beyond the margin of error against a man considered by some to be the least qualified person ever to run for president.

Clinton's loss in the Electoral College seems shocking until one considers caste. Whether consciously or not, the majority of whites voted for the candidate who made the most direct appeals to the characteristic most rewarded in the caste system. They went with the aspect of themselves that grants them the most power and status in the hierarchy. According to *New York Times* exit polling of 24,537 respondents, 58 percent of white voters chose the Republican Donald Trump and only 37 percent went for the Democrat Hillary Clinton. While she won nearly 3 million more votes than Trump by the popular count, she attracted a smaller share of the white vote than any Democratic candidate other than Jimmy Carter in his failed bid for reelection against Ronald Reagan in 1980.

"The parties have grown so divided by race," writes the political scientist Lilliana Mason, "that simple racial identity, without policy content, is enough to predict party identity."

There was perhaps no clearer measure of white solidarity than the actions of white women in 2016. The majority of them—53 percent—disregarded the common needs of women and went against a fellow white woman to vote with their power trait, the white side of their identities to which Trump appealed, rather than help an experienced woman, and themselves, make history.

"Trump was ushered into office by whites concerned about their status," Jardina writes, "and his political priorities are plainly aimed at both protecting the racial hierarchy and at strengthening its boundaries." These are people who feel "that the rug is being pulled out from under them—that the benefits they have enjoyed because of their race, their group's advantages, and their status atop the racial hierarchy are all in jeopardy."

● ● ●

The ruptures exposed in 2016 transcend a single election or candidate and go well beyond the initial theories of economic insecurity as the driver of the white vote. "In many ways, a sense of group threat is a much tougher opponent than an economic downturn," wrote the political scientist Diana Mutz, "because it is a psychological mindset rather than an actual event or misfortune."

Once in office, the forty-fifth president made no secret of his laser focus on the desires of his base. "Whether out of personal animus, political calculation, philosophical disagreement or a conviction that the last president damaged the country, Mr. Trump has made clear that if it has Mr. Obama's name on it, he would just as soon erase it from the national hard drive," wrote the *New York Times* White House correspondent Peter Baker.

Those susceptible to "dominant group status threat," Mutz wrote, will do whatever they can to protect the hierarchy that has benefited them, to "regain a sense of dominance and well-being."

The election outcome alone had his base feeling better. A couple of days after the election, two middle-aged white men with receding hairlines and reading glasses took their seats in first class on a flight from Atlanta to Chicago. They suspected by looking at each other, and knowing the polling results, that they were likely on the same team. It didn't take them long to confirm that they were.

"Last eight years," one of them said, "worst thing that ever happened, I'm so glad it's over."

"It was bigger than an election," the other one said. "It was one of the most amazing events I think we'll ever witness. I stayed up all night to watch it."

"Yeah, well, I went to bed that night thinking I'd be crying the next morning. Woke up. Best news I ever heard."

"There is justice in this world. They made a bad, bad choice with her," one said.

"The current president was a bad choice," the other said.

"He was in over his head. It's a beautiful day!"

"Yep, finally got it right. Yessiree."

CHAPTER TWENTY-TWO

The Symbols of Caste

The Confederate general who led the war against the United States over the right to hold human beings hostage for all their natural-born days, Robert E. Lee, or, more precisely, a bronze sculpture of Robert E. Lee, rose two stories high on its granite pedestal in the center of a village green in Charlottesville, Virginia. On this day in the late summer of 2017, the statue in honor of a hero of the former slaveholding states was now covered with a thin black tarp that had taken two men positioned in cranes something like an hour to stretch across the length and width of it, over the general's head and the American Saddlebred horse he sat astride.

The statue was under a shroud while city leaders tried to figure out what to do with it. The monument had drawn the attention of the world after a rally of white supremacists turned deadly just weeks before. The rally brought together disaffected members of the dominant caste in protest of the city's plan to remove the statue. It was as if the passions of the Civil War had been resurrected and had merged with a resurgent Nazism, which the forefathers of the young Americans at the rally had fought to vanquish back in the middle of the previous century. The heirs to the Confederates and the heirs to the Nazis could see how much they and their histories had in common even if ordinary Americans did not.

On that day in August 2017, Confederate flags and swastikas interfused above the ralliers, men mostly, some with haircuts as severe as their faces. Together, the night before, they had marched through the campus of the University of Virginia, extending Nazi salutes, chanting, "Sieg Heil," and "White lives matter," and "Jews will not replace us." They held tiki torches in the night air, reenacting the torchbearers' rivers of light at the old processions for Hitler. The following day, at the rally itself, the neo-Confederates and the neo-Nazis arrived well armed, which in turn drew counterprotesters bearing signs of peace. Then a white supremacist rammed a car into a crowd of counterprotesters, killing one of them, a paralegal named Heather Heyer, and wounding dozens of others.

Now the city was trying to keep the statue from public view, but every time the city covered it, someone would come and remove the tarp, releasing Lee's likeness in protest. The city would again send in the cranes to put the tarp back over it. The day I happened to visit Charlottesville, shortly after the rally, the city was prevailing.

From the center of the green, in the very middle of town, rose a jagged black trapezoid tied at the base like a giant chifforobe wrapped for protection until the movers arrive. It looked for all the world like a giant trash bag from which you could make out the crown of the general's head and the nose and tail of the horse at opposite ends. The whole effect of the giant trapezoid in the middle of a stately park brought more attention to the general, and to the monuments to the Confederacy, not less, though the tarp had been a short-term compromise to keep it from public view. Tourists came in search of it.

"Guess that's him right there," a man said, crossing the street to take a closer look. The tourists waited their turn to take their picture in front of the cloaked general. Then they made the pilgrimage to the street across from the statue, the street where Heather Heyer had been killed. It had become a block-long memorial to her, piles of dying roses and sunflowers, heartbroken messages scrawled in the pavement and on the sides of brick walls, a plea for humanity.

We are witness
Never forget
The minute we look away,
the minute we stop fighting, bigotry wins
There is no more room for hate
That all men are created equal

Across the United States, there are more than seventeen hundred monuments to the Confederacy, monuments to a breakaway republic whose constitution and leaders were unequivocal in declaring the purpose of their new nation. "Its foundations are laid," said Alexander Stephens, the vice president of the Confederacy, "its corner-stone rests upon the great truth that the negro is not equal to the white man; that slavery subordination to the superior race is his natural and normal condition. This, our new government, is the first, in the history of the world, based upon this great physical, philosophical, and moral truth. . . . With us, all of the white race, however high or low, rich or poor, are equal in the eye of the law. Not so with the negro. Subordination is his place. He, by nature, or by the curse against Canaan, is fitted for that condition which he occupies in our system."

The Confederacy would lose the war in April 1865, but in the succeeding decades would win the all-important peace. The Confederates would manage to take hold of the public imagination with gauzy portrayals of the Lost Cause. Two of the most influential and popular films of the early twentieth century— *Birth of a Nation* and *Gone with the Wind*—fed the country and the world the Confederate version of the war and portrayed the people of the degraded lowest caste as capable only of brute villainy or childlike buffoonery.

Even though the Thirteenth Amendment in 1865 ended slavery, it left a loophole that let the dominant caste enslave people convicted of a crime. This gave the dominant caste incentive to lock up lowest-caste people for subjective offenses like loitering or vagrancy at a time when free labor was needed in a penal system that the dominant caste alone controlled. After a decade of Reconstruction, just as African-Americans were seeking entry to mainstream society, the North abandoned its oversight of the South, pulled its occupying troops out of the region, and handed power back to the former rebels, leaving the survivors of slavery at the mercy of supremacist militias nursing wounds from the war. The federal government paid reparations not to the people who had been held captive, but rather to the people who had enslaved them.

The former Confederates reinscribed a mutation of slavery in the form of sharecropping and an authoritarian regime that put people who had only recently emerged from slavery into a world of lynchings, night riders, and Klansmen, terrors meant to keep them subservient. As they foreclosed the hopes of African-Americans, they erected statues and monuments everywhere to the slave-owning Confederates, a naked forewarning to the lowest caste of its subjugation and powerlessness.

It was psychic trolling of the first magnitude. People still raw from the trauma of floggings and family rupture, and the descendants of those people, were now forced to live amid monuments to the men who had gone to war to keep them at the level of livestock. To enter a courthouse to stand trial in a case that they were all but certain to lose, survivors of slavery had to pass statues of Confederate soldiers looking down from literal pedestals. They had to ride on roads named after the generals of their tormenters and walk past schools named after Klansmen.

Well into the twentieth century, heirs to the Confederacy built a monument with Lee, Stonewall Jackson, and Jefferson Davis carved in granite, bigger than Mount Rushmore, in Stone Mountain, Georgia. If the Confederacy had lost the war, the culture of the South and the lives of the lowest caste did not reflect it. In fact, the return to power of the former Confederates meant retribution and even harder times to come.

• • •

By the time of the rally in Charlottesville, there were some 230 memorials to Robert E. Lee in the United States, including the Robert E. Lee Hotel in Lexington, Virginia, Robert E. Lee Park in Miami, Florida, and Robert E. Lee Creek in Boise National Forest in Idaho, two thousand miles from the old Confederacy. There are scores of plaques, busts, schools, and roadways throughout the country—a Robert E. Lee *Street* in Mobile, Alabama, a Robert E. Lee *Drive* in Tupelo, Mississippi, a Robert E. Lee *Boulevard* in Charleston, South Carolina, a General Robert E. Lee *Road* in Brunswick, Georgia, and a Robert E. Lee *Lane* in Gila Bend, Arizona.

Students take classes at Robert E. Lee High School in Jacksonville, Florida, and in Tyler, Texas, among others, and at Lee Junior High School in Monroe, Louisiana. Eight states in the Union have a county named after Robert E. Lee: Alabama, Arkansas, Florida, Kentucky, Mississippi, North Carolina, South Carolina, and Texas. The third Monday in January is Robert E. Lee Day in both Mississippi and Alabama.

Robert E. Lee was a well-born graduate of West Point Academy, a pragmatic and cunning military strategist, a political moderate, for his times and his region, and a Virginia slaveholder who saw slavery as a necessary evil that burdened the owners more than the people they enslaved. "The blacks are immeasurably better off here than in Africa, morally, socially & physically," he once wrote. "The painful discipline they are undergoing, is necessary for their instruction as a race, & I hope will prepare & lead them to better things. How long their subjugation may be necessary is known & ordered by a wise merciful Providence."

Like other slaveholders, he made full use of the "painful discipline" of which he spoke. In 1859, three of the people he enslaved on his Virginia plantation—a man named Wesley Norris and his sister and cousin—fled north and were captured near the Pennsylvania border. They were forced back to Lee's plantation. Upon their arrival, Lee told them that "he would teach us a lesson we would never forget," Wesley Norris later recounted.

Lee ordered his overseer to strip them to the waist, tie them to posts, and whip the men fifty lashes and the woman twenty, on their bare backs. When the overseer resisted, Lee got the county constable and told him to "lay it on well," which the constable did. "Not satisfied with simply lacerating our naked flesh," Norris recalled, "Gen. Lee then ordered the overseer to thoroughly wash our backs with brine, which was done."

This was common practice and standard procedure during much of the 246 years of slavery. Had these and even more gruesome atrocities occurred in another country, at another time, to another set of people other than the lowest caste, they would have been considered crimes against humanity in violation of international conventions. But the slaveholders, overseers, and others in the dominant caste who inflicted atrocities upon millions of African-Americans over the centuries were not only not punished but were celebrated as pillars of society.

Lee was never called to account for what he did to the Norrises nor to the many families he broke apart as an enslaver, the children he separated from parents, the husbands from wives. Even after leading the war of southern secession that ended with more casualties than any other on this soil, Lee faced few penalties associated with treason. President Andrew Johnson, the Tennessee Democrat and onetime slaveowner who succeeded Abraham Lincoln after Lincoln's assassination, granted amnesty to most of the Confederates in a bid to move on from sectional tensions and to put the matter to rest. Lee did no jail time and suffered little censure, though he was no longer permitted to vote, and he was forced to relinquish his plantation, which the government coveted and converted into Arlington National Cemetery.

It turned out that, after the war, many white northerners

felt a greater kinship with the former Confederates who had betrayed the Union than with the people whose free labor built the country's wealth and over whose freedom the Civil War had been fought. The North's conciliatory embrace of the former Confederates compelled Frederick Douglass to remind Americans that "there was a right side and a wrong side in the late war which no sentiment ought to cause us to forget," adding that "it is no part of our duty to confound right with wrong, or loyalty with treason."

Robert E. Lee went on to become president of a college that would later add his name to its own, Washington and Lee University in Virginia. This granted him social standing and a worshipful legacy, and allowed him a platform to weigh in on issues of the day with authority if he chose.

His reputation only grew after his death in 1870. As the country embraced segregation, north and south, with redlining and restrictive covenants keeping black people out of white neighborhoods and the races separate, he became not just a southern hero, but a national one. He is interred at a chapel named after him on the campus of Washington and Lee, Confederate flags flanking, up until recently, a mold of the general in repose. Among the memorials in his honor well beyond the South, there came to be plaques and busts of him in the Bronx and in Brooklyn, elementary schools named after him in Long Beach and San Diego, and five different Robert E. Lee stamps issued by the U.S. Postal Service. Usually, it is the victors of war who erect monuments and commemorations to themselves. Here, an outsider might not be able to tell which side had prevailed over the other.

· · ·

At two o'clock in the morning on April 24, 2017, a SWAT team positioned its sharpshooters at strategic locations at a dangerous intersection in downtown New Orleans. K-9 units patrolled the grounds and perimeter. At the center of the targeted area, men in face masks and bulletproof vests went about their perilous duty in the darkness. Others had refused to risk their lives for this, declined even to attempt the operation, after the death threats and firebombing that preceded this moment. These men in face masks were the only ones willing to take up the mission. They were removing the first of four Confederate monuments in the city of New Orleans.

Tensions had been building since 2015 when Mayor Mitch Landrieu, a fifth-generation Louisianan whose ancestors had been in the state since before the Civil War, decided it was time for the Confederate statues to go. That June, a gunman inspired by the Lost Cause of the Confederacy massacred nine black parishioners as they prayed at the end of Bible study at Emanuel African Methodist Episcopal Church in Charleston, South Carolina. Under international pressure, the South Carolina state legislature and Gov. Nikki Haley agreed to remove the Confederate flag from the state capitol and put it in the Confederate Relic Room in the State Museum. South Carolina had been the first state to secede from the Union in the run-up to the Civil War, and this gesture opened the way for other states to follow if they could gather the will.

Landrieu was moved by this and was further awakened by his friend, the jazz trumpeter Wynton Marsalis, to the perspective of the descendants of enslaved people who had been terrorized under the Confederate banner.

The monuments in question included one for Confederate

president Jefferson Davis and one for Gen. Robert E. Lee, the latter of whom had no direct connection to New Orleans but whose statue was erected by the city as the Jim Crow regime took hold after the end of Reconstruction.

Now, more than a century later, the city was within its right to remove its own property, and Mayor Landrieu thought it would be a fairly straightforward process of public hearings and a vote by a city council as progressive as the city it represented. With the country newly reminded of the enduring nature of white supremacy, supporters came forward, including an influential citizen who pledged to donate $170,000 toward the cost of removing the monument as long as he could be assured of anonymity.

The city tested the idea with the public. At one hearing, a Confederate sympathizer had to be escorted out by police after he cursed and gave the middle finger to the audience. A retired lieutenant colonel in the Marine Corps, Richard Westmoreland, came at it from the other side. He stood up and said that Erwin Rommel was a great general, but there are no statues of Rommel in Germany. "They are ashamed," he said. "The question is, why aren't we?"

As time wore on, though, things got ugly. The city had trouble finding a contractor to remove the statues. Every contractor who considered the city's request got threatening attacks at home, at work, and on social media. It turned out that not one construction company in New Orleans wanted to touch it. Finally a contractor in Baton Rouge agreed to do it, but he pulled out, too, after his car was firebombed. The Confederate sympathizers made it clear that "any company that dared step forward," Landrieu wrote, "would pay a price."

The faithful of the old Confederacy held candlelight vigils at the monuments and clogged the city hall switchboard, cursing and threatening the receptionists. Soon the benefactor backed out of his promise of donating money for the removal effort. If it were ever discovered, he said, "I'll get run out of town."

The issue was now dividing all of New Orleans. "People who had served for years on civic boards quit," Landrieu said. "There was a deep, mean chill we felt when we entered a room for a public event." Some of the mayor's own neighbors and some of the people he thought of as friends averted their gaze when they saw him. He had not anticipated "the ferocity of the opposition."

Finally, the city found a construction company willing to take on what had become hazard duty in a virtual war zone. It could be seen as karma that the only construction crew willing to risk their lives to remove the Confederate statues was African-American. Due to the dangers of the operation, the company charged four times what the city had anticipated to remove the three largest monuments, and said the company would only go in if there was police protection. By now, the city had few other options if it wanted the statues gone.

The mayor decided first to remove a monument to a supremacist organization called the White League because white citizens seemed to have the least attachment to that one. Still, the city took no chances.

That night, the men wore long sleeves and masks both to protect their identities and to conceal their skin color. Cardboard covered the company name on its trucks and cranes and hid the vehicle license plates. Still, the pro-Confederate forces poured sand in the gas tank of one of the cranes. As the workers proceeded to remove the obelisk in pieces, drones lurked above them taking unauthorized photographs of the operation. People in the crowd trained high-definition cameras on the workers to try to identify them. Finally, the pieces of the obelisk were down and driven to a storage shed.

The next month, the Robert E. Lee monument, a larger-than-life bronze likeness, arms crossed, standing on a sixty-foot marble column in a manicured circle in the center of town, was the last of the four to be removed. His figure dangled from a crane in full daylight and, this time, to cheering crowds.

Mayor Landrieu gave a speech that day to remind citizens of why this needed to happen. "These monuments celebrate a fictional, sanitized Confederacy," he said, "ignoring the death, ignoring the enslavement, ignoring the terror that it actually stood for."

They were more than mere statuary. "They were created as political weapons," he would later write, "part of an effort to hide the truth, which is that the Confederacy was on the wrong side not just of history, but of humanity."

The day that New Orleans wrested Robert E. Lee from his column, the Alabama state legislature sent a bill to the Alabama governor, Kay Ivey. As in most of the former Confederacy after the post-civil-rights realignment, Republicans now dominated Alabama. They were now fighting to keep monuments to the very cause that the one-time party of Lincoln had fought in the Civil War. The new Alabama bill sent to the governor that day made it illegal to remove any monument that had been in place for twenty years or more, which in effect meant that nobody could lay a hand on a single Confederate statue in Alabama.

...

An ocean away, in the former capital of the Third Reich, Nigel Dunkley, a former British officer and now a historian of Nazi Germany, drove along a curve of what is left of the Berlin Wall. He pointed to the neoclassical buildings of the old Weimar Republic that were for a time run by the Nazis and have been reclaimed since the reunification of Germany. We drew near the Brandenburg Gate, which survived the Allied bombing in the Second World War, and then reached a wide-open space in the very center of downtown.

The office towers and government buildings came to a halt and gave way to a modernist Stonehenge on 4.7 acres, the size of three football fields, where once there had been the death strip to catch defectors in the Cold War. Two thousand seven hundred eleven concrete rectangles, as if a field of chiseled coffins of varying heights, stand in formation, separated by just enough space for people to walk between them and to contemplate their meaning. The stones undulate and dip toward the center, where the ground hollows out, so that when a visitor reaches the interior, the traffic noise dies away, the air grows still, and you are trapped in shadow, isolated with the magnitude of what the stones represent. This is the Memorial to the Murdered Jews of Europe who perished during the Holocaust. There is no sign, no gate, no fence, no list of the 6 million. The stones are as regimented as the Nazis and as anonymous as the captives shorn of identity in the concentration camps. Since 2005, the memorial has borne mute witness to anyone who wishes to come, day or night.

The designer of the memorial, Peter Eisenman, a New York

architect, chose not to explain the meaning of the number 2,711, or very much else about the installation. "I wanted people to have a feeling of being in the present and an experience that they had never had before," Eisenman told *Der Spiegel* the year it opened. "And one that was different and slightly unsettling."

The company that once produced cyanide gas for the concentration camps now provides the protectorate applied to the concrete stones to prevent graffiti and defacement, which might be seen as either an act of atonement from the perspective of some or the very least they could do from the perspective of others. The installation is the most imposing of a series of memorials to the people killed under Hitler's reign. "We have a memorial to everyone victimized by the Nazis," Dunkley said. "There is a memorial to homosexuals who perished. There is a memorial to the Sinti and Roma right outside the Reichstag. We have lesser memorials to lesser groups. And then we have the stumbling stones."

These are the micro-memorials of discreet brass squares the size of one's palm inscribed with the names of Holocaust victims and placed throughout the city. More than seventy thousand of these stumbling stones, known as *Stolpersteine,* have been forged and installed in cities across Europe. They are embedded among the cobblestones in front of houses and apartment buildings where the victims whose names are inscribed on them are known to have last lived before being abducted by the Gestapo. "Here lived Hildegard Blumenthal, born 1897, deported 1943, died in Auschwitz," reads a stumbling stone clustered among others outside an apartment building in western Berlin. Nearby are the stones for Rosa Gross and Arthur Benjamin, who were deported in 1942 and who perished in Riga.

The stumbling stones force the viewer to pause and squint to read the inscription, force the viewer to regard the entry doors the people walked through, the steps they climbed with their groceries and toddlers, the streets they strolled that were the everyday life of real people rather than abstractions of incomprehensible millions. Each one is a personal headstone that gives a momentary connection to a single individual. Leaning over to read the names on the stumbling stones forces you to bow in respect.

• • •

Nigel Dunkley made a slow turn near the site of the Reich Chancellery in the Mitte of Berlin and pulled his old Volvo up to a parking lot off Wilhelmstrasse. It was an asphalt square at the base of some concrete office and apartment buildings, and it had a low guardrail around it, like parking lots everywhere.

"You see that blue Volkswagen parked next to the white minivan?" he asked me.

From the car window, I looked past a recycling bin on the sidewalk and then over to the asphalt lot, the white lines separating each car, and saw the Volkswagen he was pointing to. It was parked in front of the low, straggled branches of untended barberry bushes.

"Right there, underneath that Volkswagen, was Hitler's bunker," Nigel said. The hideout had been built thirty feet underground and protected by two meters of reinforced concrete, in the event that Hitler should ever need a secure location. This is where Hitler spent the last weeks and hours of his life, hiding out from enemy shelling as the Allies closed in on them, where he heard that Mussolini had been executed and his Wehrmacht overcome on every front, where he married Eva Braun at the last minute as his closest confidants turned on him, where he shot himself in the head after biting into a cyanide pill, and where his hours-long wife had bitten into a cyanide pill just before him, on April 30, 1945. His body was unceremoniously dragged to a nearby lot and set afire.

In America, the men who mounted a bloody war against the United States to keep the right to enslave humans for generations went on to live out their retirement in comfort. Confederate president Jefferson Davis went on to write his memoirs at a plantation in Mississippi that is now the site of his presidential library. Robert E. Lee became an esteemed college president. When they died, they were both granted state funerals with military honors and were revered with statues and monuments.

An American author living in Berlin, who happens to be Jewish and to have been raised in the South, often gets asked about Germany's memorials to its Nazi past. "To which I respond: There aren't any," Susan Neiman, author of *Learning from the Germans: Race and the Memory of Evil,* has written. "Germany has no monuments that celebrate the Nazi armed forces, however many grandfathers fought or fell for them."

Rather than honor supremacists with statues on pedestals, Germany, after decades of silence and soul-searching, chose to erect memorials to the victims of its aggressions and to the courageous people who resisted the men who inflicted atrocities on human beings.

They built a range of museums to preserve the story of the country's descent into madness. They converted the infamous villa at Wannsee, where fifteen men worked out the details of the Final Solution to kill the Jews of Europe, into a museum examining the consequences of that fateful decision. The country converted the Gestapo headquarters into a museum called the Topography of Terror, a deep dive into the founding of the Third Reich. As for the man who oversaw these atrocities, Germany chose quite literally to pave over the *Führer*'s gravesite. There could be no more pedestrian resolution than that.

• • •

In Germany, displaying the swastika is a crime punishable by up to three years in prison. In the United States, the rebel flag is incorporated into the official state flag of Mississippi. It can be seen on the backs of pickup trucks north and south, fluttering along highways in Georgia and the other former Confederate states. A Confederate flag the size of a bedsheet flapped in the wind off an interstate in Virginia around the time of the Charlottesville rally.

In Germany, there is no death penalty. "We can't be trusted to kill people after what happened in World War II," a German woman once told me. In America, the states that recorded the highest number of lynchings, among them the former Confederate States of America, all currently have the death penalty.

In Germany, few people will proudly admit to having been related to Nazis or will openly defend the Nazi cause. "Not even members of Germany's right-wing Alternative for Germany party," wrote Neiman, "would suggest glorifying that part of the past."

The Germans who may "privately mourn for family members lost at the front," Neiman wrote, "know that their loved ones cannot be publically [*sic*] honored without honoring the cause for which they died."

In America, at Civil War reenactments throughout the country, more people typically sign up to fight on the side of the Confederates than for the Union, leaving the Union side sometimes struggling to find enough modern-day conscripts to stage a reenactment.

In Germany, some of the Nazis who did not kill themselves were tracked down and forced to stand trial. Many were hanged at the hands of the Allies for their crimes against humanity. The people who kidnapped and held hostage millions of people during slavery, condemning them to slow death, were not called to account and did not stand trial.

In Germany, restitution has rightly been paid, and continues to be paid, to survivors of the Holocaust. In America, it was the slaveholders who got restitution, not the people whose lives and wages were stolen from them for twelve generations. Those who instilled terror on the lowest caste over the following century after the formal end of slavery, those who tortured and killed humans before thousands of onlookers or who aided and abetted those lynchings or who looked the other way, well into the twentieth century, not only went free but rose to become leading figures—southern governors, senators, sheriffs, businessmen, mayors.

• • •

On a gray November afternoon, couples with strollers, tailored women with their shopping totes, commuters in wool and tweed, all make their way to the Wittenbergplatz subway station off Kurfürstendamm, the buzzy, neon-lit Fifth Avenue of Berlin, on the west side of the city.

They converge at the front doors to the station, and there to the right of them is the sign, nearly a story high, for every commuter, every shopper, every store clerk, every couple on a date, every backpacked student and tourist to see. Translated from German, it reads: *Places of Horror That We Should Never Forget.* Then it lists the places never to be forgotten: Auschwitz, Dachau, Bergen-Belsen, Treblinka, Buchenwald, Sachsenhausen, and half a dozen other concentration camps.

It was through these station doors that thousands of Jews took their last look at their beloved Berlin before being forced onto trains that would carry them to their deaths. This fact, this history, is built into the consciousness of Berliners as they go about their everyday lives. It is not something that anyone, Jew or Gentile, resident or visitor, is expected to put behind them or to just get over. They do not run from it. It has become a part of who they are because it is a part of what they have been. They incorporate it into their identity because it is, in fact, them.

It is a mandatory part of every school curriculum, even for grade school students, and it is never far from view for any citizen. This is not to say that everyone is in agreement as to the lengths to which the country goes to reinforce this history. What seems not in contention is the necessity of remembering. A former member of the German parliament was once talking with Nigel Dunkley and thought out loud about his discomfort with the massive stone installation to the European Jews near the Brandenburg Gate, which some have compared to a cemetery in the middle of downtown. "Why can't we have a nice park with grass and trees and a proper monument?" the former parliamentarian said. "Every time I drive past, I feel I am being punished by this higgly-piggly mess."

"If that is what you really think," Dunkley said to him, "that you're being punished, then you are being punished."

When Dunkley takes German students on tours of the history of the Third Reich, he asks them their reaction to what they have seen.

"Do you as Germans feel any guilt for what the Germans did?" he will ask them.

They will go off into groups and have heated discussions among themselves, and then come back to him with their thoughts.

"Yes, we are Germans, and Germans perpetrated this," some students once told him, echoing what others have said. "And, though it wasn't just Germans, it is the older Germans who were here who should feel guilt. We were not here. We ourselves did not do this. But we do feel that, as the younger generation, we should acknowledge and accept the responsibility. And for the generations that come after us, we should be the guardians of the truth."

CHAPTER TWENTY-THREE

The Stockholm Syndrome and the Survival of the Subordinate Caste

Over the centuries, people at the margins have had to study those at the center of power, learn their invisible codes and boundaries, because their survival depends upon knowing them as well as if not better than their own dreams and wishes. From the sidelines, they learn to be watchful of the needs and tempers of the dominant caste. They decode how those in power are getting along with one another or not, who is gaining or losing favor.

They must develop powers of perception if they are to navigate from below.

"Knowledge without wisdom is adequate for the powerful," wrote the sociologist Patricia Hill Collins, "but wisdom is essential to the survival of the subordinate."

To thrive, they must somehow adjust themselves to the expectations of the dominant caste, to play out their role upon the stage, and, while they may choose not to fully submit, they find that things go easier for them if they default to the script handed down through the ages, if they accept their assignment of serving and entertaining, comforting and consoling, forgiving any trespass without expectation of atonement from their trespassers.

The ancient code for the subordinate caste calls upon them to see the world not with their own eyes but as the dominant caste sees it, demands that they extend compassion even when none is forthcoming in exchange, a fusion of dominant and subordinate that brings to mind the Stockholm Syndrome.

Though the syndrome has no universally accepted definition or diagnosis, it is generally seen as a phenomenon of people bonding with those who abuse or hold them hostage. It takes its name from a 1973 bank robbery in Stockholm, Sweden, where the hostages came to feel empathy for the men who held them captive during the six-day siege. It is regarded as a survival mechanism in which people must become attuned to the people with power over them and learn to adjust themselves to their expectations to please them.

• • •

In the fall of 2019, a Dallas courtroom became a set piece for the display of the interlocking roles and power imbalances of caste. In a rare case in American history, a white former police officer was convicted of killing a black man who had been having ice cream and watching television in his own apartment, an apartment the officer argued she had mistaken for her own. The conviction carried a sentence of up to ninety years. The prosecutor recommended twenty-eight years, the age the victim would have been at the time had the defendant not killed him. In the end, the former officer was sentenced to ten years, with eligibility for parole in five.

The brother of the slain man extended his forgiveness to the dominant-caste woman who had killed his brother, and he hugged her in a scene that went all over the world. As the dominant-caste woman was sobbing over her conviction, the bailiff, a black woman, went over to her and began stroking the blond hair of a woman who had killed an innocent man of the bailiff's own caste. Had the inverse occurred and a black man taken the life of a white woman under similar circumstances, it is inconceivable that the murder sentence would have been ten years or the felon been hugged and his hair stroked, nor would it be remotely expected.

Many observers in the dominant caste were comforted by the bailiff's gesture, which they saw as an act of loving, maternal compassion. Many in the subordinate caste saw it as a demeaning fetishization of a dominant-caste woman who was being extended comfort and leniency that are denied African-Americans, who are treated more harshly in an era of mass incarceration and in society over all.

The judge was also a woman from the subordinate caste, and she stepped down from the bench to give the convicted killer a Bible. Then she held the dominant-caste woman close to her bosom and prayed on her and with her. No one could remember ever seeing such a thing, a judge or an officer of the court hugging and consoling a newly convicted felon. The judge's embrace seemed not so far removed from the comfort black maids extended to the disconsolate white children in their care as they wiped away their tears over the centuries.

"It's almost impossible to imagine the same level of compassion," wrote the journalist Ashley Reese, "being extended toward a black person who was just charged with murder."

...

From the moment I saw the pictures, they rattled me. It was November 2014, in the middle of the post-Ferguson protests against police brutality. At a rally in Portland, Oregon, there appeared a melancholy black boy in front of a crowd of protesters, holding a sign in the direction of the officers that said, "Free hugs."

There was something deeply unsettling about that image that I could not figure out at first. For one thing, the boy's face looked more like that of a man's on a child's small frame. His face was contorted in anguish, tears glistening down his cheeks, a wrenching emotion out of sync with the circumstances. He was wearing a fedora that seemed of another century. He did not have the carefree look of a child nor the affectionate cheer of someone offering hugs to strangers.

A white police officer responded to the sign and hugged the boy. The photograph went viral, shown on every television network. It comforted many in the dominant caste to see this gesture of compassion and grace. Here was a black child wanting to hug someone from a group that had been in contention with young black males in the months before this encounter. They were moved by the way the boy hugged the officer long and deep, as if clutching him for dear life.

What was disturbing about that picture could only be seen if one applied the same standards of human behavior to subordinated people as to others. Few black mothers, or mothers in general for that matter, would insist that their sons, and especially their black sons, go over and hug a police officer or any stranger they didn't know. And few children would willingly do so. The boy's face showed far more than discomfort but a despair of someone older than he appeared to be.

The world would not know the tragedy beneath that moment until years later. Two white women in Minnesota had adopted the boy, Devonte Hart, and five other black children from Texas, receiving more than $2,000 a month from the state for doing so. Over the course of ten years, the women essentially held the children captive, keeping them isolated in remote locations, withholding food from them.

They used them as props to attract a social media following with staged videos of the children forced to dance and sing for their captors. Off-camera, the women beat the children with belts and closed fists and held one girl's head under cold water as punishment after the women found a penny in the girl's pocket. When the children sought help and food from neighbors and teachers, the women defaulted to caste stereotypes, told the other adults not to feed them, that the children were playing the "food card," that they were lying, that they were "drug babies," whose birth mothers, they told people, were addicted while pregnant.

Authorities in multiple states inquired into reports of abuse but seemed unable to protect the children. Even after one of the women pleaded guilty in Minnesota in 2010 to misdemeanor assault of one of the daughters, the children remained in their custody. After that, whenever anyone got close enough to intervene, the women pulled the children out of school and moved to a different jurisdiction. They were able to rely on both the patchwork of disconnected social service agencies and their own caste privilege—the presumptions of competency and the benefit of the doubt accorded them—to evade state investigations and to deflect the children's pleas for help.

That day in November 2014, they posted pictures of Devonte hugging the police officer and got adulation from people all over the world. People saw what they wanted to see and not the agony in the face of a twelve-year-old boy who had the body of an eight-year-old due to starvation, his hug, on some level, a bid to be rescued. People saw a picture of black grace when what the world was actually looking at was an abused hostage.

On March 26, 2018, with caseworkers closing in, the two women put the children in their SUV and drove off a cliff in Northern California along the Pacific Coast Highway, killing themselves and the children they had held captive. Blindness to the depth of pain in the boy's face, the latitude granted these white saviors to abuse children seen as throwaways, the collective desire to solve tribal wounds with superficial gestures of grace from the wounded—all of these things contributed to this tragedy and haunt many of us still. We were all witness to a crime that ended in horror.

• • •

The act of forgiveness seems a silent clause in a one-sided contract between the subordinate and the dominant. "Black people forgive because we need to survive," essayist and author Roxanne Gay wrote. "We have to forgive time and time again while racism or white silence in the face of racism continues to thrive. We have had to forgive slavery, segregation, Jim Crow laws, lynching, inequity in every realm, mass incarceration, voter disenfranchisement, inadequate representation in popular culture, microaggressions and more. We forgive and forgive and forgive and those who trespass against us continue to trespass against us."

In 2018, as every week seemed to bring a new case of dominant-caste people calling the police on black people going about their daily lives, a middle-aged white woman in Brooklyn called the police on a nine-year-old boy who she said had sexually assaulted her as he passed her at the register at a corner deli. The boy said he had not done such a thing, had not touched her, and began to cry. What saved the boy from further action was the store video, which later went viral. It shows the boy passing the woman in the crowded deli and his bag brushing against her, unbeknownst to him as he walked by.

The woman was shamed into apologizing for the false accusation. Afterward, people wanted to know, had he forgiven her? The boy had not learned all the rules of caste yet, had not lived long enough to have read the whole script or have it completely downloaded to his subconscious. He was thinking with the still-free mind of an innocent who had not yet faced the consequences of breaking caste. "I don't forgive the woman," he said, "and she needs help."

The little boy had the X-ray vision of childhood. He had not accepted the inversion of right and wrong, had not been willing to concede a privilege that should not be extracted but granted freely at the discretion of the aggrieved.

"What white people are really asking for when they demand forgiveness from a traumatized community is absolution," Gay wrote. "They want absolution from the racism that infects us all even though forgiveness cannot reconcile America's racist sins."

...

One cannot live in a caste system, breathe its air, without absorbing the message of caste supremacy. The subordinated castes are trained to admire, worship, fear, love, covet, and want to be like those at the center of society, at the top of the hierarchy. In India, it is said that you can try to leave caste, but caste never leaves you. Most immigrants to the United States from India are among the most accomplished and well-to-do from their mother country, and thus few Dalits have the resources to get to America. By some estimates, Dalits are less than 2 percent of people of Indian descent in America. For those who manage to make it across the ocean, caste often migrates with them.

And so a brilliant Dalit from India, a Ph.D. at a prestigious university on the East Coast, paced and shifted his weight from one foot to the other, growing agitated at the very mention of the surnames of his upper-caste countrymen. These are names that might have little meaning to most Americans but which signify rank and privilege in India. The names Gupta and Mehta and Mukherjee, common among Indian immigrants in America, are among the most revered in their homeland.

"These names," said the Dalit scholar Suraj Yengde, who was at Harvard at the time, shaking his head and looking down toward the carpet. "I can't look them straight in the face. I can't look them in the eye. I don't know what to say. These were our masters. My grandfathers were the workers of their grandfathers. I would never be invited inside their homes."

He began pacing again. "I have been here three years. I still do not have the confidence to talk with them."

At the bottom of the hierarchy, the message of inferiority comes at you in whispers and billboards. It burrows into your identity. The violence and terror used to maintain the hierarchy keep you in your place without signage.

"It is a feeling of danger," the Dalit scholar said, just the thought of upper-caste people. "They are a danger to me. I feel danger with them."

Caste is more than rank, it is a state of mind that holds everyone captive, the dominant imprisoned in an illusion of their own entitlement, the subordinate trapped in the purgatory of someone else's definition of who they are and who they should be.

Back home in India, when the scholar goes into a store, they watch him and hound him like a thief, as with a black person in a store in America. He has absorbed that expectation and adjusted to it to survive. "I never ask about the quality of an item," the scholar said. "I ask the price. If I ask the quality, they will say, 'You can't afford this, why are you wasting my time?' If I say I want to see it, they will say, 'Get out. I will call the police.' So I come back with friends who are not Dalit, who can speak their language and get it for me."

It is for that reason that he stood there in the lobby of a high-end hotel after a dinner near campus and pointed to his shoes, his leather-clad sneakers. He bent down and pressed the empty toe box of his sneakers. "These shoes I bought," he said, "they are not my size. They are too big for me. I bought them because I did not want to trouble the salesman. I did not have the confidence to ask for another size. So I bought what he gave me."

He, like subordinate-caste people wherever there is caste,

has had to create an entire protocol to protect himself from insult. "If I go into a store and stay thirty minutes, I have to buy something," he said. "I have so many things that I was afraid to return."

They do what they must to avoid further insult.

"For us, it is dignity," the Dalit Ph.D. said. "If I go some-place, they might say, you can't afford this, you are wasting my time. So when I go to a restaurant, I don't want to take up the waiter's time. They might attack us, and then they say that we are hostile, when for us it is a matter of dignity. Our dignity is under assault."

He once accompanied two white American women to a store and was astonished at their behavior. "They took up the owner's time and did not buy anything," he said. "I could not imagine doing that."

The fear runs deep within his soul.

I asked him, "Is this fear of anticipated rejection or the ac-tual rejection itself?"

"It is the former caused by the latter," he answered.

"What would help you feel better in these situations?" I asked him.

"What I need is to feel better inside my own skin," he said.

CHAPTER TWENTY-FOUR

———

The Price We Pay for a Caste System

Leon Lederman was an American physicist who won a Nobel Prize in 1988 for his groundbreaking contributions to our understanding of the particles of nature. Decades afterward, when he was in his early nineties, he began to suffer memory loss and to require additional care. In 2015, he took the extraordinary step of auctioning off his Nobel Prize medal for $765,000 to cover medical bills that were mounting. In 2018, he died in a nursing home, his Nobel Prize in the hands of someone else.

Compared to our counterparts in the developed world, America can be a harsh landscape, a less benevolent society than other wealthy nations. It is the price we pay for our caste system. In places with a different history and hierarchy, it is not necessarily seen as taking away from one's own prosperity if the system looks out for the needs of everyone.

People show a greater sense of joint responsibility to one another when they see their fellow citizens as like themselves, as in the nations of western Europe or in Australia, a diverse country with a looser hierarchy. Societies can be more magnanimous when people perceive themselves as having an equal stake in the lives of their fellow citizens.

There are thriving, prosperous nations where people do not have to sell their Nobel Prizes to get medical care, where families don't go broke taking care of elderly loved ones, where children exceed the educational achievements of American children, where drug addicts are in treatment rather than prison, where perhaps the greatest measure of human success—happiness and a long life—exists in greater measure because they value their shared commonality.

• • •

In the winter of 2020, the one year in human history that would hold the promise of perfect insight, an invisible life-form awakened in the Eastern Hemisphere and began to spread across the oceans.

The earth's most powerful nation watched as faraway workers in hazmat gear tested for what no one could see, and deluded itself into believing that American exceptionalism would somehow grant it immunity from the sorrows of other countries.

Yet the virus arrived on these shores, and it planted itself in the gaps of disparity, the torn kinships and fraying infrastructure in the country's caste system, just as it exploited the weakened immune system in the human body.

Soon, America had the largest coronavirus outbreak in the world. Governors pleaded for basic supplies and test kits, were reduced to bidding against one another for ventilators. "As Usual," read a headline in *The Atlantic,* "Americans Must Go It Alone."

The virus exposed both the vulnerability of all humans and the layers of hierarchy. While anyone could contract the virus, it was Asian-Americans who were scapegoated for it merely because they looked like the people from the part of the world that the virus first struck.

And as the crisis wore on, it was African-Americans and Latino-Americans who began dying at higher rates. Preexisting conditions, often tied to the stresses on marginalized people, contributed to the divergence. But it was the caste-like occupations at the bottom of the hierarchy—grocery clerks, bus drivers, package deliverers, sanitation workers, low-paying jobs with high levels of public contact—that put them at greater risk of contracting the virus in the first place. These are among the mudsill jobs in a pandemic, the jobs less likely to guarantee health coverage or sick days but that sustain the rest of society, allowing others to shelter in place.

As the number of deaths climbed to the highest in the world, America—and those looking to it for leadership—had to come to terms with the untested fragilities of its social ecosystem.

"To a watching world," wrote *The Guardian*, "the absence of a fair, affordable US healthcare system, the cut-throat contest between American states for scarce medical supplies, the disproportionate death toll among ethnic minorities, chaotic social distancing rules, and a lack of centralised coordination are reminiscent of a poor, developing country, not the most powerful, influential nation on earth."

The pandemic, and the country's fitful, often self-centered lack of readiness, exposed "a failure of character unparalleled in US history," in the words of Stephen Walt, a professor of international relations at Harvard University. The pandemic forced the nation to open its eyes to what it might not have wanted to see but needed to see, while forcing humanity to contemplate its impotence against the laws of nature.

"This is a civilization searching for its humanity," Gary Michael Tartakov, an American scholar of caste, said of this country. "It dehumanized others to build its civilization. Now it needs to find its own."

Part Seven

———

Awakening

———

CHAPTER TWENTY-FIVE

Shedding the Sacred Thread

Near the sacred waters of the alluvial plains, east of the Thar Desert, a man born to the highest caste in India had awakened slowly to a privileged despair. He had a position of rank in civil society and a high-born wife and family. He was a Brahmin, of the priestly caste, above even kings and warriors. He was the Indian equivalent of the bluest of blood in America. Unlike ordinary men, he was twice born—first, of his mother's womb and then of the temple during the rite of passage for boys of the upper castes. The Brahmin, the Kshatriya, and the Vaishya alone have historically been granted this singular elevation. It is one of the many things—perhaps the most prized, transcendent thing—that set upper-caste men apart from lower ones as the most favored by the gods.

Many years before, on the day that he, as a young Brahmin boy, went through his second birth, his head had been shaved, and he was bathed in a ritual cleansing. The Brahmin priest read from holy text and called upon the god Vishnu for his strength and protection. At the appointed hour, they slipped a sacred thread around his neck that fell over his bare shoulders and draped it across his chest, three interwoven threads representing the body, the mind, and the tongue with which to speak wisdom. This was his initiation into Brahmin manhood, and, henceforth, he was to wear the sacred thread at all times, under his clothing by day, to sleep in it by night, and to wash in it, as it remained one with his skin. He was to keep it clean and pure as a Brahmin was to remain clean and pure, and to replace it if it became frayed or polluted, if, for example, he were by chance touched by anyone of the lower castes. When he became old enough to shave, he would have to tuck it behind his ear, or hold it under his chin as he washed, to protect it. The sacred thread was an extension of his Brahmin body, the purest of all human bodies, and a signal to everyone of his high rank in the land. He was now permitted to take meals with the men in the family and village and learn his place among the men of high caste.

But on a Sunday thereafter, his father was out surveying his land. The father came across a farmworker on his land, but the farmworker did not bid the father the respect due a Brahmin lord in the father's eyes. The laborer was a Dalit, the lowest of the castes, one whose very shadow was polluting to the boy and his father's caste. The Dalits were trained to bend in fear at the sight of their superiors. Untold thousands of Dalits had lost their lives for offending the upper castes and were at their mercy.

The boy's father took a stick and charged after the Dalit laborer. The Dalit pulled the limb of a tree to protect himself from the father. Seeing this, the father gathered his senses and retreated from the Dalit and ran away from him. But a group of fellow Brahmins witnessed the father running, saw him permit an Untouchable to chase away his master. The father had not upheld his superiority over the Dalit. He had brought dishonor to his caste by allowing an inferior to prevail over him.

The caste system had a way of policing the behavior of everyone in its wake to keep everyone in their assigned places. Now he had brought shame and humiliation to himself, to his line, and to his caste in that one moment. Seeing no option to retain his honor, the father fled the village. His family searched and searched for him and finally found him chanting in a room surrounded by images of the gods.

"I lost my father that day," the Brahmin recalled many decades later, "and I lost my childhood." Perhaps his father had been mentally unwell from the start. Perhaps the pressures to live out a role that one was born to but did not choose for oneself, and to which one's temperament was unsuited, had been too much for the father.

The Brahmin grew up and had a family of his own. He put his father's humiliation behind him. But in the anonymity of the big city, he began to see the hardships and inequities all around him, the dust rising from the streets and into the thick air, the street sweepers and the scavengers who he had been told accepted their lot beneath him. But he knew from the Dalit who had stood up to his father that they did not accept their lot, that they were not the docile, lazy creatures of caste mythology.

The Brahmin came to know and to admire the few Dalits who crossed his path in his work, who had pushed through the walls of caste to become educated, professional. He came to realize that they were as capable as he was, and, in fact, that because they had to come so far, they knew things about the world that his privilege had not required him to know. He saw that the caste system created a smooth path for some and broken-glass shoals for others, that creativity and intellect were not restricted to one group alone. These were the people whose very sight and touch was said to be polluting, and yet here he was sitting across from them, sharing and learning from them. He was the beneficiary of their gifts rather than the other way around, and he came to see what had been lost by one not getting to know the other for his lifetime and all the lifetimes before his. He began to see himself differently, to see the illusion of his presumed superiority, that he had been told a lie, and that his father had been told a lie, and that trying to live up to the lie had taken some part of his father away. For this, he bore a heavy guilt and shame over the tragedy that had befallen the family and a memory that would not leave him. He wanted to be free of it.

He shared this realization with a Dalit he had come to know and told him of a decision he had made. "I have ripped off my sacred thread," he told the Dalit, a professional man. "It was a poisonous snake around my neck, and its toxic venom was getting inside of me."

For most of his life, he had worn the sacred thread as if it were strands of hair from his head. Removing it amounted to renouncing his high caste, and he considered the consequences, that his family might reject him if they knew. He would have to determine how to manage their knowing when the time came.

He was now born a third time, the shades lifted in a darkened room in his mind.

"It is a fake crown that we wear," he came to realize.

He wished every dominant-caste person could awaken to this fact. "My message would be to take off the fake crown. It will cost you more to keep it than to let it go. It is not real. It is just a marker of your programming. You will be happier and freer without it. You will see all of humanity. You will find your true self."

And so he had discovered. "There was a stench coming from my body," he said. "I have located the corpse inside my mind. I have given it a decent burial. And now my journey can begin."

The Radicalization of the Dominant Caste

We had sat down for dinner, a family friend and I, at a chic restaurant in a hip section of a major American city. I did not know her well, but I knew that she was an artsy free spirit, kindhearted, well traveled.

She was also from the dominant caste and had grown up in a neighborhood surrounded mainly by people like herself. As we sat catching up on each other's lives, lives that each of us had known only from afar, several waiters passed by, and it was unclear which one was ours.

Finally, a waiter stopped at our table. He was blond, curt, and matter-of-fact. I ordered fish, she ordered pasta. We both ordered drinks, an appetizer or two.

While we waited for the drinks to arrive, a couple from the dominant caste, same caste as her, sat down at the table next to us. Our waiter rushed over to take their order, now charming and effusive, filling them in on the specials, chatting them up. Seconds later, he brought a basket of bread to their table. He brought them their drinks shortly thereafter, while we sipped water and waited for ours.

The family friend was growing impatient, seething actually, and turned to see where he was. She was trying to process an unaccustomed disregard. The waiter rolled around to check on the people next to us yet again and to deliver drinks and bread to other tables down the row.

Trying to keep calm, she motioned for him to come over. "We haven't gotten our drinks yet," she said. "Can you bring us our drinks, please? And we'd like bread, too," she added, looking over at the couple who had arrived after us. They were now dipping theirs in olive oil, as we stared at an empty table.

He nodded and said sure, but stopped to check on several other tables on his way back to the kitchen, which delayed him further. He reappeared later with dishes on his tray, but these were now the appetizers for the couple at the next table.

The family friend motioned to him again. "Our drinks? And we never got the bread."

"Oh, right, sure," he said, turning back again.

It was now hard for her to concentrate on whatever it was she was saying. The people next to us were remarking on how good the appetizers were and had all but finished their bread. Their table was laden, and ours was empty, and she seemed exquisitely aware of the couple beside us, that they were passing us on the escalator of dining attention.

On one of his many rounds past our table, the waiter at last brought the drinks but not the bread, and the exclusion was now impossible to ignore. Finally, he showed up with the entrées. The people next to us were on to their desserts, which were lovely apparently, from what they were saying. She stared at the pasta and jostled it with her fork, tasted it, and set the fork down.

"Pasta's cold. It's not even good. How's your fish?"

"It's okay. Not great. Mine's cold, too."

"I'm getting the waiter."

Her face was now approaching crimson. She fidgeted in her seat and looked around for him, shaking her head in disbelief. She was barely able to keep it together.

"Can you come here a second?" she called out to him as he passed again. "I know exactly what this is about. This is about racism!"

Her voice was rising, she was loud enough for the whole restaurant to hear.

"You're a racist! This restaurant is racist! We sat here all this time, and you served all these other people at all these other tables, and you ignored us this whole time just because she's African-American."

People at other tables were now looking over at me, when I had not wanted the attention. I had no interest in making a federal case out of this. If I responded like that every time I was slighted, I'd be telling someone off almost every day.

But she was just getting started. "I want your name, I want the manager's name. I will turn this place out."

She pushed the bowl of pasta to the center of the table. "The pasta's cold," she said. "I can't even eat it. Her fish is cold. She can't eat hers. I'm not paying, we're not paying. I'm telling everybody I know not to come here. This is crap."

With all of the ruckus, the manager came out to see what was going on. As it happened, the manager was a petite African-American woman, who seemed cowed by the ferocity of this newly minted anti-racist, anti-casteist, upper-caste woman, standing before her enraged at the unaccustomed humiliation. The manager apologized profusely, but my friend was having none of it.

She stormed out of the restaurant, and I walked out with her. It took a while for her to calm down.

Part of me wanted to say to her, "Imagine going through something like this almost every day, not knowing when or how it might happen. You wouldn't last very long. We can't afford to be blowing up every time we're slighted and ignored. We stand up when we need to, but we have to find a way not to go off every time and still get through the day."

Part of me resented that she could go ballistic and get away with it when I might not even be believed. It was caste privilege to go off in the restaurant the way she did. It was a measure of how differently we are treated that she could live for over forty years and not experience what is a daily possibility for any person born to the subordinate caste, that it was so alien to her, it so jangled her, that she blew up over it.

But part of me wished that every person in the dominant caste who denies and deflects, minimizes and gaslights African-Americans and other marginalized people could experience what she did. She had been radicalized in a matter of minutes. She knew full well that this was not how people treated her when she was out with others in the dominant caste. She had come to the realization on her own.

And part of me, the biggest part of me, was happy to see her righteous indignation on my behalf, on her own behalf, and on behalf of all the people who endure these indignities every day. It would be a better world if everyone could feel what she felt for once, and awaken.

CHAPTER TWENTY-SIX

The Heart Is the Last Frontier

December 2016, One Month After the Election
He smelled of beer and tobacco. He was wearing a cap like the men at the rallies who wanted to make America great again, the people who had prevailed in the election the month before. His belly extended over his belt buckle. The years had carved lines into his face, and stubble was poking through his chin and cheeks. He let out a phlegmy cough.

I had called the plumbing company because I had discovered water in the basement, and he was the one they sent. He was standing at the threshold of my front door and seemed not to have expected someone who looked like me to answer. It's a predominantly white neighborhood, with joggers and cyclists and purposeful moms in yoga sweats pushing baby strollers, ponytails bouncing, maybe a labradoodle trotting behind. Landscapers' trucks and housekeeping crews squeeze past each other on every side street. I was used to that reaction.

"Is the lady of the house at home?" a leafleteer or survey-taker will ask me—the only lady in sight, standing right there in front of them. The assumption doesn't inspire me to indulge them. I could correct them if I wanted, and they might try to play it off, or I could just spare them the embarrassment.

"No, she's not here," I'll say. They never press me, never seem to suspect.

"Do you know when she'll be back?"

"No, no, I don't," I'll say. "Who shall I say is calling?" They will hand me a card or a flyer, and I will give it a glance as they go on their way.

So the plumber checked to see if this was, in fact, the right house, then walked in with a let's-get-this-over-with look on his face. "Where's the basement?"

I was reliant on this man and others like him, now that I was both widowed and motherless, having lost the two most important people in my life within a span of eighteen months. I was having to depend on contractors to fix things in this house, people who might resent me for being here and might or might not be inclined to help me or even to do their job. And now the air had shifted after the election.

He followed me into the basement and stood there as I moved boxes to make space for him to better inspect it. I moved my mother's portable wheelchair, the one she would not be needing anymore, and a lampshade, stacks of my late father's engineering books, and an old bucket, as the plumber watched, never reaching over to help. I began sweeping water toward the sump pump as he looked down at the wet floor.

I told him that there had been three or four inches of water, that the HVAC man had helped get the sump pump restarted to drain most of the water out, that this had never happened before.

"I hardly ever come into the basement," I told him. "We had that drought, so I didn't think about water in the basement. My husband was the one who came down here." He was the one who checked the filter on the furnace, checked the fuse box, patched things in his workshop, which was exactly as he had left it, the sawhorse and drill bits untouched from whenever he'd last come down to fix something before he died. He died last year, I told the plumber. The magnitude of that statement seemed not to register. The plumber just shrugged and said uh-huh.

I was sweeping the water with him standing there, and I was remembering what had happened in the last week. I had been trying to get as far away from the grief as I could over the holidays. I would have left the planet if that had been an option, but that was not yet possible, so I had planned the next best, most convenient recourse to detach from the gravity of loss, which was a ticket to Buenos Aires. I had never been to Buenos Aires, so there were no memories to surface there, nothing to make me think of having seen or done this or that with anyone I had lost. As I was preparing to go, the HVAC contractor arrived for the semiannual check of the furnace and discovered water in the basement. He was an immigrant from Central America, and, though it was not his job, he helped to drain it as best he could.

• • •

The plumber was now surveying the boxes and stepped around a few of them, knocking a lampshade and wreath to the wet floor and not reaching over to pick them up. I kept sweeping. It appeared as if there was nothing further for him to do, or at least I would say he wasn't doing anything.

He pointed to the sink. "That's where the water is coming in," he said, looking to wrap this up.

"But the sink's never overflowed before," I said. "It had to be more than that."

"How long's it been since the water came?"

"Maybe since the rains last week. There's a drain here somewhere. I wonder if it's clogged."

I started moving boxes and was feeling more alone with him just standing there. I lifted a heavy box, and he watched, made no gesture to help. He merely said, "You got that?"

I had moved enough boxes to see where I thought the drain would be and still didn't locate it. It seemed this should be part of the troubleshooting, but he showed no interest.

"Maybe it's the sump pump?" I asked.

He went to look at it. "Nothing wrong with the sump pump," he said.

I now noticed packing popcorn floating in it. "Could that have kept the sump pump from working?"

"No," he said, "but the sump pump needs clearing out, though."

Why was he not doing that? Wasn't that what he was here for?

Instead he offered to write an estimate for a new one. But why buy a new pump if this one was working? I had called him in to fix whatever caused the water to build up. Since he'd arrived, I was the one sweeping water, moving boxes, searching for the drain. He was doing less than the HVAC guy had done.

I was steaming now. All he was doing was standing there watching me sweep (as women who look like me have done for centuries) and not fixing anything. He had come up with no answers, shown no interest, and now it appeared I was going to have to pay him for doing nothing.

Since he wasn't helping, I felt I had nothing to lose. Something came over me, and I threw a Hail Mary at his humanity.

"My mother just died last week," I told him. "Is your mother still alive?"

He looked down at the wet floor. "No . . . no, she isn't."

Somehow I had sensed that already, which is why I brought it up.

"She died in 1991," he said. "She was fifty-two years old."

"That's not old at all," I said.

"No, she wasn't. My father's still alive, he's seventy-eight. He's in a home south of here. My sister lives nearby to him."

"You're lucky to still have your father," I said.

"Well, he's mean as they come."

I contemplated the significance of that. What might his father have exposed him to when it comes to people who look like me? But I kept it to the present.

"You miss them when they're gone no matter what they were like," I said.

"How about your mother?" he wanted to know. "How old was she?"

"She was way older than yours, so I can't complain about that. But she was sick a long time. And you never get over it."

"I have an aunt in her eighties who still smokes and will ask you for a taste of beer," he said and let slip a laugh. "She's on my daddy's side."

I smiled and tried to look at the positive. "So your father's side is long-lived," I said.

"Yeah. I guess they are."

His face brightened, and he went over to the sump pump, bent down, and reached into it. A minute or two later, he stood up.

"Okay, sump pump's cleared out."

He turned to the area where the drain was likely to be.

"It's probably under this coffee table," he said. "If you get one end, we can move it and see where it is."

Together, we moved the table and, sure enough, there was the drain.

"Drain's not clogged, so that's not the problem," he said. "Lemme go get my flashlight out of the truck."

Once back, he trained the flashlight along the floor, inspecting the perimeter of the basement, past the sink and the washer and dryer hemmed in with boxes, past the sawhorse, along the base of the furnace, every corner up and down.

"I found it!" he said, jubilant.

I ran over to him. "What was it?"

"It's the water heater. Water heater's gone bad."

He shone the flashlight onto the top of the heater, onto the corroded pipes and the steam rising from the gaps. Water had been escaping from the broken heater and had risen into a low flood on the basement floor, which explained why the floodwater was clear and why my water bill was high.

I stepped back in relief. "I knew it had to be more than the rain."

"You'll need a new water heater. This one's gone."

How different things had been just minutes before. "My mother must've been talking to your mother," I said, "and telling her to get her boy to help her girl down there. 'My daughter needs your son's help.'"

We smiled at the thought of that. He shut off the water to the heater, which meant no more hot water in the house for now, but, more important, no more water escaping to the basement floor. He gave me the estimate for the replacement heater and charged me sixty-nine dollars for the visit, which I thought was fair. We wished each other a happy holiday, and he left.

The phone rang. It happened to be Bunny Fisher, whose father, Dr. Robert Pershing Foster, I had written about in *The Warmth of Other Suns*. She was calling to check on me, having kept in close touch over the years and even more so with my recent losses. I told her about the encounter with the plumber and the minor miracle that had happened, as we began to catch up.

Just then, the doorbell rang, the call cut short. It was the plumber again. He said he had driven back to shut off the gas to the water heater so it wouldn't be heating an empty tank. He knew his way around now, made his way to the basement, was lighthearted and chatty, momentarily family.

"This thing could have been much worse," he said. "Water could have burst from the top, destroyed everything, and scalded you or anybody else who tried to fix it. I've seen way worse."

As he headed back up the basement steps, he caught a glimpse of some old Polaroid photographs that I had salvaged from the wet boxes and had pulled aside to air out.

He paused in the middle of the staircase. "Oh, you want those," he said. "That's memories right there." Then he bounded out of the old house and into the light of the day.

EPILOGUE

———

A World Without Caste

In December 1932, one of the smartest men who ever lived landed in America on a steamship with his wife and their thirty pieces of luggage as the Nazis bore down on their homeland of Germany. Albert Einstein, the physicist and Nobel laureate, had managed to escape the Nazis just in time. The month after Einstein left, Hitler was appointed chancellor.

In America, Einstein was astonished to discover that he had landed in yet another caste system, one with a different scapegoat caste and different methods, but with embedded hatreds that were not so unlike the one he had just fled.

"The worst disease is the treatment of the Negro," he wrote in 1946. "Everyone who freshly learns of this state of affairs at a maturer age feels not only the injustice, but the scorn of the principle of the Fathers who founded the United States that 'all men are created equal.'"

He could "hardly believe that a reasonable man can cling so tenaciously to such prejudice," he said.

He and his wife, Elsa, settled in Princeton, New Jersey, where he took a professorship at the university and observed firsthand the oppression faced by black residents who were consigned to the worst parts of town, to segregated movie houses, to servant positions, and were, in the words of his friend Paul Robeson, forced into "bowing and scraping to the drunken rich."

A few years into his tenure, the opera singer Marian Anderson, a renowned contralto born to the subordinated caste, performed to an overflow crowd at McCarter Theatre in Princeton and to rapturous praise in the press of her "complete mastery of a magnificent voice." But the Nassau Inn in Princeton refused to rent a room to her for the night. Einstein, learning of this, invited her to stay in his home. From then on, she would stay at the Einstein residence whenever she was in town, even after Princeton hotels began accepting African-American guests. They would remain friends until his death.

"Being a Jew myself, perhaps I can understand and empathize with how black people feel as victims of discrimination," he told a family friend.

He grew uncomfortable with the American way of pressuring newcomers to look down on the lowest caste in order to gain acceptance. Here was one of the most brilliant men who ever lived refusing to see himself as superior to people he was being told were beneath him.

"The more I feel an American, the more this situation pains me," Einstein wrote. "I can escape the feelings of complicity in it only by speaking out."

And so he did. He co-chaired a committee to end lynching. He joined the NAACP. He spoke out on behalf of civil rights activists, lent his fame to their cause. At a certain point in his life, he rarely accepted the many honors that came his way, but in

1946 he made an exception for Lincoln University, a historically black college in Pennsylvania. He agreed to deliver the commencement address and to accept an honorary degree there.

On that visit, he taught his theory of relativity to physics students and played with the children of black faculty, among them the son of the university president, a young Julian Bond, who would go on to become a civil rights leader.

"The separation of the races is not a disease of the colored people," Einstein told the graduates at commencement, "but a disease of the white people. I do not intend to be quiet about it."

He became a passionate ally of the people consigned to the bottom. "He hates race prejudice," W.E.B. Du Bois wrote, "because as a Jew he knows what it is."

• • •

The caste system in America is four hundred years old and it persists in part because we, each and every one of us, allow it to exist—in large and small ways, in our everyday actions, in how we elevate or demean, embrace or exclude, on the basis of the meaning attached to people's physical traits. If enough people buy into the lie of natural hierarchy, then it becomes the truth or is assumed to be.

Once awakened, we then have a choice. We can be born to the dominant caste but choose not to dominate. We can be born to a subordinated caste but resist the box others force upon us. And all of us can sharpen our powers of discernment to see past the external and to value the character of a person rather than demean those who are already marginalized or worship those born to false pedestals. We need not bristle when those deemed subordinate break free, but rejoice that here may be one more human being who can add their true strengths to humanity.

A housing inspector does not make the repairs on the building he has examined. It is for the owners, meaning each of us, to correct the ruptures we have inherited.

The fact is that the bottom caste, though it bears much of the burden of the hierarchy, did not create the caste system, and the bottom caste alone cannot fix it. The challenge has long been that many in the dominant caste, who are in a better position to fix caste inequity, have often been least likely to want to.

Caste is a disease, and none of us is immune. It is as if alcoholism is encoded into the country's DNA, and can never be declared fully cured. It is like a cancer that goes into remission only to return when the immune system of the body politic is weakened.

Thus, regardless of who prevails in any given election, the country still labors under the divisions that a caste system creates, and the fears and resentments of a dominant caste that is too often in opposition to the yearnings of those deemed beneath them. It is a danger to the species and to the planet to have this depth of unexamined grievance and discontent in the most powerful nation in the world. A single election will not solve the problems that we face if we haven't dealt with the structure that created the imbalance to begin with.

As it stands, the United States is facing a crisis of identity unlike any before. The country is headed toward an inversion of its demographics, with its powerful white majority expected to be outnumbered by people not of European descent within two decades. This is unknown territory for everyone in the hierarchy, an ethnic distribution that could potentially look closer to that of South Africa than to what Americans have grown accustomed to.

Anticipatory fear seems already to have surfaced, but if history is any guide, a change in demographics might have less of a material effect on the dominant caste than imagined. A 2016 study found that, if disparities in wealth were to continue at the current pace, it would take black families 228 years to amass the wealth that white families now have, and Latino families another 84 years to reach parity.

Thus, as in South Africa, there would be no reason to believe that economic, social, and, in America, political dominance would not still remain in the hands of those who have held it for the entirety of the country's history.

This will be a test of the cherished ideal of majority rule, the moral framework for caste dominance in America since its founding. White dominance has already been assured by the inherited advantages of the dominant caste in most every sphere of life, and in the securing of dominant caste interests in most aspects of governing—from gerrymandered congressional districts to voter suppression to the rightward direction of the judicial branch to the Electoral College, which favors the dominant caste, whatever the numbers.

Will the United States adhere to its belief in majority rule if the majority does not look as it has throughout history? This will be the chance for America either to further entrench its inequalities or to choose to lead the world as the exceptional nation that we have proclaimed ourselves to be.

Without an enlightened recognition of the price we all pay for a caste system, the hierarchy will likely shape-shift as it has in the past to ensure that the structure remains intact. The definition of whiteness could well expand to confer honorary whiteness to those on the border—the lightest-skinned people of Asian or Latino descent or biracial people with a white parent, for instance—to increase the ranks of the dominant caste.

The devastating truth is that, without the intervention of humanitarian impulses, a reconstituted caste system could divide those at the bottom and those in the middle, pick off those closest to white and thus isolate the darkest Americans even further, lock them ever more tightly to the bottom rung.

It would be a crisis of spirit, a defeat of the American soul, because the toxins upstream eventually make their way downstream, as has occurred with the addiction crisis in America. It turns out that everyone benefits when society meets the needs of the disadvantaged. The sacrifices of the subordinate caste during the civil rights era, for instance, benefited women of all ethnicities—the wives, daughters, sisters, and nieces of every American man—women who now have legal protections against job discrimination that they did not have before the 1960s.

Many of the advancements that Americans enjoy and that are under assault in our current day—birthright citizenship, equal protection under the law, the right to vote, laws against discrimination on the basis of gender, race, national origin—are all the byproducts of the subordinate caste's fight for justice in this country and ended up helping others as much as if not more than themselves.

• • •

To imagine an end to caste in America, we need only look at the history of Germany. It is living proof that if a caste system—the twelve-year reign of the Nazis—can be created, it can be dismantled. We make a serious error when we fail to see the overlap between our country and others, the common vulnerability in human programming, what the political theorist Hannah Arendt called "the banality of evil."

"It's all too easy to imagine that the Third Reich was a bizarre aberration," wrote the philosopher David Livingstone Smith, who has studied cultures of dehumanization. "It's tempting to imagine that the Germans were (or are) a uniquely cruel and bloodthirsty people. But these diagnoses are dangerously wrong. What's most disturbing about the Nazi phenomenon is not that the Nazis were madmen or monsters. It's that they were ordinary human beings."

It is also tempting to vilify a single despot at the sight of injustice when, in fact, it is the actions, or more commonly inactions, of ordinary people that keep the mechanism of caste running, the people who shrug their shoulders at the latest police killing, the people who laugh off the coded put-downs of marginalized people shared at the dinner table and say nothing for fear of alienating an otherwise beloved uncle. The people who are willing to pay higher property taxes for their own children's schools but who balk at taxes to educate the children society devalues. Or the people who sit in silence as a marginalized person, whether of color or a woman, is interrupted in a meeting, her ideas dismissed (though perhaps later adopted), for fear of losing caste, each of these keeping intact the whole system that holds everyone in its grip.

"Caste is not a physical object like a wall of bricks or a line of barbed wire," the Dalit leader Bhimrao Ambedkar wrote. "Caste is a notion; it is a state of the mind."

No one escapes its tentacles. No one escapes exposure to its message that one set of people is presumed to be inherently smarter, more capable, and more deserving than other groups deemed lower. This program has been installed into the subconscious of every one of us. And, high or low, without intervention or reprogramming, we act out the script we were handed.

And yet, somehow, there are the rare people, like Einstein, who seem immune to the toxins of caste in the air we breathe, who manage to transcend what most people are susceptible to. From the abolitionists who risked personal ruin to end slavery to the white civil rights workers who gave their lives to help end Jim Crow and the political leaders who outlawed it, these all-too-rare people are a testament to the human spirit, that humans can break free of the hierarchy's hold on them.

These are people of personal courage and conviction, secure within themselves, willing to break convention, not reliant on the approval of others for their sense of self, people of deep and abiding empathy and compassion. They are what many of us might wish to be but not nearly enough of us are. Perhaps, once awakened, more of us will be.

• • •

As each of us came into consciousness, we learned, based on the random outward manifestation of the combinations of genes that collided at the precise moment of our conception, that because of what we look like, the world had already assigned a place for us.

It was up to each of us to accept or challenge the role we were cast into, to determine for ourselves and to make the world see that what is inside of us—our beliefs and dreams, how we love and express that love, the things that we can actually control—is more important than the outward traits we had no say in. That we are not what we look like but what we do with what we have, what we make of what we are given, how we treat others and our planet.

Human beings across time and continents are more alike than they are different. The central question about human behavior is not why do those people do this or act in that way, now or in ages past, but what is it that human beings do when faced with a given circumstance?

None of us chose the circumstances of our birth. We had nothing to do with having been born into privilege or under stigma. We have everything to do with what we do with our God-given talents and how we treat others in our species from this day forward.

We are not personally responsible for what people who look like us did centuries ago. But we are responsible for what good or ill we do to people alive with us today. We are, each of us, responsible for every decision we make that hurts or harms another human being. We are responsible for recognizing that what happened in previous generations at the hands of or to people who look like us set the stage for the world we now live in and that what has gone before us grants us advantages or burdens through no effort or fault of our own, gains or deficits that others who do not look like us often do not share.

We are responsible for our own ignorance or, with time and openhearted enlightenment, our own wisdom. We are responsible for ourselves and our own deeds or misdeeds in our time and in our own space and will be judged accordingly by succeeding generations.

• • •

In a world without caste, instead of a false swagger over our own tribe or family or ascribed community, we would look upon all of humanity with wonderment: the lithe beauty of an Ethiopian runner, the bravery of a Swedish girl determined to save the planet, the physics-defying aerobatics of an African-American Olympian, the brilliance of a composer of Puerto Rican descent who can rap the history of the founding of America at 144 words a minute—all of these feats should fill us with astonishment at what the species is capable of and gratitude to be alive for this.

In a world without caste, being male or female, light or dark, immigrant or native-born, would have no bearing on what anyone was perceived as being capable of. In a world without caste, we would all be invested in the well-being of others in our species if only for our own survival and recognize that we are in need of one another more than we have been led to believe. We would join forces with indigenous people around the world raising the alarm as fires rage and glaciers melt. We would see that, when others suffer, the collective human body is set back from the progression of our species.

A world without caste would set everyone free.

Acknowledgments

This is a book that I did not seek to write but had to write, in the era in which we find ourselves. As I embarked upon it, I was blessed to work with two legends in publishing—my editor, Kate Medina, and my agent, Binky Urban, who embraced the idea from the start and who gave me the space to follow the threads where they led me.

The first place I went, or rather felt compelled to go, was Germany—Berlin, specifically—to try to comprehend a caste system that had arisen in a terrifying space of time, in a country that has been wrestling with atonement ever since. I am grateful to Krista Tippett for introducing me to a lovely group of people in Berlin that I otherwise would never have met. My thanks to Irene Dunkley and to Nathan and Ulrich Koestlin for their kindnesses and most especially to Nigel Dunkley, who recognized my mission from the start and shepherded me through the trail of Reich history with keen insight.

For the opportunity to experience India firsthand, I am indebted to professors Ramnarayan Rawat and K. Satyanarayana, who opened the door as I planned my first trip to Delhi, who made a way for me to meet other scholars of caste, and who extended to me every courtesy. There I had the chance to talk with Dalits who had labored against the obstacles in their paths and with whom I felt an immediate kinship, along with people from a range of other castes. Among the people whose perspectives I found especially helpful were Anupama Prasad and Sharika Thiranagama, who were completing research into caste inequities.

Unbeknownst to me, word spread that I had flown to India on this mission of caste. I was soon asked to speak at an international caste conference at the University of Massachusetts Amherst, alongside Indian political theorist Gopal Guru and Indian philosopher Meena Dhanda. I was overwhelmed to later be asked to deliver the conference's closing remarks.

There, faced with translating the Jim Crow caste system for an audience focused on India, I began to draft the earliest outlines of what would become the pillars of caste. I am ever grateful to Sangeeta Kamat, Biju Mathew, and other conference leaders who embraced me and invited me into their fold and to the many other kindred spirits I met there, including Suraj Yengde, Jaspreet Mahal, Balmurli Natrajan, and also Gary Tartakov, who immediately understood the humanitarian goals of my work and encouraged me onward.

During this quest, I came to know two survivors of the Indian caste system then living in London. Tushar Sarkar gave hours of his time to describe his experiences growing up in India and his disillusionment with caste. Sushrut Jadhav shared with me the parallel burdens, blessings, and exhaustions of living a life in defiance of caste, along with his insights as a psychiatrist and anthropologist. At his home, I had stimulating conversations with his family and with the author Arundhati Roy about the absurdity of caste.

Because this project interweaves the perspectives and insights of multiple disciplines—anthropology, sociology, psychology, political science, philosophy, and history—I am indebted to entire bodies of scholarship and to those who have contributed to an archive I sought to learn from and perhaps to build upon. I am grateful for the work of historians of enslavement, particularly Edward Baptist, Daina Ramey Berry, and Stephanie Jones-Rogers, and, in the history of race-based medical experimentation, the groundbreaking work of Harriet Washington. While this book is pointedly not about racism in itself, any book that touches on the subject owes a debt to the scholarship of Ibram X. Kendi and to the mission of Bryan Stevenson, whose memorial to lynching victims sets the standard for reconciling history.

For taking a sledgehammer to the false god of race, I am grateful to the late anthropologists Ashley Montagu and Audrey Smedley and, in the current day, am appreciative of Ian Haney López for his legal genealogy of race in America. For uncovering the parallels between Jim Crow America and aspects of the Third Reich, I am indebted to the definitive research of James Q. Whitman of Yale University. His work decisively connects the history of Nazi Germany to that of the United States and illuminated what I had had reason to believe from the start. I am appreciative of the discerning analyses of philosopher Susan Neiman of the Einstein Forum in Berlin, whose book *Learning from the Germans* was published just as I completed my manuscript. Discovering their work as I neared the end of my research affirmed the course that I had taken.

Early on, I discovered scholarly mentors from the past, people who had walked this road and whose words I turned to time and again for reassurance and insight. These ancestors in the scholarship of caste include John Dollard, Hortense Powdermaker,

Lloyd Warner, Burleigh Gardner, and Gerald Berreman, in particular. Berreman studied and lived in both India and the Jim Crow South and was in a singular position to compare the two caste systems. He recognized the parallels and stood up to the skeptics with the quiet conviction that comes from deep research and firsthand experience.

Beyond these, I consider the late anthropologist Allison Davis to be a spiritual father in the quest to understanding the role of caste in America. The caste system forced him and his wife and scholarly partner, Elizabeth, to live what they studied, and they risked their lives to train a searchlight on the evils of caste. I am happy to honor and acknowledge David A. Varel's fine biography, *The Lost Black Scholar: Resurrecting Allison Davis in American Social Thought,* which thoroughly and eloquently recounts the Davises' groundbreaking work.

Seventy years after the Davises completed their fieldwork in Mississippi, I happened to be attending a gala at the New York Public Library. There, that night, I first mentioned to my editor and my agent that I planned to write this book. Minutes later, I was mingling among the thousand or so guests packed together in tuxedoes and sequins, and found myself standing near a man I had never met but who had been a fan of *The Warmth of Other Suns.* He told a bit of his background and his name, Gordon Davis. I realized, from what I knew of the late anthropologist's life, that the man I was talking to was all but certainly the son of Allison Davis. I asked if that, in fact, was true. A prominent attorney in his own right, he was heartened that I knew of his father and had held him in such deep admiration. Coming just minutes after committing to this project, I took this to be a sign that I was meant to write this book.

I have been deeply grateful to the many people whose paths I crossed who, knowing of my first book, shared unbidden their encounters with caste as they, too, tried to make sense of it. There were serendipitous moments, like running into former New Orleans mayor Mitch Landrieu just as I was contemplating the role of Confederate symbols. Over the years, I have been continually inspired by my ongoing conversations with historian and dear friend Taylor Branch, whose work and perspective often intersect with mine. I am also ever grateful to Sharon Malone and Eric Holder for the grace and thoughtfulness they have shown me.

The nature and timetable for a book under production in an era of global pandemic required collaboration and commitment on an epic level. Working remotely in a time of uncertainty, the following people at Penguin Random House, in addition to my editor, Kate Medina, made this book possible: Gina Centrello, whose support I have treasured, and publisher Andy Ward and deputy publisher Avideh Bashirrad. In copy editing, managing editorial, and production: Benjamin Dreyer, Rebecca Berlant, and Richard Elman. In the departments of art and design, overseen by Paolo Pepe, I had the pleasure of working with Greg Mollica, who could not have found a better photograph for the cover, who designed the brilliant jacket and wholeheartedly obliged my suggestions, as did Virginia Norey in designing the book's sublime interior. I am grateful for the support and enthusiasm of the publicity department—Maria Braeckel, Susan Corcoran, London King, and Gwyneth Stansfield; and of the marketing department—Barbara Fillon, Leigh Marchant, and Ayelet Gruenspecht. Noa Shapiro deftly kept me and everyone else in touch and moved the process along.

Given all that this book required, I cannot imagine completing it without the calm and steady stewardship of production editor Steve Messina. His deep commitment, attention to detail, and patience oversaw the conversion of an evolving manuscript into galleys and then into a book that you can now hold in your hands. My sincerest gratitude to him.

Special thanks also to Sarah Cook, acting dean of the Honors College at Georgia State University, who, at a critical moment, made available to me three of her brightest students—Noah Britton, Clay Voytek, and Savannah Rogers. In the final weeks and months of my completing the manuscript, they spent time and energy researching last-minute questions and leads. Noah and Clay further dedicated themselves to additional weeks of fastidious fact-checking and, by the time the work was done, had taken up the cause of the book as their own.

I would like to thank every reader of *The Warmth of Other Suns* and all of those who have written letters to me since its publication. Your support enabled the travel and work required for this book, and, while I sincerely regret that circumstances have often not permitted me to reply directly, please know that each and every letter is precious to me and each has sustained and brought joy to me as I continue this work.

Due to the toll that research of this kind takes, I cannot imagine getting through the process without the encouragement of J. Blair Page and of Bunny Fisher, who showed unflagging commitment to this book and to my well-being and who listened separately to drafts or to sections of it, rendering compassionate feedback. I am grateful to the extraordinary Miss Hale not only for sharing her story for this book but also for sharing her unmatched culinary masterpieces, her grace and wisdom, and, above all, her five beautiful children, who spark delight every time I am in their presence. My thanks to Stephanie Hooks for her ever-present optimism and for introducing me to their world.

For the compassion they have shown, I am thankful for D. M. Page and for Todd, Marcia, Leslie, Maureen, Christine, Brenda, and Dahleen; for Margie S., Michelle T., Rosie T., Rebecca, and Michael for their love and support at a time of personal challenge and loss; and, for dear Ansley and Rafe, for the eye-rolling, sidesplitting joy, wit, and laughter they bring. Thanks to the rest of the Hamilton family, and as always to Gwen and Phil Whitt, to the Taylor family, and to my extended family in Virginia.

I could not have gotten through the deepest chambers of this work without the backdrop of seemingly unrelated music that brought either the focus or the uplift I needed at various points of the writing. The nature of the task drew me for some reason to music from before September 11, 2001, and I found myself turning to: Philip Glass (specifically String Quartet no. 5), Parliament ("Flash Light"), America ("A Horse with No Name"), Prince ("7"), the Police, Thelonious Monk and T. S. Monk, and the soundtrack to the classic French thriller *Diva*. Aside from its gorgeous range of music, *Diva* is one of the few big-screen portrayals of a woman of my archetype depicted in ways that some other women can take for granted, presented as refined and pivotal rather than as subordinated stereotype or sidekick. Although there have been notable exceptions in recent years, this is a film where I need not dread the woman getting whipped, mocked, hypersexualized, killed off, cast as a servant, or portrayed by a man, a common practice in an industry that long denied black women the chance to portray themselves as they truly are. *Diva* was the kind of film that perhaps could only be imagined outside of the American caste system.

I received my first lessons in caste from my parents, who never used that word but who came into the world during what the historian Rayford Logan called the Nadir. They grew up under the ever-present threat of the southern regime, found a way to survive Jim Crow and even to flourish despite the obstacles their own country placed in their path. They prayed that their daughter might somehow escape the arrows of caste that they had endured and, although, in our country, that was not to be—it was not, nor is it still, far enough along for that dream of theirs to come true—I am ever grateful for their guiding light, their faith and fortitude, and the highest of standards they set for me and that they themselves lived. In every word I write, I can only hope to bring honor to their sacrifices.

Finally, I am grateful beyond language for the love and devotion of Brett Hamilton, the kindest and most giving husband I could have wished for, a gift from the universe. Many of the observations in this book first found a voice in our deeply fulfilling conversations and in our life together. While it breaks my heart that neither he nor my parents lived to see this culmination of what we, each in our own ways, sought to transcend, I feel his cosmic embrace as I send this out to the world, and I know that all three of them are with me now and always.

Isabel Wilkerson
April 2020

Index

silent earthquakes, 8–9
Sims, James Marion, 138–39
Sinclair, William A., 123
slavery, 35–36, 40–45, 149–52, 262
   agricultural needs and, 34
   American caste system origins
     and, 21–22
   auctions in, 135–36
   Confederate monuments and,
     259–70, 275
   cruelty and punishment in,
     37–39, 125–26, 128,
     136–37, 265
   dehumanization and, 132–36
   entertaining in, 127–29
   first Africans in colonial, 32–33
   free blacks during, 233–34
   medical experimentation and,
     137–39
   religion justifying, 92–93
   terror as enforcement in,
     140–45, 265
   upward mobility and, 196–98
   workday in, 38, 137
smallpox vaccine, 196–98
Smedley, Audrey and Brian, 34–35,
   56, 59, 147
Smith, David Livingstone, 317
Smith, Hoke, 199
Smith, Lillian, 161
Smith, Robert, 209–10
Sokol, Jason, 48
South Africa, 315
Stacy, Rubin, 84
Stampp, Kenneth M., 21, 136–37,
   141, 149, 196
Steinberg, Stephen, 123
Stephens, Alexander, 261
Stockholm Syndrome, 280

Stoddard, Lothrop, 73–74
Stowers, Freddie, 192
Stuart, Charles and Carol DiMaiti,
   171–75
Supreme Court, 99–100, 105, 113,
   200, 251

T
Tartakov, Gary Michael, 292
Tesler, Michael, 254
Thind, Bhagat Singh, 114
Tocqueville, Alexis de, 22, 72–73
Truman, Harry S., 194
Trump, Donald, 254–57
Tulsa massacre, 196
Tye, Larry, 209

U
Uncle Tom, 203
unconscious bias, 165–66
United States (US), 11–13, 20, 41,
   122–24, 139; *see also* American
   caste system
   democracy in, 93
   Electoral College and, 7
   first Africans in colonial, 32–33
   majority rule in, 315
   Nazi Germany inspired by, 72–78
   race in, 14–15, 18, 46
   racism and casteism in, 63–64
   spontaneous shrines in, 66
   2016 presidential election in,
     6–9, 254–58

V
Vardaman, James K., 122
Vaughan, Alden T., 33
Vavreck, Lynn, 254
Veeck, Bill, 211

Venter, J. Craig, 58
Verba, Sidney, 68, 121

W

Walt, Stephen, 291–92
Ward, Jason Morgan, 193
Warner, W. Lloyd, 45
Washington, Harriet A., 138, 197
Watkins, Mel, 107–108
Weiner, Mark S., 106
Westmoreland, Richard, 268
Whitaker, Forest, 96
Whitefield, George, 38–39
whites
    caste intrusions by, 181–89
    child care for, 198–99
    definition of, 15, 111–14
    as dominant caste, 15, 43,
        106–107, 109, 158–66

    as "ethnics," 227–29
    European immigrants as, 42–44,
        109–11, 206
    forgiveness and, 285
    occupational hierarchy and,
        124
    presumed superiority of,
        149–50
    racial identity of, 255
    radicalization of, 300–303
white supremacy, 21, 250
Whitman, James Q., 72, 74, 77, 80
Williams, David R., 165–66
Williams, Eugene, 106
Wiltse, Jeff, 107
Woodard, Isaac, Jr., 193–95

Y

Yengde, Suraj, 286–88

338

About the Author

Isabel Wilkerson, winner of the Pulitzer Prize and the National Humanities Medal, is the author of the critically acclaimed *New York Times* bestseller *The Warmth of Other Suns.* This, her debut work, won the National Book Critics Circle Award for Nonfiction and was named to *Time's* 10 Best Nonfiction Books of the 2010s and the *New York Times's* list of the Best Nonfiction of All Time. Wilkerson has taught at Princeton, Emory, and Boston universities and has lectured at more than two hundred other colleges and universities across the United States and in Europe and Asia.

isabelwilkerson.com
@isabelwilkerson

Underlined

Where Books Are Life

your favorite **books**

your favorite **authors**

all in one place

Share your love of reading with us!

getunderlined.com

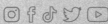